State Ideology and Language in Tanzania

State Ideology and Langage in Tanzania

Second and Revised Edition

Jan Blommaert

EDINBURGH
University Press

© Jan Blommaert, 1999, 2014

Edinburgh University Press Ltd
The Tun – Holyrood Road
12(2f) Jackson's Entry
Edinburgh EH8 8PJ
www.euppublishing.com

First edition published by Rudiger Koeppe in 1999.

Typeset in 10/12pt Adobe Garamond by
Servis Filmsetting Ltd, Stockport, Cheshire,
and printed and bound in Great Britain by
CPI Group (UK) Ltd, Croydon CR0 4YY

A CIP record for this book is available from the British Library

ISBN 978 0 7486 7579 1 (hardback)
ISBN 978 0 7486 7581 4 (webready PDF)
ISBN 978 0 7486 7580 7 (paperback)
ISBN 978 0 7486 7583 8 (epub)

Contents

Figures

Preface to the second edition

State Ideology and Language in Tanzania appeared in its first edition in 1999 and summarised research carried out since 1985. That start date is relevant: I was in Tanzania when Julius Nyerere stepped down voluntarily as President of Tanzania and handed the State House over to his successor, Ali Hassan Mwinyi. The new President promptly signed an agreement with the International Monetary Fund, thus terminating two decades of *Ujamaa* in his country and turning Tanzania into a free-market economy and, eventually, a nominal multiparty democracy. Nominal because in both cases the post-1985 period showed continuity rather than disconti-nuity. While for a time Tanzania became a bonanza for foreign investors, the social and economic structure of the country did not change much; and in politics, the ruling party of Nyerere's one-party state, the *Chama Cha Mapinduzi* (CCM), pro-vided the supreme leadership of the country until the day of writing: Mwinyi was succeeded by Mkapa and then by Kikwete – all of them CCM.

The first edition of this book was driven by a desire to document what I consid-ered (and still consider) to be a curious but telling case of language planning. What happened in Tanzania since independence, and certainly since the introduction of a formal model of Ujamaa in 1967, was an outstanding case of linguistic hegemony. It is a well-weathered sociolinguistic fact that Tanzania is exceptional in Africa because of the nationwide predominance of one language, Swahili. This fortuitous situation emerged because of reasons to be explained in this book, the most important of which was Ujamaa politics. Swahili became absorbed into the nation-building drive caused by Ujamaa, and its emblematic role as the language that incorporated and articulated independence – and, later, the socialist revolution – pushed Swahili into the most remote parts of the country and made it – to varying degrees of skill and fluency – part of almost every Tanzanian's repertoire. The story of Swahili is a story of an overwhelming political-ideological success.

What is less well-known in sociolinguistic circles is that this success was in actual fact not recognised in Tanzania itself. As I will describe in this book, the overwhelm-ing success of Swahili as a language of the nation-state was quite systematically accompanied by an elaborate culture of complaints, in which linguists, intellectuals and politicians alike presented the case for Swahili as a failure and a headache. As soon as I set foot in Tanzania and expressed an interest in the predicament of

Swahili, I was deeply exposed to this discourse of failure, expressed by people whose language repertoires in the meantime displayed the deep and lasting traces of the success of Swahili.

This curious paradox led me to investigate the phenomenon, and pretty soon I realised that the contradiction was a language-ideological effect. While the facts on the ground pointed towards massive success, the particular ideological imagination in which Swahili was captured – it ought to be the language of the socialist revolution – made assessments of success subject to impossible demands: the spread of a uniform language should have contributed to the construction of social, cultural and political homogeneity in the country. Evidently, this was not to happen – and this is why language planners never stopped proclaiming the failure of the political Swahili project.

This was easy enough to observe. As I said, my arrival in Tanzania as a researcher coincided with the formal termination of Ujamaa, and in the following years I witnessed some of the changes in the country first-hand. I witnessed the birth of new political parties and movement, of new entrepreneurial classes and, eventually, a new middle class, of new forms of popular culture rejecting the mantras of socialism, of new forms of scholarship and debate. Well, all of this suddenly very visible sociocultural and political diversity expressed itself in Swahili – in *a range of varieties* of Swahili, many of them innovative and creative and all of them testifying to the intense dynamics of language, culture and society in the country. What was thus seen as evidence of the failure of Ujamaa in the field of language was in actual fact hard evidence of its lasting success.

For me, Tanzania thus became a superb case through which some perennial problems of language planning could be exposed and explained, notably some of the language ideologies that tend to dominate language planning till this day: the assumption that linguistic engineering stands in a direct relationship with social transformation, the assumption that 'language' was the key concept in all of this, the assumption of ideally monolingual societies and so on; the chapters in this book will engage at length with these language-ideological assumptions. These assumptions obscured several critical processes in the reality of sociolinguistic life: that not 'language' but 'register' is the 'stuff', so to speak, of language in society; that language is only to a certain extent 'makeable'; that as soon as a language is distributed throughout a large number of users it will tend to explode into numerous new sub-varieties, and so on. Above all, the language-ideological fundamentals of language planning tend to obscure the duty of researchers to actually see and interpret what goes on – how real language is used by real people in real social environments.

While the 1999 edition of this book was welcomed by scholars as a useful contribution to the historiography of Swahili in postcolonial Tanzania and as an example of perhaps wider relevance, elucidating some key points in the postcolonial story of languages elsewhere, I did not think that the points made were spelt out with adequate clarity. I therefore jumped at the opportunity offered to me by Edinburgh University Press to quite thoroughly revise the 1999 edition and incorporate both new theoretical and methodological observations and new empirical material extending the historical coverage of the book to include very recent phenomena. These recent phenomena were collected during a research stay in Dar es Salaam in September 2012, and I am immensely grateful to my old Tanzanian friends and colleagues – mentioned in the preface to the 1999 edition – for welcoming me once again and bombarding me with reflections on the continuities and discontinuities in the Tanzanian sociolinguistic landscape. The fact that my good friend Koen Adam, Ambassador of Belgium in Tanzania, offered to host me provided the most gener-ous, comfortable and effective working environment I have ever had there, and I am deeply grateful to Koen, Els, Maarten and Jonathan for their hospitality and care while I was doing my work there.

While there, I realised that my interest in the socio-political history of Swahili had, if anything, become even deeper and more intense than before. To a large extent, this is the result of activities over the past decade, always performed in collab-oration with some exceptional scholars. I am thinking of Michael Silverstein, Susan Gal, Salikoko Mufwene and Rob Moore in Chicago; of Gunther Kress, David Block and Norbert Pachler in London; of Christopher Stroud, Mastin Prinsloo, Anna Deumert, Quentin Williams and Charlyn Dyers in Cape Town; of my friends in the Max Planck Sociolinguistic Diversity Working Group, Karel Arnaut, David Parkin, Steve Vertovec, Ben Rampton, Jens-Normann Jørgensen, Sirpa Leppanen, Adrian Blackledge, Angela Creese and their many stellar collaborators; and of people such as Alastair Pennycook, Piet Van Avermaet, Suresh Canagarajah, Stephen May, Gao Yihong, Lionel Wee, Christina Higgins, Sabrina Billings and many others on the conference circuit. My own team in Tilburg, of course, provided me with the most stimulating and creative environment, and I must thank Sjaak Kroon, Odile Heynders, Ad Backus, Jeanne Kurvers, Piia Varis, Max Spotti, Sanna Lehtonen, Fie Velghe, Dong Jie, Caixia Du, Xuan Wang, Jos Swanenberg, Kutlay Yağmur and the others for keeping me in good shape over the past few years and for feeding me continuously with superb data and ideas from various parts of the world. And there would have been no book without Karin Berkhout's titanic editorial efforts to turn a textual nightmare into a decent manuscript.

Finally, I express my thanks and appreciation to Dr Rudiger Koeppe of Rudiger Koeppe Verlag, the publisher of the 1999 edition, for releasing the copyright to the book and enabling me to engage with this subject in new ways – of which I hope that they will spark for my readers the fascination with this subject that I have entertained for almost three decades.

Jan Blommaert
Antwerp and Dar es Salaam
September 2013

Preface to the first edition

This book came into being in a gradual way, and its current shape is the product of a long process that started in 1985, when I first visited Tanzania and became interested in the intriguing plethora of discourses *about* language in the country. Ever since that time, the politics of language in that country has been one of my research preoccupations, as findings on Tanzania proved to be fertile points of reference for assessing situations elsewhere in Africa and indeed elsewhere in the world. I started publishing on various aspects of language, politics and ideology in Tanzania, and after a number of years the idea of a synthesis was raised by colleagues and picked up by myself as a worthwhile goal. The synthesis is this book. In no way does it terminate the process of research, let alone the curiosity I have for this topic. But it compiles material published over the years (and for which references can be found at the back of the book) and puts some order and structure in research efforts that, as so often, sometimes suffered from the fast and fragmented writing models of contemporary academic life. A first and preliminary version of this book was published as a working paper in 1997 (*LICCAP* 3, University of Duisburg, Germany); feedback and comments on this first attempt encouraged me to continue working on the manuscript and submit it to channels of wider circulation.

The topic of this book has been, and still is, a recurrent issue in conversations with many friends and colleagues, in Tanzania and elsewhere. The numerous discussions I had with them had a tremendous influence on my view on the matter. In particular, I wish to thank Mugyabuso Mulokozi, Kulikoyela Kahigi, Rugatiri Mekacha, Saida Yahya-Othman, Yohani Msanjila, Joshua Madumulla, Hermas Mwansoko, Casmir Rubagumya, Herman Batibo, Haroub Othman, David Massamba, Shaaban Mlacha, Yared Kihore and Daniel Mkude – all in Dar es Salaam – and Michael Meeuwis, Jef Verschueren, Chris Bulcaen, Sigurd D'hondt, Gino Eelen, Johannes Fabian, Stephen Neke, Sinfree Makoni, Kathryn Woolard, Monica Heller, Jim Collins and Sue Gal elsewhere and on other occasions.

Jan Blommaert
Antwerp
August 1999

Preface to the first edition

Dedicated to Stephen Neke
and Eline Adam

Chapter 1

Introduction

In the former Yugoslavia, Serbia and Croatia used to have one common language. But since Croatia became an independent republic, interviews with or statements made by Serbs are subtitled in 'pure' Croatian before they are broadcast on Croatian national television. The suggestion is: We don't understand this strange, foreign language; our language is different from that of the Serbs. The wider context for this peculiar phenomenon of creating differences out of similarities is that of nation building and radical nationalism.

Language is seen as one of the key ingredients of the construction of group identities. It is an acoustic symbolisation of politicised otherness. Since language is an intrinsically historical object, phenomena such as that described above always carry a connotation of historicity. Our language *has always been* different from that of the Croats; Tito has forced Serbs and Croats together in an artificial, multi-ethnic state and has made them use an artificial, multi-ethnic language. And so, the construction of a 'pure' Croatian language becomes part of a process of nation building which is historically motivated and, thus, politically legitimate. In the eyes of the Croatian nation builders, the Croatian language is not created, it is recreated, or even restored to its original state of ethnolinguistic purity. Modern nations require singular symbols: one unambiguous name, one homogeneous identity, one common history, one language.

But language seems particularly ill-suited for this kind of symbolisation. Language usage can be characterised by an almost infinite degree of variability and diversity. Age, gender, class, education, profession, geography, individual characteristics all shape different varieties of language use, and these varieties may themselves be controlled by situational-contextual factors. Any single language, once linguists and sociolinguists start looking at it, falls apart in a mosaic of dialects, sociolects, idiolects, jargons, slang variants, colloquial variants, registers, styles and speech events, and whenever we use 'language' we in fact use the specific bits just mentioned.

These crystallise in particular configurations, called repertoires, in the course of the life history of any individual speaker. I myself grew up using a Flemish dialect, and part of my primary-school training was in that dialect, some of the older teachers being unable to speak standard Dutch. I picked up standard Dutch during my last year in primary school, and I was repeatedly sanctioned by teachers because of my persistent use of dialect expressions. During my years of secondary-school and college training, I acquired a number of highly specific registers and jargons, and standard Dutch became my 'natural' (that is, habituated) first language. My competence in the dialect I had grown up with declined and its development halted, due to a geographical factor (my family moved to Brussels, and I went to college in yet another city) and to situational and speech-event factors (I only used this dialect when interacting with a handful of family members). At the same time, I acquired a number of register varieties: the kind of informal intellectual speech involving occasional code-switching into English or French and using a local-vernacular variety of Dutch as its basis. My dialect accent became complemented by another one, and both layers of accent are audible whenever I speak 'standard' Dutch (or, indeed, French, English, Swahili or any other language).

But still, despite this overwhelming variability, I would qualify myself as a 'native speaker of Dutch', and Dutch would have the connotation of *standard* Dutch – the variety I had to learn when I was eleven years old, and for which I got bad marks due to my struggle with the dialect with which I grew up. Strictly speaking, I am in no way a native speaker of standard Dutch, and I doubt whether many other Flemish-Belgians would be able to sustain claims to the contrary. We all acquired the varieties that count as 'standard' through institutional channels such as schools. These schools, to use a Bourdieuian frame, standardised us together with the language. They moulded us into Flemish-Belgian citizens, capable of manipulating the symbols of our Flemish identity, the most important of which was standard Dutch – we became a *language community* in Silverstein's sense: a group ideologically professing 'speakerhood' of what is understood as *one uniform particular* language – Dutch. In Silverstein's own terms, we became a group 'of people by degree evidencing allegiance to norms of denotational . . . language usage' (Silverstein 1998: 402). And most of all, schools gave us a language ideology: they persuaded us to accept that standard Dutch was our natural, native language, suggesting that what we spoke before (and outside the classroom) was an imperfect, deficient 'patois'. The school reshuffled the symbolic hierarchy of our language varieties, placing the national variety on top and framing all other varieties as things that happened within the confines of, and subject to the control of, standard Dutch.

When I moved to Brussels with my family, and thus landed in a largely French-speaking environment in which the Flemish community had a strong sense of minorisation, this ideology of language came in handy. My Flemish peers and myself heavily idealised 'our language', standard Dutch, over and beyond the different regional varieties spoken in the community. We felt like a monolithic bloc of Flemish people, confronting an equally monolithic bloc of Francophones. In contact and conflict situations such as these, standard Dutch became the emblem of our homogenised common identity (which, in all likelihood, did only emerge in contact and conflict situations with non-Flemish people).

To the extent to which all scientific endeavours have an autobiographic dimension, this is my autobiographical angle. I have never experienced language as a simple, unambiguous and self-evident instrument. Language has always been a fragmented, highly ambiguous object for me, and the deceiving simplicity of that one, clear label 'Dutch' has always mesmerised me. My overriding interest in language and language usage became that of how language is itself a meta-discourse on other topics and other areas of social life. Most of all, I became interested in how language could become a political-ideological domain, how people can be made to feel as if they derive their common identity, and the socio-political order imposed by this commonness, from the impression that they all speak the 'same' language, and this in the face of overwhelming evidence to the contrary. As Silverstein pointed out, homogeneous 'language communities' are ideological constructs rendering invisible the stunning diversity in the myriad of 'speech communities' that drive the empirically observable sociolinguistics of everyday life. Such speech communities are tied together by 'recogniz[ing] an implicit normativity to such indexical semiosis as informs and underlies communicative acts of identity and groupness' (ibid.: 407). In light of such paradoxes, how do we explain such symbolic hierarchies and ideological blind spots in our sociolinguistic imagination? And how do they fit in larger-scale social and political processes? Those fundamental questions have guided me through most of my work, including the present book.

The view of language that I want to promulgate in this book has already been hinted at above. It is non-organic, non-homogeneous, non-natural, and incongruent with stable and homogeneous identities. I refuse to accept some of the age-old folk (and scholarly) assumptions about language as a natural feature, inextricably linked to natural identities in clear-cut 'one language–one people' patterns (cf. Blommaert 2006). Instead, I want to focus on how 'language' in the sense used in 'language communities' can be *made* by clearly identifiable actors, and how language spread and language change, as well as features of concrete language usage in various contexts, can be *organised* by institutions and social structures involved in the distribution of power and control in a particular society. And I also want to show how such institutionalised ideological constructs relate to the complexities of language-on-the-ground – how the processes of homogenisation from above relate to the processes of diversification from below.

This book, thus, addresses language policy and ideology from two directions: an institutional top-down direction, oriented towards the definition, role and function of 'language' and 'language users' (the 'language community' features); and a grass-roots, vernacular bottom-up direction in which we look at the registers and repertoires deployed in actual situated language usage (the 'speech community' features). Both directions have defined the architecture of this book; but before we can comment on that, let us clarify these two directions.

1.1 HOMOGENISATION FROM ABOVE

The first half of this book will be devoted to the organisation of a language – Swahili – by the postcolonial Tanzanian State. More particularly, I will investigate the way in which Swahili was swept up in a wave of massive nation building exercises in the late 1960s and 1970s, driven by and incorporated in the state ideology of

Ujamaa. We will see how the Tanzanian state made a successful attempt at ideological hegemony (successful, at least, for some time), and how Swahili was given a prominent role in this process of homogenisation. Swahili was, thus, deliberately constructed, manufactured, and not 'just' as a language, but as an overdetermined emblem of national belonging and ideological rectitude.

There are numerous precursors to this kind of analytical exercise, and I have been particularly inspired by Johannes Fabian's *Language and Colonial Power* (1986), not merely because it treats the same language as the one I want to investigate, Swahili, but also because it takes the political process of colonialisation as the crucial factor in shaping Swahili in the former Belgian Congo. Fabian's analysis of the 'colonial appropriation' of Swahili shows how misleading the linguistic premise can be that a language that is now spoken should be a language that has always been spoken. It exposes the limits of organic views of language spread and language change. Languages do not always change spontaneously, and neither do they always change according to established laws or regularities. Change can be diagnosed best by looking into concrete processes of communication, both at the micro- and at the macro-levels, and these patterns of communication will always involve power. These power relations may be structurally asymmetrical and give language usage a dimension of control and coercion by qualifying specific forms of language usage as normative or 'normal'. These processes of 'normalising' forms of language usage (and hence of 'abnormalising' others), best understood in terms of a Gramscian version of hegemony, may be crucial factors in shaping the sociolinguistic profile of societies. This sociolinguistic profile can, in turn, be treated as an index of the processes of hegemonisation in a society. The ordering of languages or language varieties and the social domains in which they are being used can then lead us to insights into how the society is made *politically* cohesive.

This again can be illustrated by looking at my own sociolinguistic background. In contemporary Flanders, standard Dutch has acquired more than just instrumental values. The Flemish nationalist trend that has reshaped Belgium into a federalised state has also caused a reordering of the linguistic repertoire for Flemish people. Standard Dutch has now become more normative than before, to the extent where certain Flemish dialects are being subtitled on television, despite the fact that twenty years ago quite a few dialect speakers would appear in television interviews.[1] Dialects and accents have been replaced by 'standard' Dutch as the locus of Flemish group solidarity. In the old days, the Flemish dialects served the symbolic function of affirming Flemish identity as opposed to the Francophone Belgian identity. In the Belgian parliament of the early twentieth century, the language of the Flemish people was called *Vlaams* – 'Flemish'. Now that Flanders has reached a significant degree of political autonomy, this symbolic function has become redundant, and a new identity orientation is required: that of similarity to the Netherlands. The language of the Flemish people is now called *Nederlands* – 'Dutch', instead of *Vlaams* – 'Flemish'. The eyes of the Flemish nationalists are turned away from their former target, Belgium, and they now look to the nation-state with which they feel a close ethnolinguistic affinity (cf. Blommaert 2011).

At the same time, the language repertoire of the Flemish is reshuffled in another way. Whereas the 'normal' second language for Flemish people used to be French – Belgium was very much a bilingual Dutch-French state – the current tendency, more or less completed at present, is to replace French with English. The Flemish Government disseminates propaganda materials (including key holders, pins with the Flemish flag, plastic bags, and so on) that carry Dutch and English texts. Two words are printed on the key holders, pins, bags, and so on: *Vlaanderen* – the Dutch name – and *Flanders* – its English equivalent. Again, the symbolic orientation of this reconstruction of the 'normal' linguistic repertoire is away from Belgium, and in the direction of other international communities (the EU and, beyond it, the world). The anti-Belgian orientation of Flemish nationalism displays itself through a reorganisation of the linguistic resources which Flemish citizens are supposed to use, first, when communicating within their own community (standard Dutch), and, second, outside their community (English). French, the language of the former enemy, has been re-stratified and placed in a lower symbolic position than before.

Of crucial importance in this process of shaping a linguistic ideology is the role of institutional (and/or semi-institutional) discourses. The alignment of political ideology and language practice is oriented, stimulated and monitored by a number of authoritative communicating actors; first and foremost by the state and its officials, but also by 'secondary' institutional discourses such as scientific discourse, media coverage and forms of widely distributed artistic or intellectual expressions (literature, music): the mid-level and civil society actors Louis Althusser (1971) famously called 'ideological state apparatuses'. In one way or another, each of these communicating actors can and does claim authority over the message it disseminates, either by referring to group values and group interests (as with political communication), or by referring to standards of objectivity, methodological rigour, standards of quality or aesthetic canons (as with science, the media and intellectual/ artistic expressions). In each case, messages are de-individualised, they are produced and perceived as statements not pertaining to individual preferences or opinions but imbued with a surplus value that gives them higher credibility, reliability or plausibility than otherwise. The critical factor in this process of constructing authority is that of *legitimation*: referring one's statements to a higher social level, either by framing them in a particular generic pattern (the public address, the scientific paper, the novel), or simply by assuming an institutional persona (*the* politician, *the* intellectual), thereby situating one's statements in the context of an identifiable leading social category (cf. Thompson 1990). Not all communication is socially equivalent, some forms of discourse commonsensically appear to be more easily believed than others. The message, largely regardless of its content, is framed or contextualised a priori, on the basis of generic or personality features. Central in the study of language and ideology therefore are the communicative activities of 'ideology brokers' such as politicians, scientists, intellectuals, journalists, artists.

I chose to investigate these phenomena in a Third World context, that of Tanzania. The reasons for this are manifold. First, Tanzania, like any other decolonised state, has been faced with the task of nation building, and language (Swahili) has played a major role in it (explicitly acknowledged, in contrast to many other countries). Especially in the wake of the introduction of Ujamaa, the Tanzanian version of African socialism, in 1967, nation building became a top priority for the Tanzanians, and nation building went hand-in-hand with the dissemination of Ujamaa. Swahili was and is a hotly debated *political* topic in Tanzania, and literature reflecting this debate is relatively abundant. It is therefore a rather obvious target for an analysis such as this one.

Second, because of its political importance, Swahili has also been the object of intensive linguistic engineering and language planning, and it has been used as the medium of one of Africa's outstanding vernacular literatures. Therefore, the processes of constructing authoritative discourses on and in Swahili can be rather easily monitored.

Third, and on a more general level, language planning and language policy are quickly acquiring new relevance in the context of globalisation, where the nation-state is increasingly questioned as a relevant scale-level for social and political organisation. As a scale of social organisation, it is indeed becoming rapidly overtaken by the events. As a scale of political organisation, however, the nation-state is not irrelevant. Further, the more we witness the super-diversification of contemporary societies, the more we see states roll back towards procedures and institutional categorisations that exude the homogeneity of an earlier era (Blommaert 2009, 2010; Blommaert and Rampton 2011). Responses to increased diversity appear very often to deny this diversity. Language policy often plays a role in this (see, for example, essays in Blommaert 1999; Crawford 2000;). A critical re-examination of language policy attempts, therefore, can help us understand such tensions.

1.2 DIVERSIFICATION FROM BELOW

Let us be precise with regard to the tensions I just mentioned. The classic self-imagination of a nation-state as a relatively homogeneous community held together by potent symbols such as a common language, culture and tradition is crippled by what Steven Vertovec called 'superdiversity' (Vertovec 2007): new and highly diversified migration processes resulting in unprecedented forms of ethnic, linguistic, cultural and religious diversity, organised in a broad range of different forms of community and (electronically mediated) network structures, and with very diverse degrees of attachment and loyalty to the place where one lives. This, of course, is evident in the global megacities often investigated in studies on globalisation and superdiversity, and it is evident in the highly mobile world of global professionals, popular artists and businesspeople (see for example Pennycook 2007; Blommaert 2010).

Interestingly, however, similar phenomena of extreme diversification triggered by globalised mobility can be found in less metropolitan places. We find global templates directing and formatting, so to speak, language usage in the socio-economic margins of the world: rural and minority areas in Central China, villages in the Gambia, small tourist resorts in Northern Finland, the townships around

Cape Town and so forth (Wang et al. 2013). And this is not just a contemporary phenomenon: as Alastair Pennycook recently showed, very similar phenomena could be noted in the historically remote context of colonisation and imperialism (Pennycook 2012). There are good reasons to accept that the phenomena now described as features of superdiversity were, in actual fact, always and everywhere common features of social processes, and that differences between such processes in the margins and in the metropolitan centres are differences of degree rather than of substance. It is, thus, quite likely that *every* attempt towards institutional socio-cultural homogenisation was accompanied by reinvigorated processes of social and cultural diversification on the ground.

Such processes of diversification can now be described and analysed by means of a substantially more accurate and nuanced theoretical and methodological apparatus than was the case some decades ago. The work done on language ideologies, for instance, has since the early 1990s enabled us to distinguish several layers in the phenomenology of sociolinguistic processes – layers of 'pragmatic' practice and layers of 'metapragmatic' indexical organisation for instance (Agha 2007) – and such work has prompted an entirely new empirical programme for addressing language policies (Kroskrity 2000). It has also provided a range of new analytical tools for the analysis of situated speech, in which we can now distinguish elaborate patterns of indexical organisation providing social, cultural and political levels of meaning to each act of language (Silverstein and Urban 1996; Silverstein 2003; Rampton 2006; also Hymes 1996). In general, such work has deeply influenced our understanding of what communicative practices are, how they operate and how we must understand their effects. We have learned, thus, to observe the actual arrangements of communicative resources – bits of 'language', accents, stylistic features, metalinguistic features and so on, organised in registers and genres – as the actual building blocks of meaning-making, and so to dismiss 'language' in its traditional sense (the named entities such as 'English' or 'Swahili') as the compellingly relevant object of sociolinguistic analysis. People use resources, which they indexically qualify as *counting as language*, from within locally defined complexes of social and cultural normative conventions. It is with such flexible and dynamic materials that sociolinguistic lives are organised on the ground, and a study of language policy benefits from examining this level of actual sociolinguistic organisation too.

Why? Because to do so enables us to see, at least, the real effects of top-down policy, planning and implementation. The Tanzanian State invested tremendous efforts in turning the country into a Swahili-speaking society; was this, or was this not, a success? And by means of which instruments and processes was this achieved? Census data will offer us only approximations of sociolinguistic reality, so if we wish to know the answers to such questions it is sociolinguistic reality we have to directly address.

In the second part of this study, we shall see how the sociocultural and political homogenisation of Ujamaa nation building rapidly gave rise to new forms of social diversification and stratification, and we shall be able to specify the causes and reasons for that process of early fragmentation and observe its continuity and intensification in recent years. This process of diversification, it must be emphatically noted, should not obscure the tremendous success of the Tanzanian language planners: processes of diversification occurred in a society that had become effectively Swahili-speaking. To the extent that Ujamaa was expected to turn every Tanzanian into a Swahili-speaking subject, it was an amazingly successful exercise. Stressing 'Swahili', however, risks overlooking crucial aspects of sociolinguistic reality, as argued above. And indeed, processes of fragmentation become manifest as soon as one starts looking at differences *within* and *across* 'languages'. While the 'language' Swahili spread all over Tanzania, penetrating even the remotest villages and towns, the spread of *specific registers* obeyed very different rules. Swahili, one can say, was the great equaliser of Ujamaa; but specific forms and varieties of Swahili instantly became the great re-stratifiers in Tanzanian society, enabling elites and specific subcultures to self-identify, and, eventually, when Tanzania became a fully globalised consumer society, they became the emblems of particular consumption-driven network communities and consumer identities.

The outcome of this study is, therefore, paradoxical. Language planners wanted Tanzania to be entirely dominated by Swahili. They achieved that. But they also believed that the spread of Swahili would at once turn every speaker into a socialist professing the values and principles of Ujamaa. They failed: in the twenty-first century, Swahili – rather, specific registers of it – is the medium, vehicle and emblem for enthusiastic consumerism and self-confident expressions of neoliberal world-views. I believe that similar paradoxical outcomes can, and will, be observed elsewhere too.

1.3 THE ORGANISATION OF THE BOOK

I have divided this study into eight chapters. Chapter 2 provides some crucial background and discusses some general issues related to the empirical study of an African political ideology. It starts from the general observation that postcolonial politics in Africa have yielded a remarkable amount of theoretical-political writings by senior statesmen. In particular, they have given rise to a tradition of African socialism, of which Ujamaa is one (rather prominent) instance. Next, some general theoretical points will be discussed. I will offer a number of terminological and theoretical comments on the notion of 'ideology' as it will be used in this study, and, second, I reflect on the intercultural dimension in an analysis such as this one.

After this background chapter, the actual enquiry into state ideology and language begins, and, as indicated above, two separate sets of evidence will be discussed. Chapters 3 to 7, consequently, are organised in two parts. Part 1 discusses 'Swahili and the state: the macropolitics of language', and contains three chapters.

Chapter 3 will discuss some of the cultural-philosophical aspects of Ujamaa in greater detail. Ujamaa was a humanist political theory, with an important emphasis on the development of man. As a consequence, it contained (often vague or oblique) references to culture and identity. Furthermore, the introduction of Ujamaa in 1967 marked the beginning of a massive nation-building campaign, in which socialism was blended with state nationalism. The question as to whether Ujamaa was a nationalist theory is, however, not all that clear. This becomes obvious from the way in which cultural issues were dealt with. The government stood in opposition to a number of more radical intellectuals, who advocated a more theoretically elaborated concept of 'national culture'. At the same time, however, the national language, Swahili, was constructed along Herderian lines as the expression of deeper cultural and political values. Central actors in the cultural-philosophical debates in Ujamaa Tanzania are the intellectuals, whose ambiguous role places then sometimes on the side of the government, and, at other times, in strong opposition to the government.

Chapter 4 engages with the way in which Ujamaa permeated linguistic research. Linguistics is a way of thinking about language and acting on it. There was a long tradition of language planning and language standardisation in Swahili, and this tradition was continued after independence. This, however, meant that some of the basic premises of colonial linguistics were adopted in postcolonial Tanzanian linguistics. Furthermore, linguistic research after independence was guided by metaphors of 'development' and 'modernisation', and it was moulded in a narrow theoretical frame which privileged certain types of linguistic work: word-coining, dictionary making and so forth. Next to that, linguists were actively engaged in promoting a Swahili identity, as one important aspect of nation building. The new language created through their research efforts should contribute to the development of a new man in a new nation. But the language-and-identity debate proved perilous, because it invoked conceptions of culture that were rooted in history and tradition. This created a conflict between those scholars who saw Swahili as the expression of a new, postcolonial identity and a culture that was being constructed, and other scholars who emphasised the past greatness of Swahili and its connection with Muslim coastal societies.

Chapter 5 turns to Swahili literature. Literature is again seen as a way of handling language, and it is clear that the introduction of Ujamaa has altered the literary profile in Tanzania. First, writing in Swahili was in itself more highly valued than before. Second, literature was seen as an important propaganda asset, and it was explicitly politicised. As a consequence, a number of new genres emerged, and literary production was boosted, both qualitatively and quantitatively. The connection between literature and politics also triggered an interesting debate on aesthetics and ideology, in which similar contrasting positions were taken as in the linguistic debate on language and identity. Traditionalists defended the coastal and Muslim perspective on Swahili, and modernists defended the postcolonial, innovative dimension of Swahili. In the meantime, however, Ujamaa penetrated literature in a more implicit way. A case study of a folk novel shows how Ujamaa became a frame of reference for discussing aspects of one's society. This frame of reference guaranteed the clarity and comprehensibility of the story plot, of the character description, and of certain tropes and attributes used in the story.

Chapter 5 concludes the first part of the study in which I examine the top-down and homogenising direction of the Tanzanian situation. Next, I turn towards language from below. Part 2 addresses 'Swahili and society: the micropolitics of register and repertoire', and contains two chapters.

Chapter 6 examines 'Campus Swahili', a variety I recorded in the 1980s and early 1990s among the academics on University Hill. The intellectuals make use of a very exclusive symbolic resource: 'High' English, which they mix with equally-elaborate 'High' Swahili. In this way, their speech becomes an unambiguous expression of elite consciousness, and thus runs counter to the classless ideals of Ujamaa. Other forms of code-switching were also present in urban Dar es Salaam; what set the academics apart, however, was a set of intra-language differences, the 'quality', so to speak, of the Swahili and English resources they blended. Campus Swahili so becomes an index of early class fragmentation in the Ujamaa system, of an incomplete hegemony for which flawed aspects of language policy were, if not the instant causes, at least critically important factors.

In Chapter 7, I bring on the analysis to a later point in history – 2012. We thus acquire a kind of *post hoc* vantage point from which we can look back on about half a century of Swahilisation in Tanzania, decades after the official end of Ujamaa, at a time in which a city such as Dar es Salaam has been turned into an economic boomtown in East Africa ruled by a neoliberal and business-class government, in which a new economic elite has emerged and articulates new forms of consumer behaviour and identities, and in which parts of that middle class have gone online. The fragmentation observable in Chapter 6 can now be read back as the onset of a tremendously dynamic system of social differentiation and fragmentation, which brings Tanzanian society at least partially in line with almost every other contemporary society: Tanzania has become a hub for globalisation in the margins.

Chapter 8 concludes the book and summarises the various arguments put forward in the different chapters, and attempts to combine them in a refined picture of how state ideology becomes *de facto* hegemonic in the domain of language, but is perceived as non-hegemonic because of the parameters it has used to measure its own hegemony. From a realistic point of view, Ujamaa has firmly permeated, structured and influenced thinking about language and language usage in Tanzania, yet the monolingual and monocultural connotations in the idea of nation building used by Ujamaa politicians ultimately defeated its idealistic aims: to construct a nation which was characterised by singular symbols. Pragmatically, this project was a success – Swahili is the language that defines the country and its citizens. But metapragmatically it failed: these citizens do all sorts of things with Swahili not initially anticipated by the architects of Ujamaa and Swahilisation. The language-political score board of Tanzania, therefore, shows what perhaps can best be seen as an uneasy draw.

1.4 NOTE

1. Dialects can, however, still be used for humorous effects or for typifying characters in television shows and soap operas.

Chapter 2

The empirical study of an African ideology

2.1 A LABORATORY OF POLITICAL IDEOLOGIES

Postcolonial Africa has produced a remarkable amount of political-ideological writings. In the early years, Ghana's Kwame Nkrumah and Guinée's Ahmed Sékou Touré gave shape to African socialism – a readaptation of socialist theories to the context of the newly independent African states, with special attention to the looming problems of neocolonialism and neo-imperialism. African socialism was very influential, but more as an idea than as a doctrine, and one can hardly speak of a formalised and coherent theory of African socialism. Nkrumah's later writings (as well as some of Sékou Touré's) have a strong Leninist ring. But the spectre of political theories using the label of African socialism also includes Nyerere's Ujamaa, the early Harambee philosophy of Kenyatta, Kaunda's Christian-inspired socialism, and even some of Senghor's less esoteric writings. Socialism was also the dominant rhetorical scheme of a number of postcolonial revolutionary movements (for example, Mulelism in Zaïre, but also in the post-revolution writings of Burkina Faso's Thomas Sankara) and in the organisation of prolonged anti-colonial struggles, especially in the Portuguese colonies (Amílcar Cabral, Agostinho Neto, Eduardo Mondlane and Samora Machel were all prolific writers). Finally, a number of independent African states (for example, Congo-Brazzaville, Somalia, Benin, Madagascar, Ethiopia) proclaimed themselves Afro-Marxist states during the decades following independence (see Young 1982: Chapter 2).

A second category of attempts to construct more or less coherent political ideologies is more disparate in bias, and ranges from appeals to ideologically flexible 'pragmatic leadership' to soft forms of liberalism. Most of the writings in this category are nationalist (but that criterion, when taken broadly, also applies to, for example, Nkrumah, Sékou Touré and Nyerere). Some only exist in writing (for example, Nguza Karl i Bond's 'Integrated Nationalism'); others to some extent have become the basis of state organisation in African countries: Mobutu's 'Authenticité' in Zaire (Congo), Arap Moi's 'Nyayoism' in Kenya, Paul Biya's 'Libéralisme Communautaire' in Cameroon.

This is a fascinating phenomenon. All these writings are explicit attempts at formulating political ideologies with their own particular name, and to varying degrees adopting and rejecting ingredients of existing political theories. Their common characteristic is a particularist perspective on political ideology. Most authors agree that it is not enough simply to copy an existing political theory, but that existing theories should first be adapted to, and to some extent modified by, the particular historical, economic and cultural contexts of the African countries to which they should be applied. Many of the politicians involved in the production of these ideologies reject straightforward Western-based classifications of their doctrines as either 'left' or 'right', 'Marxist', 'socialist' or 'liberal'. Paul Biya, for instance, echoes the opinions of many other African politicians, both from the generation of his predecessors (for example, Nyerere) and from his own generation (for example, Sankara), when he states:

> On the basis of this book, some will undoubtedly want to situate our view of the world in this or that ideological camp, by sticking a well-known label on us, or, at least, a fashionable label. We do not dispute the interesting nature of an analysis of our personal views vis-à-vis ideological currents that are well known and have been tried out with varying degrees of success throughout the world. But our aim is not to associate Cameroon to any ideology whatsoever, however fascinating the ideology may be. (Biya 1986: 13; my translation)

The most common line of argument is that the peculiar situation of postcolonial Africa, or of the particular state, calls for peculiar political theories, generated by local people on the basis of insights drawn from the local situation and targetted at a local audience.

Many of these explicit attempts to construct a political ideology occurred *after independence*, as part of the strengthening of the postcolonial state structures and the consolidation of power for the ruling party or individuals. This is at the same time a strong caveat. The proliferation of political ideologies in postcolonial Africa should not lead us to regard ideology as widely shared by the masses of the population. Articulated ideologies are typically the prerogative of the elites; and to the extent that they are successfully spread and implemented, the successes are mostly institutional and restricted to the urban masses. The rural peasantry, largely not integrated in the political process, often couldn't care less. A second caveat, but related to the previous one, is that despite the particularist tendency of most of these writings many of them are in fact written for an international overhearing audience, among whom the author wants to establish some degree of legitimacy as a political thinker, or among whom the author wants to create a favourable image of his or her regime. Thus, many appeals to particularism have a legitimising or apologetic dimension. The former Kenyan president Daniel Arap Moi, for instance, describes his rather heavy-handed approach to state security in these terms:

> In the African context, patience pays, because we have problems galore! Our available resources, capable manpower and proven faith are all in short supply. Working with these fundamental imperfections one is bound to be imperfect; one is bound to make mistakes. Therefore, one must be especially watchful, critical

and unassuming. That means continuous vigilance, flexibility and readjustment. That is pragmatism. (Arap Moi 1986, quoted in Blommaert 1991: 190)

This urge to write canonised versions of new and particularised political ideologies is a remarkable phenomenon. After all, we have grown up with a frame of reference which contained relatively few political -isms, most of them universalist in nature and ambition: capitalism, liberalism, socialism, Marxism-Leninism, Maoism and nationalism (a fuzzy term for non-universalist political theories). We have also learned to think in terms of a very limited set of political systems: democracy, dictatorship, absolutism, totalitarianism, anarchism. From this restricted viewpoint, the attempts of African leaders to create a new -ism, and to write books and papers formalising this doctrine, are at best expressions of optimism about the capacity to create something new. We tend to regard their attempts at formulating new ideologies as reinventions of the wheel, as mostly questionable ambitions to go down in history as creative political thinkers.

Some of the intentions we thus impute to the authors of such new doctrines may indeed be correct. On the other hand, we may also try to look upon these attempts to design new ideologies as genuine expressions of political analyses and perspectives. They may point towards a deep dissatisfaction with the kind of restricted political frame of reference which prevails in our common thought about politics, and they may express the desire to enlarge this repertoire of political-ideological categories with new political -isms that were not invented by Westerners and tried out in Europe before being exported to other parts of the world – a 'chtonic' desire, so to speak, to create an 'autochthonous' doctrine uninfected by the West (cf. Arnaut and Blommaert 2009). From that perspective, the question of how original these writings are is of secondary importance. Central to our concern would be that they are part of a more general process of self-definition in contrast to others. Finding a new -ism, or a new adjective to an existing -ism, expresses the uniqueness of the system thus described, and the fact that even though it may be partly similar to the -isms of other countries, this one is still particular and different. It is a way out of totalising generalisations that are often experienced as oppressive or unfair.

The fact that Africa has produced a remarkable number of such writings may also serve as an index of a more fundamental phenomenon. Through lack of control over 'hard' domains such as economic power, military power or monetary leverage, power and influence are pursued in 'softer', symbolic domains. Africans may be poor economically, politically and militarily, but they may be rich in political ideas. Their politicians may not count as world players in the hard fields, but they count as political thinkers. The field of political theorising and political discourse thus becomes a surrogate for real power, as Ali Mazrui once noted (1978: 72). To some extent, it may also express a belief in the power of ideology to gain control over society. It is not uncommon to read elaborate confessions of mistakes made in the past, followed by a set of new political-ideological principles that must serve to avoid the same mistakes in the future. The temerity of such drastic ideological changes, in which society is redefined almost overnight from, say, a socialist to a market-capitalist system, is often baffling to the Western observer raised in a context of political stability and indoctrinated with an unshakable belief in the basic principles of his or her political system. But it may point precisely towards the relative powerlessness of African leaders, and to the absence of a more or less streamlined coordination of politics, the economy and civil society in their countries.

In this sense, it may well be that the output of political-ideological writings in Africa is a typical Third World phenomenon – a companion of the lack of stability and power facing African politicians. If Africa is a laboratory of political ideologies, that phenomenon in itself may indicate how difficult the struggle for modern statehood is. The ideologies then become a privileged inroad into the deeper ambitions and frustrations of African leaders, and rather than as a misguided expression of personal grandeur they may be read as expressions of the weakness of state systems and their leaders in the face of overwhelming pressures and forces. Every African political ideology, even those written by dictators, could in that sense have the meta-dimension of a resistance ideology, aimed at shifting power from outside to inside their state system.

2.2 AFRICAN SOCIALISM

I will be concerned most with the development of socialist ideologies, since Ujamaa is commonly classified as a form of African Socialism. Ujamaa, the Swahili term for 'familihood', is in fact shorthand for *Ujamaa na Kujitegemea*, commonly translated as 'socialism and self-reliance' and used as such to denote the Tanzanian state ideology. And the strange jump from 'familihood' to 'socialism' instantiates a general issue. The term 'socialist' when applied to several forms of African Socialism may be misleading, for many of these political ideologies do not qualify as 'socialist' in a narrow interpretation of the term. Doom (1980: 149) characterises them as nationalist ideologies using socialist phraseology, but rejecting essential features of socialism. In many cases, the concepts of class and class struggle are rejected, alongside the base-superstructure model and economic determinism (see for example Metz 1982; Young 1982: Chapter 3). More often than not, socialism became merely the dominant lexical and rhetorical instrument of the rulers, while the pre-independence economic and social inequalities remained in place.

Nevertheless, a theoretical core can be distinguished in the various forms of African Socialism. This core revolves around a mystification of African culture history, in which traditional African village life is presented as inherently socialist in nature and structure. Politicians such as Senghor, Mboya and Nyerere repeatedly stressed the fact that precolonial Africans lived in close-knit solidarity-ruled communities in which wealth as well as poverty were equally shared by all, and in which deeply democratic forms of decision making prevailed. Affinities with the tradition of utopian socialism are evident: the precolonial African society was an ideal socialist system. In the preface to *Freedom and Unity/Uhuru na Umoja* (1966), Nyerere summarises this anthropological theory of African Socialism in the key terms of his early socialist conviction:

Despite all the variations, and some exceptions where the institution of domestic slavery existed, African family life was everywhere based on certain practices and attitudes which together meant basic equality, freedom and unity. (Reprinted in Nyerere 1969: 10)

These utopian-socialist practices and attitudes, often formulated on the basis of very fragmentary evidence, were seen as Pan-African, and were in that sense a by-product of Négritude thinking; the mixture of utopian socialism and Négritude influences provides the soil in which several varieties of African Socialism would grow.

Whereas the cultural Négritude had stressed the existence and the commonness of an African 'soul' or 'spirit' and an African mode of thought and expression, African Socialism complemented this Pan-African 'spirit' with a Pan-African natural political system. With its anticolonial bias and its emphasis on self-esteem and authenticity, it became a wonderful instrument for constructing a rhetoric of shared values, experiences and ambitions. At the same time, it also provided a wonderful populist slogan: equality was the natural model of African community organisation, and oppression by the white colonialists – probably experienced on much more objective grounds also – was presented as something that ran counter to basic African values and norms. The emphasis of this African Socialism was on group solidarity as part of the spiritual legacy of African culture.

'Hard' concepts such as class and class struggle, as well as the 'hard' economic bias of doctrinaire socialism, were disqualified as theoretical concepts adapted to and only valid for Western societies that had undergone an industrial revolution. For the largely rural and pre-industrial African societies, these concepts were irrelevant. Thus, some of the crucial ingredients of orthodox socialist theory were moved from the centre of the theory to its periphery, and what remained was a strongly utopian, humanist and populist version of socialism as a state of mind, as a natural attitude of people towards each other and society.

This made African Socialism a user-friendly political ideology. All kinds of existing policies could be covered by the term, which at the same time maintained its populist and egalitarian appeal. For instance, drastic nationalisations of industries were not necessary to have an African Socialist state. Also, an African Socialist society should not be built. It was already there, in the minds of the Africans, and all that was needed was a restoration of these values and attitudes, a decolonisation of the Africans' mind. They had to *feel as if* they lived in a socialist society, and this was basically a rhetorical matter: if politicians repeated often enough that everyone was equal, then everyone would in effect be equal.

Needless to say, this minimalistic and soft interpretation of socialism contained a number of gross idealisations. It shaped an impression of Pan-African spiritual unity that did not match the differences at the level of political system, state structure, and the different colonial legacies of the various states. The common rhetoric often hid important differences in the way in which socialism actually took shape in various countries, and this became clear as soon as politicians attempted to turn rhetoric into reality by forming regional federations. Tanzania, Kenya and Uganda, for instance, appeared to share little beyond their socialist rhetoric as soon as an East-African Federation was attempted. Beyond the level of socialist phraseology, there was ample space for experimentation, 'transitory' policies, or even autocratic rule. In Mazrui's words, the impression of African oneness derives from a Western stereotype of Africa, rather than from any kind of historical or sociological reality:

> ... the African image of their own indivisibility is a reflection of the image of Africa that the outside world has tended to hold – going back to the days when Africans were classified together as 'all backward' or 'all primitive' with little regard for the enormous variations of social and political development in different parts of the continent. It is significant that the reflection has become more real than the original before the mirror of time – and empty European generalizations like 'They are all Africans' are becoming less empty as the Africans themselves, in fellowship, affirm that so they are indeed. (Mazrui 1967a: 52)

The critique of these political systems has often been directed against the gap between rhetoric and political practice. Socialist rhetoric in some countries was used to cover up the massive introduction of foreign capital and international aid; in other words, to enhance monopoly capitalism rather than the appropriation of production forces by the masses. These critiques were often accompanied by calls for more genuine, that is Marxist, analyses of African societies and political processes. Authors such as Shivji (1976) tried to demonstrate that the concepts of class and class struggle were not that irrelevant for an African country such as Tanzania, but that they had to be redefined and adapted to the local conditions. His suggestions were followed by many other authors, and Ahmed Mohiddin, for instance, concluded his comparison of Kenyan and Tanzanian socialism by stating that '[t]he articulated view that a sophisticated or "silent" class struggle has been going on for a while, and possibly now intensified, should not be dismissed as the denouncements of young armchair revolutionaries' (Mohiddin 1981: 217). The same exercise was performed by Wallerstein (1961, 1971), who emphasised the insertion of African states into the world economic and political system and its repercussions on the structure of African societies.

These theoretical and empirical criticisms notwithstanding, African leaders have insisted on the epithet 'socialist' for their regime, and some postcolonial African regimes have been identified by the international community as belonging to the socialist camp. Lumumba's Congo was a case in point, and in spite of Lumumba's essentially moderate socialism, his insistence on non-alignment and the refusal of neocolonial economic ties with Belgium earned him the label of 'commie' among US and Belgian politicians, and led to his assassination (De Witte 1996).

It must be noted here that not all 'socialist' regimes in Africa were thrown into the 'communist' basket. Senghor's regime, for instance, but also that of Kenyatta and a few other African socialist leaders, were almost always treated as reliable Western allies, despite their own emphasis on the socialist nature of their policies. Note also that, certainly in the 1960s, postcolonial leaders had a wealth of choice of 'socialisms'. The Comintern had ceased its operations and the pre-World War

II Soviet hegemony over world socialism had been successfully challenged by the likes of Tito, Ho Chi Minh and Mao Zedong. Less doctrinaire forms of socialism, ranging from Fidel Castro's Cuban socialism through Nehru's social-democratic nationalism to Nasser's version of Pan-Arabism, had evolved successfully from a variety of corners and had gathered in the Non-Aligned Movement. European social democracy was an inspiration as well. More radical leaders eagerly observed Mao Zedong's China, especially because of the overwhelmingly rural and poorly developed character of China, and the Great Proletarian Cultural Revolution of the 1960s and 1970s was a considerable source of inspiration for many African socialists, including, as we shall see, for Nyerere. Radical thinkers in Africa saw in Mao's 'socialism with Chinese characteristics' a template for radical socialism adjusted to African realities, and Okot p'Bitek was not the only intellectual calling for an 'African cultural revolution' (Okot p'Bitek 1973).

Consequently, African Socialism in practice came in a wide range of forms, and the crucial element in the international categorisation of postcolonial African regimes, therefore, seems to have little to do with the type of national policies pursued by African leaders and more with the way in which international alliances were shaped. When these alliances were undesirable from a Western point of view, and when the local politicians used socialist rhetoric, the regimes would almost certainly be qualified as 'anti-Western' and therefore 'pro-communist'. This fluidity and arbitrariness in the classification of African regimes was, of course, partly resolved as soon as genuine Afro-Marxist regimes came to power, which proclaimed full adherence to doctrinaire Marxism-Leninism and established formal ties with communist countries.

African Socialism had some attraction to Western intellectuals, who sometimes saw it as a 'third way' between market capitalism and Soviet-style *Panzerkommunismus*, or who detected a genuine new development strategy in African Socialist texts. The emphasis on Pan-Africanism, anti-imperialism and cultural rehabilitation also struck a sensitive chord with other Third World leaders such as Nasser (who for some time aligned with the Pan-Africanists of Sub-Saharan Africa) and Nehru. The founding fathers of African Socialism also provided a number of classic texts, quoted over and over again because of their idealistic beauty and romantic radicalism. But the ideology (or ideologies) was rarely analysed as an ideology. More often than not, it was seen as just a component of a larger political process of state building, the creation of an economic and political infrastructure, the development of a foreign policy, and so on. Texts were often attributed a programmatic role in this process: in their speeches and booklets, the leaders explained what they were going to do, why, when and how. The details of the ideational and semantic network created in these texts, and the way in which it was being picked up by other groups in society, were rarely the object of an in-depth scrutiny in their own right. A number of questions about African Socialism have therefore remained unexplored, despite the huge amount of writings on the subject.

2.3 IDEOLOGY

When analysing political ideologies, one is often confronted with the dual nature of the concept of 'ideology' itself (see Blommaert 2005: Chapter 7). On the one hand, people talk about '*an* ideology', as a complex of ideas, mostly codified in books or speeches, and bearing a name mostly ending with -ism. This is one meaning of 'ideology', and when I refer to Ujamaa as a political ideology, this is the meaning I use. Another meaning of 'ideology' refers to the semiotic process of instilling ideas about society in the minds of members of that society. 'Ideology' in its first meaning is often just part of the process denoted by that second meaning of 'ideology'. Ideology in the semiotic sense uses ideological materials such as the writings of a great leader, but mostly complemented by numerous other forms of expression of the same basic messages. At the same time, any attempt to diffuse *an* ideology must make use of these ideological semiotic processes. It must seek to create *hegemony* for the ideas, values and meanings contained in the ideology, and this hegemony is nothing else but the outcome of a successful semiotic process.

In order to structure this potentially confusing dualism a number of distinctions are in order. It is clear that my ultimate target is *an* ideology in the first meaning of the term: Ujamaa. But I study this ideology by looking into a number of aspects of the process of ideology in the second sense: ways in which Ujamaa has penetrated or influenced other areas of social life. Terminologically, this may be clarified by distinguishing between various objects of study. The study of an ideology through ideological processes involves *formal and informal objects*. The formal objects are the codified, canonised texts of the leader(s). They represent the dogma in all its shapes and variations, and they are the sources to which other actors in the process refer. The informal objects have to do with the transformation of the dogma into various other discourses and representations; in other words, with the various ways in which the dogma is handled, translated, applied and transformed in everyday practices. These informal objects may fall apart in various categories:

1. The way in which the dogma is being used and applied in the institutions and structures of society (for example, the way in which it is being put into practice in educational programmes, in legislation, in popular mobilisation).
2. The way in which it is being used by secondary communicators such as the media, artists, intellectuals and so on.
3. The way in which it is being used in popular consciousness and popular political action.

The formal and informal objects are rarely perfectly identical, in the sense that the informal handling of the political ideology is rarely 100 per cent orthodox. But those in power will benefit from keeping the various versions of the ideology as similar as possible, and from erasing or denouncing interpretations of the dogma that are all too deviant from theirs. This process of trying to keep the various ideological objects as close together as possible is what I understand by hegemony. Hegemony stands for the way in which the formal ideology is superimposed on all informal ideological expressions as the single valid interpretation.

Two further qualifications are in order. First, in studying ideological processes the connection between symbols and symbolic practices on the one hand and power relationships on the other is crucial for understanding the nature of the process. This connection, advocated in John Thompson's work, involves a selective view: symbols are only ideological inasmuch as they are connected to power relations (cf. Thompson 1994: 135; cf. also Barthes 1957). There are no intrinsically ideological symbols, all symbols having the potential of serving ideological purposes in certain circumstances. Although this aspect will not be elaborated further in this study, I hold ideologies and the symbols they use to be non-autonomous. Ideologies are embedded in the socio-economic structure of society, not merely in the Althusserian sense of superstructure, but as aspects of what E. P. Thompson called 'experience' (Thompson [1963] (1991); see also Kaye 1984: Chapter 6). Experience indicates that power relations are not just economic but also social phenomena, observable not only in objective facts but also in subjective expressions. People actively experience power relations and weave a web of perceptions, opinions, attitudes, explanations, beliefs and so on around their experience. Therefore, this web is not just a reflection of material relationships between social actors but an agentive force: it is the human, subjective factor in power relationships.

Second, ideology is also a domain of conscious political action. It was Gramsci who identified the phenomenon of hegemony as an answer to the question as to why the economy, being the principal actor in history, could not in itself bring about revolutions and other political changes. Paraphrasing Gramsci, people have to know and understand the conditions in which they live in order to be able to act upon them (Gramsci 1971; cf. Bellamy 1994: 33; see also Ransome 1992). Hegemony exists in the development of a world-view by a group wanting to acquire or maintain power. This world-view legitimises the power relationship, and has to be propagated and imposed on those who are subject to that power. If hegemony fails, the power relationship may be endangered; if it works, the power relationship will be maintained and people will be successfully mobilised for the political purposes of those in power.

As will become clear throughout the book, the picture I present is that of a relatively successful case of hegemony. The Tanzanian leaders have succeeded in establishing, at least for some time, a formidable degree of agreement about the political and economic aims of their government among their citizens. There are several reasons for that, and some will be discussed in the following chapters. But one important factor contributing to the success of the Tanzanian state ideology is the near-monopoly the state (that is, the party and the government) had over all instruments that could be used to massify their ideology. Being the sole political power in a monofocal political system, both historically (the struggle for independence) and contemporarily (the postcolonial state), the Tanzanian leadership had full control over all kinds of political communication channels, and could mobilise substantial material means to disseminate its views and programmes.

They formed the undisputed centre of politics, and there were no contenders for that status.

2.4 CONCLUDING REMARKS

African political ideologies, as an essential ingredient of modern African politics, are historically contingent phenomena which crystallise at the crossroads of an African society (or a complex set of societies) and a modern state structure. They represent attempts at grasping the realities of the postcolonial African situation, at getting power over the conditions under which these states have to function, and at influencing them in the sense of structuring power relations in ways that can be legitimised by reference to the ideology. They cannot be seen as mirror images of current or past Western -isms; on the contrary, even when they explicitly credit Western -isms their introduction in a postcolonial African state is the outcome of local decisions, judged to be an answer to local questions and needs. The phenomenon of new ideologies itself teaches us something about perceptions of local socio-economic, cultural and political conditions. It is a feature of the struggle to come to terms with a task that carries hybridity in itself: to find a suitable modern state organisation in which an African society can be moulded, and which can at the same time provide maximum guarantees for stability and social and political cohesion, and provide optimal conditions for socio-economic development – that is, change.

Investigations of these ideologies cannot confine themselves to a study of the doctrinaire texts, the formal objects as I called them. In order to assess their impact, and thus to fathom the way in which they fulfilled (or failed to fulfil) the function for which they were conceived, one has to investigate the historical background of their origin, the process of their introduction, and the way in which they became hegemonic in other, informal objects. All this must be done in a way that emphasises the historiographical and reconstructive purpose of such a study.

In the next chapter, I will first sketch the cultural philosophy (often implicitly) promoted in Ujamaa. Ujamaa placed great emphasis on the humanistic dimension of development, and thus contained a view of man and of society that has received little attention in scholarship. I will mainly deal with formal objects, namely Nyerere's basic doctrinaire texts. The following chapters, however, will focus mainly upon informal objects, such as scientific texts, literature and everyday speech. The focus in those chapters will be on how Ujamaa became a frame of reference for Tanzanian people – literate elites, in my restricted analysis, by means of which they thought and talked about their society. I hope to demonstrate in those chapters how Ujamaa became 'naturalised' to some extent and in some spheres of social life, in such a way that it could serve as a rhetorical, semantic and symbolic backdrop that guaranteed clarity and provided shared background knowledge and a common vocabulary among Tanzanians. As such, the naturalisation of Ujamaa provided some of the conditions for a cohesive society, or a 'nation' as some would prefer to call it.

On the other hand, the success of the naturalisation process can be called into question by other types of evidence. When the everyday speech of intellectuals is examined, non-hegemonic or anti-hegemonic features such as English code-switching appear abundantly, and a different picture of the pervasiveness of Ujamaa emerges than that provided by analyses of science and literature, where the hegemonic process appears to have been outstandingly successful. The final impression of this exercise is ambiguous: Ujamaa ideology seems to have been hegemonic in some forms of practice, but less so in others, although both complexes of practices are performed by the same social formation (and, in my data, often even by the same individuals).

In sketching this picture, it must be kept in mind that we are dealing with hybrid disciplinary objects. The evidence is textual, but the disciplinary practice by means of which the evidence is approached carries traces from historiography as much as from anthropology, ethnography or sociolinguistics. The object of analysis changes accordingly, and shifts in status from historical object to sociolinguistic object or anthropological object. The result may be a quite idiosyncratic blend of methods and concepts, highly eclectic and sometimes less than respectful for existing mainstream approaches. But I have found that investigating ideologies means investigating a wide range of social practices that cannot be reduced to simple categories or schemes, and that have to be fed back continuously to other practices, contextual features, structural details and so on in order to retain their informative value. If ideology permeates the totality of social life and politicises social life, as Gramsci (1971) suggested, then the complexity of social life should be mirrored in a study of ideology.

Part 1 Swahili and the state: the macropolitics of language

Chapter 3

The cultural philosophy of Ujamaa

3.1 INTRODUCTION

It is common practice to discuss Tanzanian politics (and Ujamaa in particular) in ways that put great emphasis on the role of Julius Nyerere, the first President of Tanzania and founder of its ruling party, TANU (Tanganyika African National Union). To some extent, this is justified. Nyerere was the towering figure in Tanzanian postcolonial political history. He was by all standards a charismatic leader, whose speeches and writings (an impressive oeuvre in itself) gave shape and direction to almost any meaningful political development in his country. He dominated the political process in Tanzania from the 1950s – when TANU started to become the single most powerful independence movement – until 1985 when he voluntarily stepped down from the presidency, with 1967, the year of the Arusha Declaration in which he codified his Ujamaa doctrine, as the pinnacle of his power.

Discussing Nyerere cannot be avoided, and his name will appear many times in this chapter. Still, Tanzanian politics, including the way in which Ujamaa ideology came into being and gave shape to the present-day Tanzanian society, is not the story of Nyerere alone. True, he was the one who produced the crucial texts, the dogma, or, as I called it in Chapter 2, the formal objects of the ideology. But as soon as these texts were produced they gave rise to numerous informal objects. They became the topic of an exegesis by a variety of groups in society, each of which defended its own political agenda and interpreted Nyerere's speeches and writings according to their own preferences. The story of Ujamaa is as much the story of these varying and often conflicting interpretations as it is the story of the texts themselves. The texts themselves were, as all texts are, vague at certain points, ambiguous at others, and therefore presenting Ujamaa as a dogma articulated in the political oeuvre of its main architect would be misleading. The dialectic of conflicting interpretations of Nyerere's texts forms an axis of interpretation, which is not necessarily linked to stable and identifiable groups in society. The poles of this axis are formed by conservative and radical interpretations, but those who voice them need not always be the same ones. It is not the case, for instance, that the higher cadres of TANU were always the conservatives, and intellectuals always the radicals.

What do we understand by the labels 'conservative' and 'radical' in the context of interpretations of Nyerere's texts? First, it has to be understood that Ujamaa was a policy aimed at changing the country from top to bottom. It was, in other words, a project for revolutionary transition. 'Radical' interpretations of this are the easiest ones to identify. They use a more or less orthodox socialist or Marxist-Leninist and/or Maoist frame of interpretation, and hence a profoundly different theory of revolutionary transformation than those contained in pre-Arusha rhetoric by Nyerere. They will use a different epistemology, a different perspective on the stages of the transition and on the forces involved in that process than usually contained in the rhetoric of African Socialism, of which Ujamaa is one particular outgrowth. 'Moderate' interpretations, in turn, adhere to the tenets of African Socialism and neglect theoretically 'pure' socialism. Their view is at the same time more idealist (in the Marxist sense of the term) and pragmatic, and their sources of theoretical inspiration can be highly diverse.

The dialectic of those two groups of interpretations displays a historical development. In the struggle for independence and in the first five years of independence, the 'conservative', African Socialist interpretations of Ujamaa dominate. Nyerere was a convinced anti-communist and Marxism-Leninism was rejected by Nyerere in the early 1960s as just another Western ideology alien to Africa. Thus the focus was put on the Africanisation of society (intra-nationally) and Pan-Africanism (internationally). The 'radical' type of interpretations arose and grew stronger from the mid-1960s onwards, and a number of influences contributed to their growth. The violent Zanzibar Revolution of 1963-4 was a first influence, as it brought to power a government which, in the eyes of the West, looked Marxist-Leninist. Through the union with mainland Tanganyika into the United Republic of Tanzania in 1964, it rehabilitated more radical socialism as part of the political landscape (as least rhetorically), and it brought in some support from countries such as the German Democratic Republic. Second, the intensifying relations with the People's Republic of China since the mid-1960s, during the intense phase of the Chinese Cultural Revolution and culminating in the construction in 1970 of the TAZARA Railway connecting Dar es Salaam and Lusaka in Zambia, also granted more respectability to orthodox-socialist views of society. And, third, the first decade of independence witnessed the emergence of a new class of intellectuals and cadres, which will be discussed in greater detail below.

All this crystallised around the 1967 Arusha Declaration (*Azimio la Arusha*), the canon of Ujamaa. The text itself paid enough lip service to radical views of society and attempted to generate a similar kind of revolutionary energy as Mao's Cultural Revolution, by which it was clearly inspired. But, as will be explained in greater detail below, it conspicuously avoided any use of the term Marxism-Leninism, and remained vague and unorthodox on certain crucial points. But it certainly allowed for radical interpretations of Ujamaa as an African version of Marxism-Leninism and created hopes in that direction among a growing group of intellectuals in Tanzania and elsewhere.

The Arusha Declaration created a watershed, and we can talk about the 'pre-Arusha' and 'post-Arusha' developments with some confidence, because the

Declaration defined a sharp historical discontinuity – a revolutionary moment. The Declaration itself, however, was the product of a gradual process of reformulations of Ujamaa and socialism (see Pratt 1976). Nyerere himself stressed heavily the continuity of his thoughts on socialism. A Swahili booklet on Ujamaa published in 1969 has a TANU text of 1962 (called 'Ujamaa') as its first chapter, followed by the Arusha Declaration itself (Nyerere 1969: Chapters 1 and 2). Apart from clear statements on the socialist nature of Tanzanian society, the main innovations in the Arusha Declaration and subsequent policy documents were the emphasis on nation building and on an increased control of social and economic life by the state. In the wake of the Arusha Declaration, Tanzania embarked on a post-independence nationalism, in which the target would be the total hegemony of TANU and its Ujamaa doctrine.

In the remainder of this chapter, I will discuss a number of aspects of Ujamaa which have a bearing on the relationship between ideology and language. These aspects are, first, the question of whether Ujamaa must be seen as a socialist ideology rather than a nationalist ideology (see section 3.2), second, the question of a National Culture (see section 3.3) and the role of Swahili (see section 3.4), and, finally, the role of the intellectual elites in the process of nation building, and in particular the way in which they engaged in contests with the government for ideological leadership (see section 3.5).

3.2 SOCIALISM OR NATIONALISM?

Was Ujamaa a socialist theory? Or was it a socialist-flavoured form of nationalism? These questions are not easy to answer. In the first place, Ujamaa promoters self-identified with both labels. They called their TANU party a 'nationalist' party or movement, and saw Ujamaa as a socialist revolutionary programme. When the party was renamed in 1977, it became CCM – *Chama cha Mapinduzi*, the 'party of the revolution'. So an analysis of Ujamaa in terms as abstract as 'socialism' and 'nationalism' can only proceed by using comparative yardsticks. The ones I will use here are doctrinaire socialism or Marxism-Leninism on the one hand, and current European forms of nationalism (as known in Flanders and Catalonia, for instance) on the other hand.

A lot has been written on the socialist qualities of Ujamaa, and the conclusions of most authors are unambiguous: when Ujamaa is measured against doctrinaire socialism, then it certainly does not deserve to be called orthodox socialism, let alone communism (see, for example, Mulei 1972; Mohiddin 1981; Metz 1982). Although the Arusha Declaration offers more precise statements on the socialist structure of society than previous texts on socialism, the basic thrust of pre-Arusha socialism is unmistakably still there. The rhetoric is surely more radical, but the text itself – as well as post-Arusha statements by Nyerere and other leaders – remains conspicuously silent when it comes to defining basic socialist analytical concepts such as class or class struggle. The socialist dimension, if any, is to be situated at the level of economic policy. The Declaration introduced a thoroughgoing economic transformation, in the sense that the country would basically withdraw from the economic world market and focus its economy on national self-reliance ('*Kujitegemea*').

Another socialist element in the Declaration is the increased power of the party and the state. From 1967 onwards, TANU and its state apparatus become the near-exclusive players in the field of economy, banking and trade, and the exploitation of natural resources (including tourism). The state apparently reinforces its legitimacy by reinforcing the state (a process already noted by Wallerstein 1961). And, finally, Tanzania, by its emphasis on non-alignment and support for the liberation struggles in other African countries, effectively ended up on the left-hand side of the international political spectrum. Although the Western powers kept huge embassies in Dar es Salaam, the splendour and the prominent location of embassies of countries such as the German Democratic Republic, China, Bulgaria and the Soviet Union testified to the importance of socialist states in Tanzania's foreign relations.

These elements, together with the distinct increase of Leninist and Maoist influences in the rhetoric of some party leaders and in their proletarian appearance (Nyerere wore the simple and uniform-like *Kaunda suit*, similar to and probably modelled onto the *Mao suit*), allowed for a revolutionary reading of the Arusha Declaration. The Soviets, for instance, noted with approval the shift to the left which was codified in the Declaration, and they gave Nyerere the benefit of the doubt when it came to socialist purity. On the other hand, nobody could have missed how carefully Nyerere and other prominent party and government officials avoided qualifying the Arusha Declaration as a Marxist-Leninist programme. The term Marxism-Leninism is as good as absent in texts and speeches on Ujamaa. Nowhere is it used as an epithet or a qualification of the Declaration, and neither is the term socialism. The contrary is also true: Marxism-Leninism nor socialism are not used in contrast to Ujamaa. The authors of the main Ujamaa texts remain silent about it. Another striking observation is the fact that after the union with Zanzibar, the ultra-left was purged from the party and the state apparatuses (cf. Mulei 1972; Tordoff and Mazrui 1972; Shivji 2008). Marxism was launched as a rhetorical frame and as a pattern of outward appearances for state officials, and it was eagerly adopted by parts of civil society, but it was not given any leeway inside the state power structure. This left a space of ambiguity which, as we shall see, dominated much of the debate after the Arusha Declaration.

Ujamaa itself, however, as a term and as a trope, was constantly emphasised as the Tanzanian innovation in the field of socialist theory. Ujamaa, though used since the early days of TANU, had acquired a new referential meaning through the Arusha Declaration. It now covered the specific policies introduced in the Declaration and subsequent major policy documents, and it stood for the new model of society projected in the Declaration. The term Ujamaa is used in an autonomous way, without positive or negative reference to other political categorial terms such as Marxism-Leninism or socialism. Part of the reason for this must be sought in the history of the socialist strategy in Tanzania. Ever since the early days, TANU (and Nyerere in particular) had stressed the particularism of African and Tanzanian politics, and the fact that Western concepts and models were not completely applicable to their society.

In that sense, the Arusha Declaration continues the tradition of political-ideological particularism, a kind of Négritude social democracy, of TANU and Nyerere.

Another part of the reason for this may lie in the pragmatism and the diplomatic skills of Nyerere and his associates. They must have been aware of the negative, possibly dangerous, impact caused by an alignment of Ujamaa with communism. Although the Zanzibar Revolution has been understood as the first communist revolution in East Africa, the days of the Afro-Marxist regimes had not yet arrived, and the proclamation of a policy programme that paid too much lip service to Marxism-Leninism would have closed the doors to Western allies and supporters. And, finally, other reasons may lie in the internal balance of power within the party hierarchy and its wider audience. Put under pressure by an ultra-left wing minority of intellectuals and party cadres, a shift to the left was a move that could rally some support. On the other hand, the moderate, African Socialist majority could not be antagonised. Ujamaa was the formula which carefully balanced moderate and left-wing tendencies, and which could muster maximum political and popular support. As a result, Ujamaa became known as a political theory in its own right, classified as a left-wing ideology, but devoid of the geopolitical connotations given to Marxism-Leninism (and to a lesser degree to socialism). Because of its African particularist bias, it also became a non-imitable political system, which could only be adopted by other parts of the Third World if it was thoroughly adapted to the local conditions. This particularist dimension made it a non-threatening ideology with very little chance of exportation and with no ambitions to become the revolutionary philosophy of oppressed Third World societies.

In contrast to the issue of socialist orthodoxy, the nationalist characteristics of Ujamaa are relatively poorly documented. Many authors simply adopt the Tanzanian self-qualification of Ujamaa as a form of nationalism.[1] The evidence used in favour of this qualification is mostly the element of *Kujitegemea*, economic self-reliance. It is seen as a form of economic autarky and hence as a nationalist economic programme.

However, the issue is not all that clear. There are good reasons to suggest that Kujitegemea was in fact quite the opposite of nationalism, and to see it as an economic measure inspired by Pan-Africanism. As we know, Nyerere was an ardent supporter of Pan-Africanism, and efforts towards regional or subregional integration have marked his entire career (Shivji 2008: 69).[2] The view he held on the matter can be summarised as follows: independence must mean the abolition of all forms of dependencies that characterised the colonial period. Thus, African states should be independent monetarily and economically. No neocolonial economic (or aid) relations should be allowed. But economic independence could not be gained by individual African states alone, since all of their national economies were colonial in structure, and thus oriented towards the former colonial powers. Therefore, African states should strive towards greater economic and political cooperation and possibly unification, either into a 'United States of Africa' (Nyerere [1963] 1975), or into subregional unions. The prerequisite was that each African state would have an economy in which foreign influence had been minimised. Kujitegemea was just that: the abolition of all forms of economic dependency of Tanzania from the outside world.

Nyerere appeared to be determined to set the example for the rest of Africa, despite the fact that realistic prospects for African integration had already been lost in the early 1960s. The Congo Crisis of 1960–1 (the first great international crisis to hit the newly independent African continent) had brought the Cold War to Africa and had divided Africa into two camps: a moderate, pro-Western camp led by statesmen such as Fulbert Youlou and Félix Houphouët-Boigny, and a more radical Pan-Africanist and non-alignment camp led by Nkrumah, Sékou-Touré and Nasser. But Nyerere could not be discouraged by these events. The union with Zanzibar in 1964 was largely symbolic. The two small islands of Zanzibar and Pemba could not be said to be a major new economic asset for Tanzania. Furthermore, the socialist inclination of the Zanzibar leaders led to severe diplomatic difficulties with Western countries. To Nyerere, it was an exemplary case of African subregional integration. Furthermore, it represented a break in the colonial map of Africa: here was an African political entity that had been created by Africans themselves, and not by Europeans.

Despite the huge disproportion in size and economic weight between Zanzibar and mainland Tanzania, Zanzibar secured a relatively large and powerful presence in the Tanzanian government and parliament. It was clearly not a case therefore of usurpation or re-colonisation, but a fair and equitable agreement between two previously independent states. Furthermore, coinciding with the shift towards Ujamaa, Nyerere sought closer contacts with Kenya and Uganda, and tried to unite the two countries into an East-African Union. But although Kenyatta of Kenya and Obote of Uganda both nominally professed to socialism, they were never really enthusiastic about a union with a state which had by then become stigmatised as being a bit too socialist.

It is not implausible to see Kujitegemea in the light of these attempts towards subregional unification. Nyerere wanted to prepare his country for any kind of African (sub)regional integration. He wanted to shape its economy in such a way that there would be no burden of international debt nor commitments to foreign trade partners, both of which would jeopardise the projected union with other African states. This also explains the radical non-alignment in foreign policy pursued by the Tanzanians. Although they were sought after as preferential trade partners by countries from the Soviet bloc and by China, they consistently refused to ally themselves openly with one or another power bloc. In that sense, Kujitegemea could only be interpreted as a nationalist strategy in a Pan-African sense, but not in a strictly national sense. Nyerere was a nationalist in as far as Africa, not Tanzania, was concerned (a point strongly emphasised by Shivji 2008). This does not mean that Kujitegemea was *not* a nationalist measure. It may have been nationalist, but it was not exclusively nationalist, it was much more than that.

So what does the qualification of nationalism pertain to? Most texts use it strictly in the sense of 'liberation nationalism': a collocation between 'struggle for independence' and 'nationalism'. Anticolonial movements in the Third World are seen as nationalist movements, according to this interpretation of the term 'nationalism', because they fought for *national* independence from foreign dominance. But the nation, as noted by Mazrui (1967b), is something quite awkward in this context. It is not the historically imagined congruence between a people and a territory central to European nationalist conceptions, but an entity of which the historical arbitrariness is well understood. There were no historical nation-states in Africa that had become colonies, all colonies having been a coincidental agglomerate of various ethnic groups and political units on a territory which was defined on the basis of all sorts of criteria except that of ethnic, cultural or linguistic homogeneity. The common bond used by Africans in their struggle for independence was their joint colonial experience as oppressed people, ruled by a minority of foreigners. The notion of a 'nation' used in this sort of nationalism is hardly comparable to that currently used in, for example, Flanders, Québec, Brittany or Catalonia. It has a history that begins with colonisation, the moment at which *foreigners* defined them as a unified people belonging to one specific colonial territory (ibid.: 6–7).

So if this liberation nationalism is a nationalism at all, it is certainly not the kind of nationalism professed by the Flemish, Catalans and other 'modern' nationalist movements. That the issues central to the liberation struggle in Tanzania were not strictly national can be judged from Tanzania's unswerving commitment to liberation movements elsewhere in Africa. Tanzania hosted FRELIMO cadres and fighters from Mozambique and SWAPO cadres from Namibia during the liberation wars, and for many years it harboured ANC militants in training facilities outside Morogoro and Bagamoyo. The commitment was not only to Tanzanian liberation but to the liberation of all Africans. If 'patriotism' is a more neutral term, devoid of ethnic or cultural connotations, then Ujamaa can certainly be called a patriotic ideology. It contained an appeal to all the citizens of the country to contribute their share to the burden of constructing a new society. Tanzania was the main target of political action, although as noted above, this in itself had a Pan-Africanist dimension. If Tanzanians were called upon to be patriotic, this meant that they should support the cause of independence of all Africans or indeed of all oppressed peoples. Tanzania was only one piece of a larger part of the world, and when one would say that Ujamaa was an inward-looking ideology, then surely the Tanzanians' horizon was very broad.

There is one way in which the label of nationalism could be secured for a political ideology such as Ujamaa, and it would consist of an equation between nationalism and all forms of political-ideological particularism. In that sense, many postcolonial African political ideologies would qualify as nationalist theories, to the extent that they claim to present a political model which is rooted in African traditions and customs, not copied from existing Western models, and as such not transferable to other times and places. Political-ideological particularism (even when it is universalist in ambition) would in this definition be intrinsically nationalist. In the case of Ujamaa, this dimension is clearly there, and it would allow for a qualification of nationalist ideology were it not that the Pan-African bias of Ujamaa (as well as that of many other postcolonial ideologies) clashes with the received view that nationalism and internationalism are opposites, or if they are not, then they are at least sequentially ordered phases in a political process. National and international causes are narrowly intertwined in Ujamaa, and they create a picture strongly different from those of modern European nationalisms.

3.3 THE NATIONAL CULTURE

Ujamaa was sensed to transform the country culturally. Yet the history of the cultural project of Ujamaa – in my view one of its most crucial aspects – remains largely unexplored. It is unquestionably a complex domain, touching on issues such as self-definition and its relationship to power. Moreover, the cultural philosophy of Ujamaa has not been the object of codification or dogmatisation. In Nyerere's own writings, and in those of other main figures, it has to be read between the lines. It is, as are many other things in Ujamaa, something that crystallises in the informal objects: the writings of a variety of individuals, whose interpretations of it vary according to the position they take with regard to Ujamaa in general. The major policy texts only serve as the point of departure here. The architects of Ujamaa were very well aware of the importance of culture. One of the core elements of Nyerere's rhetoric since the inception of TANU was the emphasis on *man*. Socialism was only partially a matter of altering the economic relations in society; more than anything else it was a way of life, a belief similar to religious belief, and an affair of the heart rather than of the brain. A socialist society would grow as soon as people started thinking and feeling in a socialist way. Hence, society should not only be reformed in its surface structures but also in its deeper layers; society should be altered *culturally*, in relation to people's consciousness and outlooks on life.

Yet culture was a delicate subject. In its traditional meaning (culture as a traditional way of life and as a set of inherited ideas, customs, values and so on) it could be interpreted as something typical of ethnic groups. A discussion of the role of (this kind of) culture in society would then inevitably become a discussion of ethno-cultural pluralism, and this had to be avoided at all costs. 'Tribalism', or ethnic consciousness in general, was one of the main enemies of Ujamaa, and TANU had always combated the British policies of multiracialism in which such sentiments were fostered and made into political principles. Whenever Nyerere sketched his idea of a classless society he would not only refer to the absence of social class distinctions, but also to the absence of *kabila*, ethnic groups and affiliations. The dogma has it that the question: *Wewe kabila gani?* ('Which ethnic group do you belong to?') has altogether disappeared from the Tanzanians' repertoire.[3] To Nyerere, the concept of ethnic group was linked to that of *ubaguzi*, 'discrimination'. As long as ethnic consciousness would continue to exist, forms of discrimination and nepotism would exist. National unity could only be attained when people forgot their old distinctions and took on a new common identity, that of the Tanzanian *mwananchi* ('countryman, citizen'). Therefore, despite its frequent use in speeches and writings, 'culture' was never really spelt out; it was taken to be part of the more general concept of ideology. But in practice, ideology could be reduced to policy: ideological training consisted of the study of the TANU dogmas, summarised in introductory course books. Cultural unity, therefore, was sensed to be a companion of political unity.

The picture is thus somewhat ambiguous. On the one hand, 'culture' is an important ingredient of the rhetoric of Africanhood, freedom and independence. On the other hand, it is carefully avoided in the definition of the process of revolutionary transformation because of its ethnic connotations, and it is assumed to be a full ingredient of socialism as a way of life. But in spite of this ambiguity and vagueness, national culture was a recurrent element in a variety of post-Arusha developments. I shall now examine some specific usages in some detail.

Culture or ideology: Elimu ya Kujitegemea

Being a former teacher himself, Nyerere was inclined to attribute a central role to teaching and educating people in the process of revolutionary transformation. *Maendeleo maana yake ni maendeleo ya watu* ('the meaning of development of the development of people') or *shabaha ni mwanadamu* ('the target is man') were common tropes in many of his speeches and writings. He believed that the first index of real independence would not be the industrial output or the growth in per capita gross national product, but rather the increase in literacy, schooling and the political consciousness of the people. Like in many socialist-inclined new states, therefore, massive efforts were spent in the elaboration of the education system and in mass literacy campaigns in Tanzania. The results in that field were truly astonishing. The primary schools' intake rose dramatically even before the Arusha Declaration. In the wake of Arusha, the education system was thoroughly transformed through the unique *Elimu ya Kujitegemea* project ('Education for Self-Reliance'), launched in March 1967.

Education for Self-Reliance reformed the hierarchical structure of education which Tanzania had inherited from the colonial system. From then on, primary schooling would be a self-contained programme offered to all Tanzanians. In that programme they would learn the basic skills required for living and functioning in an Ujamaa society. They would learn to read and write, to use basic mathematics, to become politically aware, and to work the land.[4] The primary school programme would be taught in Swahili. The idea was to dissociate primary schooling from its status as a preparatory phase for further education, and make it a complete form of schooling in its own right. Thus, children who finished primary school would be equipped with everything they needed to live the lives of 90 percent of their countrymen: that of farmers in an Ujamaa-organised country. Adults who had missed their education due to the restricted entrance to primary schools during the colonial days would be offered adult education. Adult Education Year was declared in 1970, and mass education schemes were developed. During the National Literacy Campaign (1972–5), an estimated 5.2 million Tanzanians enrolled for literacy courses, and approximately 2 million people passed the literacy test (Hall 1975; Kassam 1979).

Under Education for Self-Reliance only the best pupils, selected though national examinations, would go on to secondary education. The secondary education system, as well as post-secondary education at higher institutes and at the university, would remain as good as intact, including the fact that teaching would be carried out in English.

Education for Self-Reliance was inspired by economic motives as well as by ideological ones. On the economic side, TANU felt that the existing system of education placed too much emphasis on the post-primary levels of education, which in practice were only accessible to a small minority of the people. Millions of Tanzanian Shillings were wasted, as the leaders saw it, on elite education and the teaching of topics that had little or no value for the lives of Tanzanian citizens. Therefore, Education for Self-Reliance shifted the balance in favour of primary education. Tanzania's limited resources would from then on be used for the masses and not for the elites. On the ideological side, Education for Self-Reliance was a classical attempt towards hegemony. The new education system (which bore some resemblance to Paulo Freire's consciencisation theory) would be one of the main vehicles for transmitting Ujamaa values to the citizens, and to rally them behind the targets set by the government and the party. The new education project (including the adult education and mass literacy campaigns) was set explicitly against the background of nation building. Being the national language and the 'language of liberation', Swahili naturally was to be the medium in which this education programme would be implemented.

The curriculum gave ample space to political education, and even basic literacy classes had an ideological dimension. Nyerere believed, and expressed in many speeches and articles, that people cannot be developed, they can only develop themselves, and in order for this to happen they should be able to understand their own predicament and the goals of Ujamaa policy. Literacy was a prerequisite for participating in the discussion of crucial policy papers in the now-literate Tanzanian political system. This certainly had its effect. Tanzanian citizens were in general more politically conscious and knowledgeable than many other Africans. Although the degree of impact should not be overestimated (in the domain of literacy for instance), Tanzanians at least knew aspects of their national history and of the history of their ruling party, and they had learned to see the world through the looking glass of their political leaders. Terms like *beberu* ('imperialist'), *bepari* ('capitalist') and *ubaguzi* ('discrimination') were household words used not only by the educated or politically interested elites. Lwaitama, in assessing the impact of Nyerere on Tanzanian society, states:

> A young *chipukizi* ('pioneer') in Tanzania is likely to know more about what is going on in South Africa, Nicaragua and Palestine than most children of her age in Britain for instance. All these things are not visible but they will be, should Uncle Sam do a Grenada on Tanzania! These Nyerere inheritances will certainly make Tanzania very expensive to rule in a completely right-wing way. (Lwaitama 1988: 24–5)

So in the eyes of Lwaitama and others, some degree of unity among Tanzanians was created through Education for Self-Reliance. The unity consists of a widely shared knowledge of how Tanzanian society holds together and how it relates to the rest of the world. The unity thus sought and attained in the Tanzanian education system is *political*: all Tanzanians have a common political background and can be rallied behind patriotic endeavours such as the war against Idi Amin or the fight against apartheid in South Africa. But has this created a new *man* in cultural terms? To some extent, but not entirely. The ideological homogenisation attempted in the education policy avoided culture as an issue.

Socialism and African culture

A consistent element in the development of post-independence politics in Tanzania is the association of socialism with aspects of African traditional culture. As mentioned in Chapter 2, socialism was seen as part of the African legacy of the newly independent states by some leaders. Reflecting on the meaning of socialism during his relief from office in 1962, Nyerere associated the communalism he saw as central to a socialist system with African tradition:

> For when a society is so organized that it cares about individuals, then, provided he is willing to work, no individual within that society should worry about what will happen to him tomorrow if he does not hoard wealth today. Society itself should look after him, or his widow, or his orphans. This is exactly what traditional African society succeeded in doing. Both the 'rich' and the 'poor' individual were completely secure in African society . . . That was socialism. That is socialism. (Nyerere [1962] 1975: 512)

Therefore, socialist education should be aimed at rediscovering these basic African values:

> Our first step, therefore, must be to re-educate ourselves; to regain our former attitude of mind. In our traditional African society we were individuals within a community. We took care of the community, and the community took care of us. We neither needed nor wished to exploit our fellow men. (Ibid.: 513)

In this line of argument, capitalism is defined as un-African, as something that was imported by the Europeans when they colonised Africa. Capitalism here stands not only for a certain mode of production of wealth – with it comes a cluster of concepts and phenomena absent from African traditional societies, such as class concepts, individual ownership of land, forms of exploitation, meritocracy instead of respect for the elders, individual accumulation of wealth, and so on. In rejecting capitalism and opting for a socialist state structure, Nyerere introduces an idealisation of the traditional African 'tribe' or village as the model for the construction of the modern state.[5] The source from which socialist strategies will be drawn is 'tribal socialism': the way of life (seen by Nyerere as socialist) of traditional African societies.

This idea of a society modelled on the African village was also put into practice. One of the important measures introduced after the Arusha Declaration was the 'villagisation project' – *Ujamaa wa Vijijini*. In the villagisation project, peasants were encouraged (or sometimes forced by means of *Ujamaa kwa bunduki*, 'Ujamaa through the barrel of a gun') to live together in self-reliant villages that were at the same time economic, political, educational and social units. The villagisation project met with fierce criticism, mainly because it was perceived as a form of Soviet-style or Maoist collectivisation, and the project was stopped in its tracks in the late 1970s because of local resistance and economic setbacks (see Von Freihold 1979; Hyden 1980).

The line of argument in which socialism is associated with African tradition is not exceptional, as we have seen earlier. The general tendency in African socialism was to associate what is in socialist theory a matter of conflicting relationships between social classes with a totally different sociocultural tradition: that of traditional preco-lonial Africa, in which classes (and hence class struggles) were unknown. This quest for traditional Africa was an essential ingredient of all decolonisation struggles in Africa. The trend was initiated by the Francophone Africans and black Caribbeans gathered in the Négritude movement from the 1930s onwards. They constructed a romantic and nostalgic mythical image of the African past 'as a lost paradise, as a stolen paradise on which the foreign invader is a parasite' (Kesteloot 1972: 76). This image of Africa was constructed to demonstrate the equivalence of African sociocultural systems to those imported and propagated by the colonisers. It was used to argue that precolonial African societies were not as chaotic, dysfunctional or 'primitive' as was commonly believed by the colonisers.[6]

Although Négritude was largely a Francophone-African affair and although it was vehemently attacked (both as a cultural philosophy and as a political pro-gramme shaped by Senghor) by Anglophone-African intellectuals such as Soyinka – 'does a tiger have to prove his *tigritude?*' – as well as by leftist Francophone leaders such as Sékou Touré, the gist of the Négritude ideas was shared by many. The essential message was that African tradition contained a treasure of social, politi-cal and cultural elements that should be revitalised and made part of present-day, contemporary African social and political structure. In this essential form, the most eminent anthropologist from Ivory Coast, Georges Nyangoran-Bouah, turned it into a 'chtonic' social-scientific paradigm; radical East African intellectuals such as Ngũgĩ wa Thiong'o advocated it; and a number of African leaders who were not usually associated with Négritude (Kenyatta, Kaunda, and Mobutu for instance) made it part of their political vision. The motive of 'cultural decolonisation' became an important ingredient of their domestic politics.

To Nyerere also, the basic Négritude ideas had some appeal. During his classic speech at the inauguration ceremony of the Republic of Tanganyika, on 10 December 1962, he announced the creation of a Ministry of National Culture and Youth (*Wizara ya Sanaa ya Taifa na Vijana*). This initiative was motivated in the following very Négritude-like terms:[7]

> Of all the crimes of colonialism there is none bigger than the attempt that was made to make us believe that we had no traditional culture of our own, or that those forms of culture that we had were primitive things about which we should be ashamed, and not things to take pride in [applause]. (In Loogman 1967: 210)

Which particular kind of culture this ministry should promote was not really made clear in the speech. Nyerere first referred to the fact that during the colonial days children were taught British songs, not those of the Nyamwezi, the Hehe or other Tanzanian ethnic groups. He also remarked that many Tanzanians could dance the foxtrot, the waltz or the twist, but that very few people had ever heard of traditional ethnic dances from their own country. He then concluded: 'I have set up this Ministry to help us regain pride in our traditional things. I would like it to look for all the useful things from every tribe, and to make these into things for the whole Nation' (ibid.).

This statement, which would suggest that local traditions would be revitalised and placed at the centre of cultural activity, was quickly mitigated in the next sentence however:

> I don't want anyone to think that reviving our own things would mean to reject foreign things. A country which refuses to adopt foreign things is a country of idiots and fools. The progress of man is impossible if we refuse to adopt things. But to adopt things does not mean to leave our traditional things. Meaningful adoption is that which helps us to improve our own traditional things. (Ibid.)

So, in the same breath, Nyerere advocated a revitalisation of local traditions and an 'improvement' of these traditions by means of the adoption of Western elements.

What we see here is that the association between socialism and African culture steers one into a collocation of culture and tradition. Even if such things demand updating and upgrading, the respectable, legitimate African culture is that of the old days, for it provides the basis for modern African political thinking. But culture-as-tradition in Tanzania exists only in its ethnic form: the traditional cultures were not unified, they were tribal – there was no Tanzanian *traditional* culture. One could invoke a mythical *African* tradition as a foundation for African socialism; but not a *Tanzanian* one for Tanzanian socialism. Stimulating culture-as-tradition, therefore, could open the gates to 'tribalism' and defeat the socialist ideal of unity. It was thus avoided.

Radical national culture

So far, we have seen that culture was either (1) an eroded concept in the educational system, overshadowed by and supposed to be a companion of political unification, or (2) an idealised and abstract concept used in advocating African Socialism, referring to precolonial traditional forms of social organisation. As a separate and structured domain of discourse, it only emerged in the wake of the Arusha Declaration and in the sphere of public debate, when radical intellectuals schooled in Marxist-Leninist philosophy discovered culture as a forgotten aspect of Ujamaa and as an under-theorised aspect of African socialism.

Texts such as those quoted above were the object of a thorough exegesis by various Tanzanian intellectuals, artists, administrators and scholars, and consequently there rapidly emerged a variety of opinions on what 'Tanzanian culture' was or should be.

Whether at the same time the concept was given a more or less well-defined shape by the activities of the Ministry and other government bodies is unclear, although the suggestion that it was *not* is more than just an educated guess. Radical intellectuals drew inspiration, ambition and energy from the example offered by Mao Zedong and his Red Guards in China; they saw the Arusha Declaration as a decisive revolutionary moment for Tanzania and demanded a Tanzanian cultural revolution. Thus, reviewing the cultural policies since independence in their influential paper, Mbuguni and Ruhumbika expressed their dissatisfaction over the fact that national culture, 'even among our leaders and promoters of culture' (1974: 275–6) is too often associated with traditions and tribal customs. Using an interpretation of the fragments of Nyerere's inauguration speech used above, they contested this dominant interpretation. In their view:

> National culture . . . is the sum total of a people's ways of life in their effort to live, to continue living and to develop as a nation. The sum total of all their ways of national life: their political system, their customs and traditions, their juridical system, their religious beliefs, their literary and artistic manifestations, their games and amusements. All that which marks out a nation as a nation and helps it to continue developing as a nation. (Ibid.: 275)

The traditional, tribal cultures can at most become *part* of the national culture, but they can never be national culture in itself. Mbuguni and Ruhumbika stress the fact that national culture will be modern culture, transmitted and expressed by Swahili, and they do not attempt to hide their contempt for tribal traditions:

> The country was exceptionally fortunate in that by the time it got to independence its numerous tribes were already in the process of being swallowed by a new and homogeneous culture identified by the whole country's use of Kiswahili. It was necessary and urgent to aid and guide this development. (Ibid.: 277)[8]

Thus, Tanzanian national culture should not consist of a renaissance of traditional African art and folklore, nor of an Africanisation of Western art, both tendencies being instances of naive and bourgeois Négritude. Mbuguni and Ruhumbika take a radically socialist stance on this issue. They cite Trotsky and Fanon in support of their view (and keep Lenin and Mao approvingly in the background) and emphasise the unity between art and society: 'In a socialist society all art is seen as a servant of society. A tool to help man better understand and shape his society according to his collective needs' (ibid.: 280). The model for this development, according to them, is Nkrumah's Ghana, where new revolutionary forms of popular theatre, art and music were actively promoted by the government and the ruling party. The anti-model is Senghor's Senegal, where:

> . . . miserable youth waste their talents trying to play Mozart on *Cora* and *Balafong*, the inevitable result being that the Africans think that perhaps Europeans understand the stuff and the Europeans on their side are absolutely convinced that it must be some wild African stuff. (Ibid.: 282)

Of course, that was an opinion of 1974, long after the Ujamaa revolution, when the critiques had been nourished by new socialist radicalism and fanned by China's Cultural Revolution. In the wake of a renewed and reinvigorated interest in revolutionary societal change, questions of cultural norms and values became more pertinent and pressing. The revolutionary moment and TANU's own humanist bias created a new sphere of political debate and action: that of culture and its relations to the structure of society. This, however, did not lead to the construction of a coherent cultural policy by TANU or the government. Cultural institutions were set up but they acted in an *ad hoc* fashion, lacking theory and vision. There were occasional eulogies of African culture, and every now and then Nyerere stressed the importance of culture to human life, but the connection between a political and a cultural strategy was not made by him nor by any other authoritative body, but by (often dissenting) individuals.

In the post-Arusha revolutionary socialist radicalisation, attempts to emphasise traditional (ethnic or 'tribal') cultures were associated with conservatism and reactionary attitudes. The more radically socialist factions, of which Mbuguni and Ruhumbika are exponents, adopted *Proletkult* theories of cultural transformation, in which the African ethnic groups substituted the pre-revolutionary social formations of Leninist analysis. They believed (echoing Mao Zedong) that the new national culture – a synonym for proletarian revolutionary consciousness – would be built on the rubbles of the pre-revolutionary ethnic cultures. The transition to Ujamaa, because it marked an important economic transformation of the country, would mean the destruction of ethnic cultures which, after all, were remnants of a pre-Ujamaa society. In the Ujamaa society, ethnic languages would be replaced by Swahili and local customs by a socialist way of life. Education, one of Ujamaa's central concerns, offered great hopes to the supporters of the new revolutionary culture. The fact that people (also those in peripheral rural areas) would become literates in Swahili, trained in agricultural skills, living in Ujamaa villages and well-informed about their political system would transform them from isolated autarkic groups into integrated parts of the Tanzanian polity. In the process, they would be absorbed into a larger sociocultural unit: that of the nation, characterised by a common commitment to Ujamaa and by the use of Swahili.

It is clear that this revolutionary perspective hinged on a number of weak points. First, it overestimated the impact of Ujamaa. Sometimes, Ujamaa villagisation seemed to have only superficial effects: the presence of party officials in the village, and some new village routines. Also, villagisation mostly developed within existing ethnic contexts, inter-ethnic villages being rather exceptional. Second, the implementation of the literacy and adult education campaigns – crucial ingredients in the strategy of cultural transformation – left much to be desired. Although the statistical results were baffling, the depth to which literacy and education had penetrated was difficult to estimate. As Mekacha (1994) argues, it certainly did not result in the Swahilisation of peripheral groups. Swahili became an additional language, superimposed on a repertoire that remained otherwise intact.

And, third, the commitment of TANU and the government towards building a truly revolutionary society was dubious. As noted above, the radical Left was marginalised together with its doctrinaire and theoretically elaborated version of socialism. The party and government were dominated by moderates, who verbally professed to radical socialism, but who did little to implement it through their policies. So the concept of national culture became something of a mirage: those who wanted to see it saw it everywhere; others didn't see anything of the kind.

The empty national culture

The practical result was that national culture never became more than a rhetorical commonplace. Most people knew what it was not: it was not ethnic, not traditional, not Western. But what it was remained unclear. In practice, it meant that local cultures were selectively revitalised. Prototypically 'cultural' elements – most would call them folklore – such as percussion music or traditional dances, combined with some elements of traditional dress, were used in new, often state-sponsored '*Ngoma* troupes', where they were part of syncretic performances including Chinese-style acrobatics and modern African pop music. This combination of old and new local and imported cultural expressions was then supposed to express or exemplify the new national culture (cf. Askew 2002).

Still, the concept of national culture had a significant impact on cultural life in Tanzania, especially among intellectuals. Ujamaa's humanism – man as the objective of all development activities – combined with the enthusiasm of a revolutionary moment in which social transformations could be engineered from the top downwards, granted intellectuals a central place in the culture-political debate. This combination of ideological frames allowed them to argue that the Ujamaa revolution should also be a revolution of the minds of the people, and that new knowledge would be needed for that. They would provide this new knowledge, and it would contain elements of Western scientific and rationalist thinking together with what they perceived as the core elements of Ujamaa philosophy. For them, national culture was an important political target, for which they were willing to work hard. They had a strong belief in the capacity of the state to transform society and its culture, and their criticism was therefore mostly directed against the leaders. As becomes clear from the fragments of Mbuguni and Ruhumbika's article, they had a clearer image of national culture than their political leaders and indeed than Nyerere himself, and they expressed it in debates, papers, comments, poems, novels and plays. But theirs was a minority stance, mostly too radical to be appreciated by the political establishment and the common man, whose cultural resilience was greatly underestimated.

One final remark must be made with regard to the concept of national culture. It was only loosely associated with the broader concept of *kujenga taifa* ('nation building'). *Kujenga taifa* stood for any type of activity that could be motivated in terms of the promotion of Ujamaa: building a school, digging a ditch, collecting money to buy school books for the children, harvesting sisal were all 'nation building activities'. In fact, the concept was often ridiculed because of its passe-partout character. People would greet each other with this question-and-answer sequence: *Unaenda wapi? Naenda kujenga taifa!* ('Where are you going? I'm going to build a nation!'). But nation building did not have the cultural connotation it has in contemporary European nationalisms. The cultural dimension of Tanzanian nation building, focused on the concept of national culture, only gained some prominence in the post-Arusha years, and mainly as an ingredient of radical interpretations. Cultural nationalism never really took hold in a coherent way. People rallied around a political agenda, not a cultural nor ethnic agenda. The concept of a 'nation', in Ujamaa, was that of a society in which culture (to be read here as the complex of traditional world-views and artistic expressions) was an epiphenomenon.

3.4 UJAMAA AND SWAHILI

Despite the vagueness surrounding the concept of culture in Ujamaa, the role of language was clear enough. In fact, language was the only issue on which absolute clarity reigned; the connection between the new nation and its new language, Swahili, was a fixed trope that was never challenged: in the independent Tanzania, the national language would be Swahili. In the transformation to a socialist state, Swahili would be one of the main instruments. It would (1) facilitate the spread of Ujamaa ideas and values; (2) allow maximum democratic participation of the masses in the process of decision making, and (3) become the particular mark of the Tanzanian citizen, who spoke an *African* language instead of the European languages adopted as official languages by most fellow Africans in other countries.

Swahili had been strongly idealised, even mythologised, since the early days of TANU. Swahili was constantly labelled as the 'language of liberation', the 'language of national independence', the 'language of freedom', and so on. Political rhetoric by Africans in Swahili during the colonial period was seen as a doubly rebellious act: first, it was an intrusion into the domain of politics, which was the monopoly of the colonial authorities, and, second, it also challenged the linguistic hegemony of the colonisers by placing an African language in the privileged position of a language of politics – a position normally assumed only by 'civilised' languages such as English or French. This metapragmatic dimension was frequently made clear to the audience: Tanzanians were told how Swahili had now become the instrument of opposition against the British, as well as the common language of all the colonial subjects, regardless of their ethnic or class affiliations. So there was not only a growing tradition of political talk *in* Swahili, but also an amount of political talk *about* Swahili.

The idealisation of Swahili, and the creation of Swahili itself as a topic of political discourse, did not mean that an articulated philosophy of language was spelt out. But the hundreds of statements, speeches, newspaper articles and papers about Swahili allow us to distinguish a number of relatively stable features of the idealisation of Swahili in Ujamaa.

1. The view of the relationship between language and what it was supposed to stand for was romantic and Herderian. Language was the carrier of a specific

set of values, a genius or a *Geist*. More concretely, Swahili was the carrier of African and Tanzanian values such as racial pride, freedom, Ujamaa and anticolonialism. Therefore, it would become a central instrument for nation building, the vehicle for expressing the non-ethnic, egalitarian, African values of Ujamaa. This romantic view functioned as a doxa, and it was never challenged, certainly not by linguists as we will see in the next chapter. The promotion of Swahili to the status of national language was perceived as linguistic decolonisation, and this was too big an achievement to be treated critically. The image of Swahili as a Herderian language-with-a-spirit was to a large extent sustained by the enthusiasm of decolonisation and of social reform through Ujamaa. If national culture had any sort of reality, then Swahili was certainly one of its characteristic features.

2. Swahili was identified with a limited number of qualities, which are at the same time seen as qualities of Ujamaa in general.

First, Swahili is seen as a symbol of *national unity*. It was the language of all Tanzanians, rich and poor, and it acted as an effective tool against centrifugal forces in society. During his last speech as chairman of CCM in 1990, Nyerere still formulated this dogma in virtually the same way as he did in the 1960s: 'If every Tanzanian had stuck to using his tribal language or if we had tried to make English the official language of Tanzania, I am pretty sure that we would not have created the national unity we currently enjoy' (quoted in Laitin 1992: 92).

Second, in line with the above point, Swahili is seen as a *non-ethnic* language. It was perceived and constructed as a language that originated through culture contact along the East-African coast and had been spread over vast portions of the Tanzanian territory even before colonisation. In combination with the first element, Swahili came to stand for anti-tribalism.

Third, Swahili was perceived as an *egalitarian* language. Since it was taken to be ethnically unmarked, there was no one group in society who had easier access to it than other groups; it was, in other words, a commodity that could be equally and evenly distributed and made accessible to all. It was an element of *democratisation*: in days past, only those who spoke English had access to power; now it was sufficient to have some proficiency in Swahili to be able to participate fully in the affairs of the state.

Fourth, Swahili was also perceived as a *modern* language, in contrast to ethnic languages which were perceived as features of a backward, traditionalist society. Swahili was the language of modern Tanzania and the new Tanzanians, those who had been forged into a nation by the joint experience of colonisation.

In line with the idealisation of Swahili, the government never paid any attention to local ethnic languages (see Topan 2008: 263). No effort was made to translate political materials into local languages, no printed or audio-visual media reporting was done in ethnic languages, and no teaching was performed using them. As will be explained in the next chapter, a huge amount of effort went into the spread and standardisation of Swahili, to the detriment of local ethnic languages. Still, they did not disappear – probably because of the reasons given above. The impact of Ujamaa-cum-Swahili was not as deep as was predicted by the political architects (a fact also noted by Laitin 1992: 80). And so the new language, the new culture and the concomitant identities became superimposed on Tanzanian villagers' language, culture and identities, but didn't really replace them. The efforts in favour of Swahili resulted in the Tanzanian citizens' development of more complex multilingual repertoires.

3. Tanzanian politics itself is conducted in Swahili. Ujamaa is a Swahili ideology, which has created its own vocabulary and frame for talking about Tanzanian and world politics. The creation of this vocabulary itself was carried out very scrupulously and rigorously, since foreign influences had to be stripped (as far as possible) from the new Swahili political lexicon (Kiimbia 1971; Temu 1971), and this lexicon was to reflect the new political culture of independent Tanzania (Ohly 1976). This lent a particular effect to Swahili political rhetoric. The fact that it was performed in Swahili, a heavily symbolic language, almost automatically placed any instance of political rhetoric in a patriotic frame. Talking politics in Swahili was in itself, irrespective of what exactly was said, an act that indexed freedom, independence and the values of Ujamaa. Swahili imposed a very strong metapragmatic frame on whatever was being said in the language.

These three features of the idealisation of Swahili can be found in a massive number of documents, and they seem to transcend the conservative-radical divide. Conservatives and radicals shared the view that the institutionalisation of Swahili was an important symbol of national independence, and they all expressed their delight in being able to work in Swahili rather than in English. This exaltation of Swahili was epitomised by the oft-quoted poem *Kiswahili* by the great twentieth-century Swahili poet Shaaban Robert: *titi la mama litamu, hata likiwa la mbwa* ('the mother's breast is sweet, even if it is that of a dog').[9]. What was previously regarded as a sign of backwardness was now a mark of pride and self-esteem, something that enabled Tanzanians to recapture their own past and culture which had been taken away from them by the colonisers (see, for example, Kombo 1972). The fact that their adoration was for what was after all a monolingual ideal of an extremely multilingual society may seem surprising and contradictory, and indeed it was to a certain extent. But the country had been unified by means of singular symbols: one nation, one party, one language.

3.5 IDEOLOGICAL LEADERSHIP: INTELLECTUALS AND SOCIETY

A central place in the nation building ambitions of Ujamaa was given to, and taken by, intellectuals, and reference to the intellectuals' interventions has been made repeatedly in the previous sections. In many ways the intellectuals were the first respondents of the government, its main collaborators, and its most enthusiastic propagandists. But it is precisely in the role and contribution of intellectuals that some of the basic paradoxes of Ujamaa as an egalitarian humanist ideology become clear. In particular, intellectuals represented a challenge to conceptions of leadership and authority.

The intellectuals are a group, or social class, which came into formation after independence. There were, of course, intellectuals before independence. But as a powerful or influential local social formation, their existence is a correlate of that of the independent state-system. Of course, the term 'intellectuals' itself is a slippery one. The substance of the group's definition may not reside so much in a clearly identifiable socio-economic profile, but rather it may be derived from a specific set of social practices: the intellectuals come into being as a distinct group in society by occupying a set of 'intellectual' symbolic domains and by assuming an intellectual role, distinct from that of other groups in society. But apart from this substantialist definition, the intellectuals crystallised around a number of institutions in the country, most prominently around the University of Dar es Salaam. The University was (and remained for decades) the prime locus for producing intellectuals, and it was often metonymically used for the whole class of intellectuals, both by intellectuals themselves and by government officials or other people. 'The Hill' – a reference to the spatial location of the university in Dar es Salaam – was a metaphor for everything that was good and bad about intellectuals.

The relationship between the political leaders and the intellectual elite has always been a difficult and ambiguous one in post-independence Tanzania. It revolves around a contradiction with regard to the intellectuals' role in Tanzanian Ujamaa society. Intellectuals were, on the one hand, a source of pride for the government, but at the same time they assumed a highly critical attitude towards the government. The intellectual class, in the sense of a minority trained in higher forms of Western-style formal education and in possession of skills derived from that training, was part of the colonial legacy (see Mazrui 1978 for an extensive discussion on this). In the colonial enterprise, the development of a small minority of well-trained Africans served a symbolic function, among a number of more practical functions. The rise of an intellectual elite, firmly under the control of the colonial authorities and almost completely modelled on archetypes from the metropolitan culture, was seen as the apex of the colonial venture, and as the ultimate proof of its utility and success. If Africans could be brought from a state of savagery to one of finesse and intellectual sophistication, then surely the work of the colonialists was good. But at the same time, of course, the colonial authorities were creating their own Frankenstein. The highly literate elites, once created, would form the spearhead of anticolonial resentment, because although they were made similar to the whites, they would never be treated as equals. And, at the same time, they were capable of competing with the whites in all fields: they were skilful debaters, capable scholars and writers, and polyglot orators.

As soon as independence was obtained, the symbolic perception of the intellectual elites changed, albeit in a paradoxical way. From the hallmark of colonisation, they became the flagship of independent development. Especially in countries such as Tanzania, where human capital development was central to all development plans, the construction of a broader, academically trained elite came to be seen as proof of the maturity and the capacity for self-reliance of the independent state. Tanzanians were now training and grooming their own leaders, their own cadres who would be able to take charge of the political, economic and educational development of the country. The qualifications for membership of such an elite, however, changed little. The intellectuals were still people who had gone through the entire cycle of 'modern' formal education, preferably including a degree obtained abroad. Their paraphernalia were still their Western-style degrees, and their highly valued skills were still those obtained through Western-style training. What changed was the social ranking of the intellectual class in society: from tightly controlled allies of colonialism, to leaders of the independence struggle, they had now become the central elite class in the independent societies.

The Tanzanian leadership poured massive support into the enlargement of the intellectual elites after independence (see, for example, Kaduma 1974; Sumra and Ishumi 1980), and attempts at regional inter-university integration between Dar es Salaam, Makerere and Nairobi were set up during the 1960s. However, the philosophy of education was still the one left behind by the British, and the products of higher education were still *wazungu weusi*, 'black-skinned whites'. Furthermore, they gave proof of an intolerable elite consciousness and an aspiration to be recognised as intellectual leaders with a matching social status, as well as of criticism against various forms of incompetence and lack of integrity among the political and bureaucratic leaders. So, just like in the colonial days, the system of elite construction through formal education proved to be a mixed blessing. On the one hand it did create an output of constructive intellectual work for the benefit of the nation, but on the other it created a group of dissident, dissatisfied elite members who criticised or opposed government policies.

The introduction of *Elimu ya Kujitegemea* in 1967 also affected the university. TANU was adamant with regard to the role of intellectuals and academically trained elites in Ujamaa society – from then on, they should not be seen as an elite in the sense of a privileged top class in society, but rather as an instrumental elite in the service of the masses. In a speech entitled 'The intellectual needs society', delivered at the University of Liberia in February 1968 (Nyerere 1974), Nyerere stressed heavily the fact that educated elites were what they were by virtue of sacrifices made by the rest of the population.[10] Consequently, since 'poor people cannot afford financial altruism . . . [w]e have a right to expect things from university graduates and others who have had higher education of any kind' (ibid.: 5). These things include: (1) a proportionally greater service to the country than that given by the uneducated masses, and (2) a non-elitist attitude *vis-à-vis* the masses. The latter – attitudinal – aspect is especially heavily emphasised by Nyerere. Real service to the country can only be given if 'the educated people of Africa . . . identify themselves with the uneducated, and do so without reservation' (ibid.: 8). And 'this acceptance of equality regardless of education is essential' (ibid.: 9). Further, the inter-class relationships, and the ensuing questions of intellectual authority, leadership and relevance are also dealt with:

> But this means that university studies, and the university itself, are only justified in Africa if they – and it – are geared to the satisfaction of the needs of the society, the majority of whose members do not have any education. Work at the university must, therefore, be so organized that it enables the students, upon graduation, to become effective servants. For servants they must be. And servants have no rights which are superior to those of their masters; they have more duties, but no more privileges or rights. And the masters of the educated people are, and must be, the masses of the people. (Ibid.: 11)

With this definition of the social status and role of the educated elites, Nyerere responded to two main criticisms made by intellectuals before the Arusha Declaration: (1) that of the lack of involvement by intellectuals in government projects, because, from then on, intellectuals would be closely involved in public services, they could feel more useful, and they would be called on to remedy the lack of intellectual capacity they observed so often in the bureaucracy and the state apparatus; (2) that of party and bureaucracy elitism, which was to be countered by an egalitarian vision of society in which both the political and the intellectual elites would be seen as servants rather than as privileged groups.

However, this upbeat message also contained sobering undertones. The encouragement came with unambiguous warnings, for Nyerere brought about a crackdown on elite consciousness among intellectuals, and exposed himself to new criticisms because of the heavily politicised view of academic training and performance. Intellectuals, from then on, were clearly given an instrumental role in the grand political project of Ujamaa. That meant, inevitably, a loss of academic freedom and a tightening of political control over the education and research activities and the public services of academics. They had been incorporated into the state apparatus, and pushed to orient exclusively towards nation building and development targets formulated by the political leaders who rhetorically identified with 'we, the uneducated masses'.

The definition of the intellectual's role by Nyerere was, as so often, ambiguous. On the one hand, it clearly involved an increase in power and political status for intellectuals. They were now given the role of revolutionary vanguard of crucial importance in the elaboration and implementation of political projects. In short, they had been granted political importance and political relevance; their work would now be part of the large-scale transformation of Tanzania into an Ujamaa state. On the other hand, their contribution would be closely monitored and sanctioned by the political leadership, and the authority relationship between the two was unambiguously unidirectional: political initiatives were taken by the government, and then further developed by the technocrats (the intellectuals) and the bureaucracy. This meant that the whole array of central political concepts, perspectives and long-term goals remained firmly within the hands of the political leaders.

The ambiguity of the power relationship described by Nyerere was epitomised by the 100 Shilling note introduced in 1985, which depicts an academic procession led by the then Chancellor of the University, Nyerere. The academic procession and the university buildings both document the high social status of the academics; but the leader of the procession is none other than Nyerere, because the state president is *ex officio* also the chancellor of the university. He is the one who grants the degrees to graduates, and he is a politician, not an academic.

This ambiguous relationship need not be problematic as long as intellectuals remain within the boundaries of their prescribed role. But a series of developments made intellectuals look for a more central ideological impact on Tanzanian society. From the mid-1960s onwards, and partially due to the impact of the union with Zanzibar, Marxist influence had increased among academics in Dar es Salaam. On the one hand, this was stimulated by the presence of left-wing expatriate scholars such as Giovanni Arrighi, Walter Rodney and Colin Leys, who seemed to have had considerable influence on social and political thinking among intellectuals. On the other hand, it had to do with the increasing possibilities for studying in socialist or non-aligned countries such as the German Democratic Republic, the Soviet Union, Yugoslavia or China (cf. Sumra and Ishumi 1980: 50–1). Although educational exchange programmes with Western countries remained important sources of advanced training, training in Marxist countries grew in quantity and influence, and it fertilised an intellectual climate at home already veering to the left. The university became the breeding ground for a radically socialist and theoretically orthodox interpretation of Ujamaa.

Academics became involved in a series of disputes with the government, including the debate on national culture already mentioned above and some debates on language and literary style that will be examined more closely in later chapters. In these debates with the government, the intellectuals challenged the political leaders' ideological leadership by means of arguments based on theoretical consistency, erudition and objective scientific research. Most often, this placed them on the left of the government because they took the socialist principles voiced in Ujamaa to their theoretical limits, and inevitably discovered that the socialism put into practice by the government was often inconsistent, undermined by factional interests, theoretically shallow or incomplete, or mere rhetoric. A consistent feature of the development of this critique was the use of the academic persona (or habitus, to use the well-known Bourdieuian term). The intellectuals assumed a political position by means of intellectual symbolic instruments, and much of their criticism revolved around the apparent lack of penetration of these intellectual skills in government policy. The tone of their critique was often patronising: 'we *know*' because we are intellectuals trained to know. And their frustration often stemmed from the feeling that government agencies did not always pay enough attention to those who knew.

Also remarkable is the fact that the intellectuals, in their disputes with the political leadership, used a particular, socialist, view of society. The intellectuals seemed to have a clear picture of the nation they were trying to build. But their 'nation' seemed to be a different one from that built by the government The government was often presented as an antisocialist, bourgeois or divide-and-rule force in society, and the intellectuals assumed the status of the true nation builders.

This ambivalent relationship between the intellectuals and the political leaders, embedded in Nyerere's statements about the relationship between intellectuals and society, was constantly enacted and re-enacted in the intellectuals' interventions in ideological debates. They certainly tried to be responsive to the call for socially constructive intellectual work, but they were often confronted with the limits of their constructive power. They were often called upon by the government for expertise, and some of the government's fiercest critics were given high executive government posts (and were thus, to some extent, silenced). But as soon as they articulated what they saw as the political-ideological consequences of their work, they were rebutted and sent back to their quarters on The Hill. Ujamaa penetrated deeply into the theoretical and methodological foundations of their scientific work, as will be shown in Chapter 4, and the fact that academics actively tried to adapt to the criteria of social and political relevance cannot be contested. But at the same time it can be shown that this adaptation to political goals did not automatically increase the political impact of their work. They had no control whatsoever over the basic ideological principles to which their work was supposed to respond, and battles over ideological fundamentals between them and political leaders invariably turned into a defeat for them.

At the root of this conflict lies a different perception of authority and status. For intellectuals, authority is derived from their superior intellectual skills; for politicians, these skills seemed to matter little since they were subordinate to political control. Among intellectuals, superior skills may lead to elite consciousness and elite behaviour, but in other cases they may also be viewed as completely at the service of the masses. In fact, intellectuals very often assumed an arrogant and patronising stance because they claimed to be at the service of the people. For politicians, however, claims to authority based on superior training are often given a class ring, and interpreted as class elitism and antisocialist behaviour. Authority, for them, is a structural matter, and it resides in a fixed hierarchical superiority. Better ideas cannot challenge this power structure. The frustration and impatience of intellectuals (for example in the field of language planning) continuously increases with every new rational argument they offer to government agencies, and with every refusal from the part of the politicians to accept rational argumentation as a reason to review government policies.

A remarkable aspect of this ambiguous relationship is the fact that, apparently, the dissident activities of the intellectuals, though often of a fundamentally ideological nature, could be easily neutralised both by politicians and by the intellectuals themselves. In contrast to political dissidents, scholars have rarely been the target of persecution or repression in Tanzania (as opposed to in Uganda or Kenya for example). There are various reasons for this. One reason is utilitarian: the political leaders needed local expertise for the elaboration of political projects. Another reason is ideological-symbolic: the humanistic bias of Ujamaa needed a sufficiently broad and active class of highly trained intellectuals as evidence for its educational successes. A third reason is social-psychological: intellectuals can be 'defined away' as a political force in society by using their identification as a separate class. In other words, tolerance for the dissident ideas of intellectuals may stem from social stereotypes about intellectuals as esoteric, unrealistic, too rigid and so on. A degree of radicalism or dissidence may even be seen as expected behaviour, and may be explained – and neutralised – as a feature of the successful creation of an intellectual class of Tanzanians. The same stereotypes can be used by intellectuals as a shield against the danger of appearing as politicians, rather than as intellectuals. In other words, intellectuals may stress their own neutralised public perception as a means to defend themselves against charges of real dissidence. Their dissidence is then presented as the product of a sense of duty, rather than as political malevolence or subversion.

Throughout this process, we can observe how structural and symbolic features interact in the genesis and development of a social class. The intellectuals were pre-defined as a class, both by institutional means (their access to higher forms of education) and by ideological means (the allocation of social status). But their class identity was constantly recreated by means of the practice of being intellectuals, namely by engaging in open disputes over fundamental ideological issues. They attempted to give shape to their pre-defined social status by filling it with forms of discursive practice that reflect exclusive features of their group identity: a sense of innovation in political and social thought, a sense of duty and public service, specific and theoretically elaborate interpretations of central concepts in the public debate, and, above all, a sense of intellectual leadership in society. By performing these practices, they could assert their elite identity and simultaneously protect themselves against charges of politically inappropriate behaviour.

The servant status of intellectuals has proved to be largely utopian. The intellectual class is a socially upwardly-mobile class consisting on the one hand of people whose aim it is to make the best use of their exclusive capacities, and, on the other hand, consisting of radical revolutionaries disappointed about the country's lack of progress in building a socialist society. Both tendencies are fundamentally destabilising for the state, although they tend to result in inertia. Even when they are called upon by the state to perform crucial nation building tasks, as with the Swahili linguists in Chapter 4, they only cooperate to a certain point. As soon as their efforts and advice run counter to government preferences and are rejected or disqualified, they become a rebellious or a disillusioned class.

3.6 CONCLUDING REMARKS

Three main themes emerged in this chapter. The first theme was of Ujamaa as a socialist or a nationalist political theory, involving different approaches to 'culture' as an ingredient of the ideology and of cultural action as an ingredient of ideological hegemonisation. There is a complex dynamic of appropriation and re-appropriation at play here, in which theoretical systems such as Ujamaa are being played off against African, 'local' traditions and Western, imported traditions. Culture, evidently, is a crucial target in such a dynamic, and in the case of Ujamaaa, with its emphasis on human capital and education, it became a site of struggle.

This struggle manifested itself most clearly around the concept of national culture, the second theme of this chapter. A humanist, socialist (egalitarian) and African ideology such as Ujamaa required political action in the field of culture; it required an elaborate view of national culture. Yet it failed to develop such a clear and stream-lined concept due to weaknesses in the way in which 'culture' was conceptualised. The dynamic of interpretation which lies at the heart of the politics of Ujamaa in Tanzania provided two sources for conceptualising culture: one 'traditional' in the literal sense, and the other radical and Marxist-inspired. In the traditionalist conceptualisation, 'culture' belonged to the realm of the celebrated source of African socialism: the local ethnic groups with their customs and traditions. Despite the homogenising aspirations of Ujamaa, attitudes towards the 'tribe' remained ambivalent: on the one hand 'tribal 'diacritics were seen as centrifugal and destabilising in a modern African socialist society; on the other hand these 'tribes' provided the raw cultural material for building the new society, which was claimed to be deeply African. In the radical conceptualisation, there was no obstacle to interventionism in the field of culture. 'Tribal' traditions were pre-revolutionary traditions that needed to be abolished as part of the socialist revolution. National culture was theorised in the radical tradition as discontinuous with the pre-revolutionary cultures; blending both was seen as a denial of the revolutionary character of Ujamaa.

This is where Swahili comes in. Swahili was one of the central nation building instruments, and its institutional metapragmatics emphasised the egalitarian dimension of the generalised use of the language, thus formulating it as a precondition for building a socialist nation. It had also been symbolised as a *new* language, characterising a new society, a new political system and new citizens. The metapragmatics of Swahili, both in the phase of anticolonial mobilisation and after independence, better fit the radical scheme than that of the more moderate African socialists. Emphasising the value of precolonial 'tribal' traditions on the one hand, while advocating the generalised use of a 'non-tribal' language on the other, shapes a paradox that was detected and exposed by a radical intellectual faction.

This brings us to the third theme of this chapter. The development of the cultural philosophy of Ujamaa was not so much state-controlled or dogmatic; it was largely caused by interventions from outside the political *nomenklatura*, and in particular from the country's emerging intellectual elite. Further, such interventions in which intellectuals engaged in critical dialogues with the state actively shaped the intellectuals as a recognisable class in Ujamaa society. In such debates, intellectuals tried and tested their discursive, intellectual and political tools; they found their niche in Ujamaa society by engaging constructively in the development of Ujamaa as they saw it: a theoretically coherent, left-wing political ideology. Their niche was that of the political and ideological opposition; of a vociferous minority whose vocation consisted in bringing *intellectual dimensions* to the fabric of Ujamaa ideology, against what they often saw as populist Ujamaa rhetoric.

The cultural dimension of Ujamaa is the field in which we can perhaps best witness Ujamaa as a 'struggle to entextualize authoritatively' (Silverstein and Urban 1996), a struggle over texts and their preferred readings. It is there that one can see that Ujamaa is not just a textual complex, but a social-semiotic process in which the official, doctrinaire texts were battlefields. Culture appeared between the lines of the important texts of Ujamaa. Reading between the lines (something in which intellectuals became specialised) was politics, and this contributed to the ideological elaboration of Ujamaa.

3.7 NOTES

1. Hobsbawm observes: 'The actual definitions of "nations" fighting for their freedom . . . was generally taken over from such nationalist movements as existed without much enquiry' (Hobsbawm 1990: 152).
2. Shivji's book, unfortunately not widely available, offers to my mind the clearest and most persuasive discussion of Nyerere's Pan-Africanist inclinations.
3. But I heard exactly that question in Dar es Salaam in 1989 and 1992. Note that ethnic affiliations are used frequently in discussing people and their characteristics, and that some ethnic stereotypes still prevail (for example, 'Chagga are clever businessmen'). Two ethnic groups have always been perceived as problematic: the Indians and the Zanzibari (Shivji 2008: Chapter 2).
4. In order to save money on school supplies, all schools were supposed to become self-reliant in their food production. Children would work in the school farm – the *shamba* – as part of their practical agricultural training. The measure was also ideologically motivated: by working in the shamba children would learn to work hard for the community and to share the fruits of their labour.
5. Note that the term 'tribe' is often used in Tanzanian discourse, including that of scholars and politicians, instead of its politically correct alternative 'ethnic group'.
6. This point of view was also adopted by European scholars such as George Balandier. See his *Afrique Ambiguë* (1957).
7. Note that Nyerere uses the term *sanaa* ('art' or 'cultural skills') in this statement, instead of *utamaduni*, the more abstract and general term for 'culture' or 'civilisation'.
8. Or even: 'It is indeed only logical to foresee cases where it will be our political duty to speed up the dying out of some of these *ngoma*' (that is, traditional ritual dances) (Mbuguni and Ruhumbika 1974: 281).
9. Shaaban Robert, who died in 1962, was himself a staunch advocate of Swahili, which he saw as an important unifying force in East Africa (see Robert 1962). The poem, *Kiswahili*, was first published in 1947.
10. Many elements in this text were foreshadowed in earlier texts. Themes such as the necessary usefulness of science for development purposes, as well as the anti-elitist attitudes of intellectuals, were, for instance, also emphasised in a 1965 speech entitled 'The role of universities' (Nyerere 1969: 179–86).

Chapter 4

Ujamaa linguistics

4.1 INTRODUCTION

As seen in the previous chapter, Swahili was heavily symbolised by the leading politicians of postcolonial Tanzania, and it was made into a politically salient symbol by its promotion to the status of national language. As a consequence, linguistics became an ideologically important occupation, deemed of national importance. This gave rise to a very remarkable development of linguistic work, concentrated around the Institute of Kiswahili Research (*Taasisi ya Uchunguzi wa Kiswahili – TUKI*), founded in 1964 to succeed the East African Inter-Territorial Language Committee and integrated into the University of Dar es Salaam in 1970. TUKI was assigned a scientific task – that of proposing all kinds of linguistic measures to improve the standards of Swahili and enhance its spread and absorption by the people. TUKI's advice would be submitted for approval and implementation to the National Swahili Council (*Baraza la Kiswahili la Taifa – BAKITA*), a political bureau in charge of official language policy. Together, TUKI and BAKITA formed the scientific instrument by means of which the Tanzanian government was going to back up its political decision to make Swahili the language of all Tanzanians. Both institutions were state institutions; Swahili was, after all, an affair of the state. For many years, Tanzania was seen as an exemplary case of language planning and language policy development, and the Swahilisation efforts attracted the attention of many well-known sociolinguists (see, for example, Harries 1968, 1969; Whiteley 1968, 1969, 1971; Abdulaziz 1971; Ansre 1974; O'Barr 1976; Myers-Scotton 1978). Groundbreaking research on language standardisation was carried out, and creative literature, as well as the development of mass media, in Swahili were boosted.

In this chapter, I shall concentrate on the gradual process through which a local type of linguistic discourse came into being, which I will call Ujamaa linguistics. I will discuss some of the theoretical and ideological foundations of types of linguistic research carried out within the context of official Swahili research in Tanzania. Much of it, I will argue, can be characterised as *political* linguistics: linguistics was part and parcel of the general political project of Ujamaa. As a consequence, some of the problems encountered by Swahili researchers may be interpreted in terms of internal contradictions or weaknesses in Ujamaa theory. The nation-building ambitions of Ujamaa, translated into an attempt at the ideological hegemonisation of all activities in society, also penetrated linguistic scientific practice and gave rise to a *local* scientific tradition.

First I will give a brief historical survey of language planning in Tanzania (in section 4.2). Then I will discuss three important features of Ujamaa linguistics: the colonial legacy (in section 4.3), the metaphors of development and modernisation that dominate the discourse of Swahili (in section 4.4), and the problem of cultural identities associated with the new national culture and the role of Swahili therein (in section 4.5). Finally, the insights gathered from the various sections will be combined and placed in a wider perspective (in section 4.6).

4.2 A BRIEF HISTORY OF SWAHILI LANGUAGE POLICY AND PLANNING

Preliminary remarks

The history of Swahili language policy and language planning, since it came into full swing in the 1930s, has been dominated by a partly functional, partly symbolic opposition between Swahili and English. The local 'ethnic' or 'tribal' languages in general received very little attention, because they were seen as an obstacle to national development.

Also, all efforts were based on two taken-for-granted language-ideological assumptions. The first assumption was that of the correspondence between efficiency (taken in a very general sense) and sociolinguistic simplicity: the fewer the number of languages spoken in a society, the more efficiently that society will function. We could call this the *efficiency assumption*. When slightly reworded and placed in a more political perspective, a widespread and well-known second assumption emerges: sociolinguistic complexity parallels social problems and the absence of what is so often called 'social integration' (see Bamgbose 1994). It is assumed that sociolinguistic diversity is one of the sources of social divisiveness in African countries, and that therefore a single national language – or, if impossible, the smallest possible number of languages – should be promoted in order to stimulate the sociopolitical cohesion of the country. We could call this the *integration assumption*.

A comprehensive critique of these assumptions is beyond the scope of this study (see Williams 1992: Chapter 5; Blommaert 1996). But it may be pointed out that both assumptions are related to a model of society and culture which takes monolingualism and a one-language-one-culture pattern to be normal features. A monolingual country is seen as more likely to be economically prosperous, more democratic, and less subject to emotional upsurges of ethnic feelings (cf. Williams 1992: 126-7). Diversity and linguistic-cultural pluralism are seen as abnormal situations and potentially problematic in themselves. The assumptions therefore fit the ideological pattern of *homogeneism*: homogeneous societies are to be preferred over societies containing a significant degree of (ethnic, cultural, linguistic) diversity (see Blommaert and Verschueren 1992, 1998). Bamgbose puts it quite simply: '[i]n

Africa, it seems that we are obsessed with the number "one"' (1994: 36). He further argues that multilingualism is the 'natural' state of all African countries, a point supported by Laitin's (1992) game-theoretical analysis of language repertoires and state construction in African countries, which concludes that the default language repertoire in Africa consists of three plus/minus one languages. The recognition and institutionalisation of linguistic pluralism is, however, a recent phenomenon (see Fardon and Furniss 1994). It is also something which requires a laborious struggle against the colonial homogeneistic linguistic ideology which has often been adopted by postcolonial governments to sustain nation-building efforts, as Spitulnik's analysis of language use in Zambian radio broadcasting shows (Spitulnik 1992).

When discussing language policy and language planning, it may also be interesting to keep in mind Neustupny's old distinction between two types of linguistic treatment of language problems: the 'policy approach' and the 'cultivation approach' (Neustupny 1974). In Neustupny's view, language policy and planning are dominated by the policy approach, while activities aimed at the 'quality' of the language and its relation to culture (often less institutionalised and performed by intellectual elites) are characteristic of the cultivation approach. Of particular interest to the discussion here are the parallels drawn by Neustupny between these approaches and levels of socio-economic development. Thus, although he acknowledges that the cultivation approach will be of some importance in developing countries, Neustupny deems it typical of the developed world, while '[i]t is the less developed modern (or modernizing) societies in which the policy approach prevails' (ibid.: 43). As will become clear in later sections of this chapter, the Tanzanian case is somewhat more complex than this, to the extent that the difference between a policy approach and a cultivation approach becomes very difficult to establish.

One final preliminary point should be mentioned. According to Polomé's (1980) survey, well over 100 languages are spoken in Tanzania. They belong to the Bantu, Nilotic, Cushitic, Khoisan, Indo-European and Semitic language families. It goes without saying that the number of speakers of each language differs significantly, as does the association of particular languages to power and status groups in Tanzanian society. Keeping such background data in mind, we can now look more closely at the history of language policy and planning in Tanzania.

The pre-independence period

During German and British colonial rule, efforts were made to spread and standardise Swahili as a lingua franca for East Africa (Wright 1965; Kihore 1976). The motives for these efforts were pragmatic: to improve – or make at all possible – communication between colonial officials and members of the local population. The choice of Swahili was based on the fact that, apparently for centuries, varieties of Swahili were widespread throughout East Africa, due to the existence of extensive commercial networks running inland from the coastal mercantile communities of Zanzibar, Mombasa, Kilwa, Lamu and Malindi (see Middleton 1992 and Le Guennec-Coppens and Parkin 1998 for surveys). The German colonisers who entered the Tanganyika territory must quickly have noticed the advantages this already established lingua franca offered for communication and the organisation of administration in the Tanganyika colony, because 'from 1890, as the vehicle of political communication with the ruled in German territory, it became the language of power' (Wright 1965: 40). German civil servants were trained in Swahili at the Seminar for Oriental Languages in Berlin before they were allowed to work in the Tanganyika colony. The Germans started standardisation efforts, or, better, canonisation efforts (Wright calls it 'the policy of Latinised Swahili' [ibid.: 44]), and encouraged the establishment of a written press in Swahili, of which the newspaper *Kiongozi* ('*The Leader*'), first published in 1905, was the most important product. The First World War, which was also fought in Tanganyika, gave a particular stimulus to the spread of Swahili, to such an extent that when the British assumed the mandate over the former German Tanganyika territory in 1920, they 'found almost a *fait accompli* with respect to the status of Swahili' (Abdulaziz 1980: 140). By that time the language was firmly established as the lingua franca in large parts of the territory, and it was used for inter-ethnic communication between colonisers and colonised as well as between various local ethnic groups. It had also acquired a considerable degree of codification due to the pioneering efforts of scholars such as Velten, Sacleux, Seidel and Krapf (see, for example, Seidel 1900). By that time, it was also used in primary-school education and local-level administration.

In 1930, an official body for the standardisation and promotion of Swahili was founded by the British: the Inter-Territorial Language Committee. The Committee made a far-reaching decision: despite the predominance of the Mombasa variety of Swahili in the northern parts of British East Africa (Kenya), the Committee selected the Zanzibar variant as the basis of further language standardisation in the whole of East Africa. Throughout their rule over Tanganyika, the British maintained the German language policy principles: Swahili was the medium of local political and administrative organisation, as well as of the primary level of school education (cf. Wright 1965; Kihore 1976; Abdulaziz 1980).

When in the mid-1940s early African nationalist movements started their activities, Swahili almost naturally became the medium of mobilisation and political education. Throughout its continued use in nationalist activities, it also acquired the symbolic load of nationalism, and was presented and perceived as a non-tribal, egalitarian and democratic medium. As a symbol and an instrument of the struggle for independence, Swahili proved to be a language with great rallying force. Abdulaziz (1971: 165) narrates the following episode from the 1947 annual meeting of the Tanganyika African Association (TAA, the forerunner of TANU):

> Delegates from all parts of Tanganyika had attended the meeting. The Chairman made his introductory address in English, whereupon a number of delegates protested and demanded that the speech be translated into Swahili.

When TANU was founded in 1954, Swahili had already acquired such political weight that the promotion of Swahili in education was one of the resolutions adopted by the founders of TANU at their first meeting (Kaniki 1974: 3). Apparently, already at that time, there was a large degree of consensus among the founders of TANU that Swahili was the 'national' language of the black Tanganyikans, and that it should either remain that way or even be further elaborated.

In the meantime, the British continued their efforts to standardise Swahili, and to stimulate the rise of a Swahili newspaper press. The publication of E. O. Ashton's *Swahili Grammar* (Ashton 1944) and *A Standard Swahili-English Dictionary* by the Inter-Territorial Language Committee under the direction of Frederick Johnson (Johnson 1939) were landmarks in the process of Swahili standardisation; both books are still standard reference material for any Swahili student today. Of particular importance for the emergence of creative writing in Swahili were the prose competitions organised by the East-African Literature Bureau in the 1950s. Supported by the Committee, it enabled the publication of important literary works by authors such as Shaaban Robert and Mohamed Said Abdullah. Nonetheless, and this is the bottom line for the pre-independence period, English remained the language used in the higher, more powerful spheres of society. As soon as one left the realms of village-level politics, petty commerce, primary education, or local-level administration and moved into those of justice, regional politics, higher education or senior managerial and administrative levels, English became the medium of communication.

The early years of independence

As soon as TANU came to power in 1960–1, its party policy on Swahili became state policy. One of the first decisions made by the newly independent government was the promotion of Swahili to the status of national language. This act was highly symbolic, but little more than that: 'the decision to make Swahili the national language of Tanzania was more a decision of intention than of fulfilment' (Harries 1968: 419), and '[t]he politicians declared Swahili the national language only as a means of achieving their own ends' (Mwansoko 1990b: 55). The colonial bifocal language policy was maintained throughout the first years of independence: Swahili, though the national language, remained confined to lower education and lower-level state institutions, while English was still used in the higher spheres of social and political life. No attention was given to the other local languages.

However, there was one notable exception: the decision to make Swahili the medium of communication in parliament. Again, this was again a highly symbolic measure, indicating the fact that politics, from then on, would be a Swahili-speaking business, such as to enable every citizen of the newly independent state to be fully informed about the political debates and to participate in them. It was also a decision of great emotional impact. When Nyerere delivered his Republic Day speech in Swahili in the *Bunge* (House of Parliament) on 10 December 1962, the then Minister of Education and Culture Sheikh Amri Abedi (also a prominent Swahili poet) reacted as follows:

> an unprecedented thing that happened on that day was that His Excellency delivered his speech in Swahili. That moment is truly the beginning of a new era in

the history of the development of this country in the fields of language, national development, and the running of the affairs of the government . . . Today we have been given the freedom to talk in our own language. We shall now enter the field of discussion with confidence, with no doubt as to the real meaning of what we are saying, nor, whether we are being correctly understood by others . . . (Quoted in Abdulaziz 1971: 166)

The decision further stressed TANU's emphasis on Swahili as a marker of African nationalism and of the new culture and identity of the independent Tanganyikans. Still, as said above, the most important function of this decision was symbolic; in the practice of education and administration, English remained a force to be reckoned with.

Attitudes toward Swahili and English changed in 1964, when the Zanzibar Revolution and the subsequent union between Tanganyika and the islands of Zanzibar and Bemba introduced radically socialist and radically pro-Swahili elements into the Tanzanian government. One of the first actions of the revolutionary government of Zanzibar after the revolution had been to ban the use of all foreign languages (namely English and Arabic) from public life, and to make the use of Swahili obligatory in all public and official business. Such radicalism had hitherto been absent from TANU's policies, and, in a way, it was somewhat out of place in the context of language use in the new United Republic. Swahili was widespread in Tanganyika, but not as a first language; it was most people's second or third language. In Zanzibar, however, the Kiunguja variety of Swahili was the mother tongue of the majority of the population. So the call for complete and radical Swahilisation may have been a return to their roots for the Zanzibari, but certainly not for the Tanganyikans.

Overcoming this problem was greatly helped by other international events, causing a deterioration of relations between Tanzania and Great Britain. The union was not welcomed by the West Germans nor the British, and they reduced or discontinued their development programmes in Tanganyika. The upheavals surrounding the unilateral declaration of independence of the white minority government in Rhodesia, and Britain's less than dynamic response to it, further strained the international relations of the new Tanzanian government and finally caused a rupture in diplomatic relations between Tanzania and its former colonial metropole in 1965. The propaganda effect of these events consisted of the creation of an ideological-metonymic opposition between Swahili and English. More than ever, Swahili became the symbol of independence, Africanhood, Tanzanian citizenship and freedom, whereas English became more and more a symbol of neocolonialism, oppression and imperialism.

After the Arusha Declaration

The Arusha Declaration – itself a Swahili text – consolidated the more radical socialist course taken after the union with Zanzibar and Pemba, and again placed Swahili at the forefront of the ideological battle. The egalitarian, classless society projected in Ujamaa would be constructed by means of and through new forms of socialisation that would all use Swahili as their medium. *Elimu ya Kujitegemea* (Education for Self-Reliance) was the most important element in the plan for the development of a socialist society. Importantly, the new curriculum (both the primary-school curriculum and the adult education programme) would use Swahili as its medium of instruction. Higher education (henceforth restricted to a small group of selected candidates) would be geared towards providing intellectual cadres who would become experts and government officials at the service of the people. Their training would be in English '"for a long time to come", until such time as Kiswahili would have "developed" enough to take over the functions of English in secondary and higher education' (Mulokozi 1986: 2).

A crucial issue in Swahili language planning had been raised: that of introducing Swahili in post-primary education. Although the Tanzanian government developed a programme for the gradual replacement of English by Swahili in secondary schools – to be implemented from 1971 onwards – it never materialised. The only secondary education course taught in Swahili was, significantly, the obligatory course on political education; but even now, the rest of the secondary school curriculum as well as that of higher learning, is still taught in English. The reasons for this, according to Mulokozi (1991: 8), are not technical but political. Despite the fact that experts (linguists, educators, curriculum developers) carried out extensive preparatory work in view of the changeover to Swahili (see the survey in ibid.: 9–11), the government refused to implement the full Swahilisation of post-primary education (Mwansoko 1990b; Massamba 1987a). In the eyes of many, the result is 'a pedagogical absurdity' (Mulokozi 1991: 9). Children are taught in Swahili during their primary-school training. They study English as a subject, but the degree of proficiency in English thus acquired is often lamentable. Yet, when they continue their education they are confronted with English as a medium of instruction, often used by teachers whose competence in English also leaves much to be desired.

We should not forget the ideological-metonymical dimension of the opposition between English and Swahili mentioned earlier. English was still the mark of neo-colonial dominance and became still more associated with anti-revolutionary forces after 1967 due to the more radical course taken by the Tanzanian leaders. Therefore, to put it mildly, very little effort was made to stimulate exposure to English in the early post-Arusha years up to approximately 1975. The radio broadcasting system was almost completely Swahilised; exposure to Anglophone literature and music was severely restricted to only those categories that could not avoid it: higher education students, higher cadres, and people in the government business establishment. Those Anglophone media that were available – a small handful of local and foreign newspapers and magazines – were not accessible to the large majority of the population, who were insufficiently competent in English to be able to read them. The ideological opposition between Swahili and English also stretched to the domain of language planning and research: all decisions related to Swahili taken in the early post-Arusha years and implemented by institutions such as TUKI or BAKITA were presented as elements of the struggle for what Ngugi wa Thiong'o (1981b) called the 'decolonisation of the mind'. The development of Swahili was invariably linked to the elimination of English; progress in Swahili would automatically entail a decline in the status of English in Tanzanian society. Later sections of this chapter will return to this issue, and discuss it in more detail.

Why did Swahilisation not take place, given the fact that it was consistently proclaimed an important political target, that it had already acquired considerable status in Tanzanian society, and that institutions such as TUKI and BAKITA had spent tremendous efforts in 'developing' the language by coining massive amounts of new terminology, drafting school books, and so on? The reasons are, at least partly, political. First came the renewal of friendly relations with Great Britain, which apparently made Nyerere and other TANU leaders realise that it would be unwise to continue the radically anti-English course their country had taken. In an interview in *The Times* in December 1974 Nyerere declared that his country was aiming for bilingualism, because: 'Tanzanians would be foolish to reject English. We are a small country. English and French are African languages, and so one we have. It is a very useful language' (quoted in Kihore 1976: 50).[1]

With statements such as this, Nyerere took away the *raison d'être* of Swahilisation. Language policy had always been aimed at a monopoly situation for one language, Swahili; now Nyerere advocated a bipolar situation in which English and Swahili would both enjoy a similarly high status. So why spend further efforts on the promotion of Swahili? Second, the oil crisis of the early 1970s had struck economically vulnerable countries such as Tanzania particularly hard. The already scarce resources of the country were sapped even further, and an appeal to foreign aid became unavoidable. There also, a radically anti-Western attitude, articulated, for instance, in an aggressively anti-English language policy, may have been perceived to be an obstacle for a smooth relationship between the donor countries and the receiver, Tanzania. And finally, the language planning results themselves were not always encouraging, as we will see shortly.

The net result with regard to Swahilisation was that from the late 1970s onwards Swahili was no longer a national priority. In 1982, despite all that had been said before, it was decided to maintain the existing language situation: Swahili would remain the national language and the medium of instruction in primary education, while English would remain the language of post-primary education. The Swahilisation project was finally shelved by the Ministry of Education in 1984 (Mulokozi 1986; Mwansoko 1990a). Since then, the *status quo* has become official. Both TUKI and BAKITA continued their efforts towards promoting Swahili, standardising it, and developing new terminology and teaching materials in it. Three important works produced by TUKI appeared in the period of decline of the Swahilisation project: the *Kamusi ya Kiswahili Sanifu* (*Dictionary of Standard Swahili*) appeared in 1981 (TUKI 1981); the *Sarufi Maumbo ya Kiswahili Sanifu* (*A Morphology of Standard Swahili*) in 1983 (Kapinga 1983); and the *Swahili-English Dictionary* – a monumental project – went into print in 2000 (TUKI 2000).

In 1985, Nyerere stepped down as President of Tanzania. His successor, Ali

Hassan Mwinyi, accepted an IMF debt-rescheduling programme shortly after his inauguration. Self-reliance gave way to an increased (and increasing) influence from international organisations on domestic economic policies, all of them using English as their medium of communication with the Tanzanian people and authorities. Mwansoko (1990b: 57) consequently notes an ideological shift from the early 1980s, defined as 'a gradual retreat from total anti-capitalist tendencies in the country and a move towards "relaxed" socialist principles . . . a return to the pre-Arusha Declaration policies', both in the economic sphere and in that of language usage.

After Nyerere

The economic liberalisation policy involved the gradual erosion of state power and the loss of the ideological hegemony of Ujamaa and TANU (now CCM) (Campbell and Stein 1992). After a long period of preparation, the first multiparty elections were held in October 1995 and won by CCM (probably due to the superior and battle-hardened party organisation in the rural areas of the country). Similarly, the state monopoly in the domain of education had been abolished, and a number of private colleges and universities were founded in different parts of the country. The most successful one, the Open University of Dar es Salaam, somewhat paradoxically broke the monopoly of English in higher education by introducing courses taught in Swahili. One of the old arguments against full Swahilisation, the idea that Swahili was 'not yet' a medium appropriate for advanced scientific discourse, was thus falsified in practice.

Together with the loss of hegemony for Ujamaa, a more relaxed attitude towards language matters has set in. New publications now appear in Swahili as well as in English, there are commercial television stations that broadcast news, sports and commercials in Swahili alongside programmes in English, there continues to be a flourishing popular music business in Swahili, and as we shall see in greater detail later in this book, the Internet has arrived in Tanzania. The disappearance of the ideological polarisation of Swahili and English appears not to have resulted in the disappearance or loss of impact for either language.

The contrast with the 1970s could not be greater: English is now more than ever a prestige language. In the now liberalised society, the free market determines the role and status of languages. But in 1997, the Ministry of Education and Culture published its new 'Cultural Policy Statement' (*Sera ya Utamaduni*). Two ingredients of this document drew the attention of linguist and language planners: first, the Sera mentions (and favourably qualifies) local ethnic languages, albeit in very general terms, thus breaking a long tradition of silence on this topic; second, the Sera advocates the Swahilisation of the state education system across the board, that is from primary school up to university level. Here also, and paradoxically, the difference with the previous periods could not be greater.

The arguments used by the Ministry in favour of Swahilisation deserve a closer look. First, the Ministry starts by observing that the present system of language in education (Swahili at the primary level, English at the post-primary level) has weakened Swahili as well as having weakened the development of the education system. Next, it is argued that attempts towards building national unity are doomed to fail if the national language (that is, Swahili) is not used in the official education system: cultural traditions would be wasted and poverty would increase because of the incompetence of a majority of the citizens in the medium of instruction (English). Only those who have access to English will benefit from progress and development. The first argument is more than just an echo of the criticism voiced against the language in education policy by linguists and intellectuals (criticism which, if possible, became even more outspoken during the 1990s, see for example papers in Rubagumya 1990; Mulokozi 1991; Roy-Campbell and Qorro 1997; Yahya-Othman 1997).

The second argument is an interesting class argument. Clearly, maintaining English in post-primary education undoubtedly resulted in social effects that ran counter to Ujamaa principles. The distribution of English parallels a crucial criterion for upwards social mobility, higher education: 'if you can speak English, you are assumed to be educated' (Yahya-Othman 1997: 15). Especially in the period 1967–75, when exposure to English was highly restricted and its use highly negatively marked, the educated elites were given a symbolic instrument, the exclusivity of which provided a means of marking elite membership. English became entrenched in Tanzanian society because it was an elite feature (cf. Mazrui and Mazrui 1998: 133). This phenomenon had already been noted in the late sixties and early seventies by Whiteley (1968, 1971) and Harries (1968). Harries emphatically warned against the social repercussions of maintaining English as a medium of higher education: '[it encouraged] the development of class on the strict basis of the English-speaking intellectuals and the Swahili-speaking workers and peasants' (ibid.: 420).

A detailed and more nuanced discussion of these issues will be given in Chapter 6. In the meantime, it is interesting to see how the Tanzanian government of 1997, well after the official abolishment of Ujamaa as a state doctrine, reached back to *socialist* arguments in an attempt to motivate Swahilisation. The prima facie paradox is that after the collapse of Tanzanian socialism, full Swahilisation suddenly becomes a realistic prospect. In other words, when Swahilisation was no longer an ingredient of a general socialist strategy, its homogenising – one could say socialist and nation-building – effects might become true.

Surveys of relatively long historical periods allow us to see the *durée* behind particular events: slower patterns of development that give meaning and structure to events, concrete struggles, policy decisions. In the case of Tanzania, full Swahilisation now will be different from full Swahilisation in the 1960s or 1970s. It will no longer have the effect of the massification of education and information envisaged by its champions in the years of Ujamaa – the instruments for such purposes have been privatised in the meantime. For one thing, Swahilisation would only be applicable to state schools, and the state-school system now has to compete with private school systems. The democratisation inherent in the old Swahilisation project is now impossible; hence the socio-political importance of Swahilisation has significantly diminished, and the government seems to have no difficulty in doing something that looked quire impossible for three decades. It is not that the government 'at last' agrees on Swahilisation. The country has changed: Swahilisation is now a far less threatening and politically empowering measure than when it would have been inserted into a general socialist strategy.

Some observations

In view of the discussion in the following sections, a few summarising observations should be made. As should become increasingly clear, language policy and language research are held together by attitudes towards Swahili and English and how they should function in the Tanzanian state:

1. The post-independence attitudes towards Swahilisation and other language planning measures can be divided into five periods:
    1. 1961–7: the pre-Arusha period. English and Swahili coexist. Swahili is ideologically constructed as the language of African nationalism and pride.
    2. 1967–75: the heyday of Swahilisation. English and Swahili become more and more symbolised as antagonistic value-complexes. This is the period of 'the struggle for Swahili' against English.
    3. 1975–82: the period of confusion. Politics and linguistics start taking divergent courses. Political decisions effectively prevent further Swahilisation; in the meantime linguistic purism reaches its peak with the publication of *Kamusi ya Kiswahili Sanifu* (TUKI 1981).
    4. 1982–6: the period of decline. The government's decision to maintain English as the medium of higher education brings the prospect of Swahilisation to an end. Efforts in that direction are stopped.
    5. After 1986: the period of relaxation. The introduction of economic liberalisation and the abolishment of the one-party state render irrelevant the old oppositional schemes of English versus Swahili, and new sociolinguistic patterns emerge.
    From 1982 onwards, the situation is virtually identical to the one that prevailed before 1967. The ideological opposition of Swahili and English has weakened considerably, especially after 1986. English has regained its pre-1967 prestige, while Swahili has attained an unprecedented level of spread and importance in use.
2. Language policies and language planning efforts were overwhelmingly monofocal. They were aimed at the promotion of one language, while, of course, acknowledging the existence of other languages. These other languages, the 'ethnic' or 'tribal' languages, received remarkably little attention both in the colonial era and in independent Tanzania. The question was reduced to an either/or formula: either Swahili becomes *the* language of the country, or English does. The argument used in favour of this monofocal

approach is twofold, and corresponds more or less to the two assumptions outlined at the beginning of this section: the efficiency assumption and the integration assumption. On the one hand, the discourse of Swahilisation concentrates on its practical advantages: Swahili would facilitate communication, it would enhance understanding between various groups of people, it would improve pupils' school performance, and so on (for an example of practical reasoning see Mulokozi 1991: 11–12). On the other hand, Swahilisation is placed against the background of the development of a new national culture, a *nation*, of which it would be the natural vehicle. This new culture was a monist concept in which pluralism – especially linguistic and 'cultural' pluralism – had little or no place. The consequence of this, however, is that most children in non-urban inland areas, where Swahili was not the mother tongue of the population, were faced with a 'hidden' language barrier when they entered primary school: that of Swahili. For them, Swahili was as foreign a language as English (a fact already observed by Khamisi 1974: 290) – in spite of the fact that it had become the national language and in spite of the widely heard argument that 'everyone spoke and understood Swahili'.

3. In debates on the English versus Swahili issue, both languages were strongly abstracted, and language-internal variability was not taken into account. Thus, the fact that different varieties of English, but also different varieties of *Swahili*, would be observed in the linguistic repertoires of Tanzanians, was hardly ever discussed (some cursory references notwithstanding, as in Khamisi 1974). Only in the late 1990s was the issue of difference and inequality *within* languages raised. Saida Yahya-Othman (1997: 24–5) emphasised the exclusivity of standard Swahili (a 'laboratory variety' in her view); by no means all Tanzanians have access to this status variety of Swahili, a fact to which the 'elitization of Kiswahili varieties among the "experts"' (ibid.: 24) contributes substantially. Thus, the generalised spread of Swahili does not automatically result in generalised equality among speakers because Swahili would come in many shapes and forms, some of which would carry status while others would be stigmatised as 'bad' or 'deficient' Swahili. This is truistic from a sociolinguistic point of view (see, for example, Hymes 1996), and ethnographic observation of social discourse practices (as in Yahya-Othman's work) would reveal that Swahili is just as much an object of struggles for authority, normativity and status – and hence an object of social differentiation and stratification – as is for instance English (including one of the characteristics of such situations: experts lamenting the 'declining standards' of Swahili usage) (Neke 2002; cf. Milroy and Milroy 1985). It looks as if Tanzanian language policy and language-political debates not only showed a blind eye towards ethnic languages, but also towards variability within Swahili. The importance of this level of variability will be the topic of Part 2 of this book.

4. Underlying the struggle between Swahili and English was the (apparently widely accepted) assumption that Swahili was an underdeveloped language,

in need of development. 'Development' and 'modernisation' then, became the guiding metaphors and the fundamental ideological grid for all language planning and research. The implicit theory here is one in which some kind of scale for measuring the degree of 'development' of languages is applied. On that scale, English ranks higher than Swahili, because English is associated with a higher level of societal and cultural development. On this point both colonialism and Marxism seem to concur: the degree of technological and economic development of a society will reflect on its culture, and hence on its language. Transforming a society – development – logically and legitimately entails transforming its symbolic repertoire, most prominent of which is its language. A more detailed discussion of this language-ideological basis will be given later.

5. Throughout the debates on the status of Swahili, one encounters various perspectives and opinions about the history of Swahili. Two points – almost stereotypes about Swahili – are constantly attacked: the view of Swahili as a language created by the Arabs, mainly in the context of the slave trade; and the impression of Swahili as not being a 'pure' Bantu language but rather a foreign, almost colonial language on a par with English, French or Portuguese. Authors such as Kihore (1976) devote copious paragraphs to a culture-historical analysis which shows that the Arab influence on Swahili society was typically imperialist or colonialist. To Kihore, the Arabs had conquered the Waswahili and forced their influence upon them. Other authors, notably Abdallah Khalid (1977), advocate a view in which the Arabs are seen as an immigrant minority who never really affected the Bantu roots of the Swahili language and culture. So despite the Arab influence, Swahili is and remains a 'pure' Bantu language. These points are not irrelevant. In view of the symbolism of Swahili as a mark of Africanhood and African self-esteem, it would be convenient if the language could be demonstrated to be 'purely' African (or Bantu), untouched by un-African (Arab) elements, and even less affected by imperialist or colonialist stigma. Diachronic or genetic-linguistic analyses demonstrating that Swahili originated as a contact language (see, for example, Heine 1970) are treated with extreme contempt by, for example, Abdallah Khalid, who insists on a 'pure' and 'complete' status for Swahili. In this respect also, the decision by the Inter-Territorial Language Committee to adopt the strongly Arab-influenced Zanzibar variant as the basis for further standardisation was perceived as a mistake, because it produced an unfavourable impression among up-country groups. Kihore (1976: 60) sees the Committee's policy to use Bantu words where possible while paying enough attention to Arabic terms as 'the biggest setback the language has ever experienced'. The Arabic-sounding terms in the newly standardised language gave rise to 'provocative adjectives like being "a bastard language" and an "inferior hybrid" (of Arabic and Bantu, the reason used by the Baganda to reject Kiswahili)' (ibid.). An argument often kept implicit in this respect is that of the connection between Swahili and Islam. From an historical and

ethnographic perspective, Swahili is the mother tongue of coastal sedentary and partly urbanised groups who, by and large, are Muslims (see Khamisi 1974: 293–4; Lacunza Balda 1991; Topan 1991, 1992; Middleton 1992). Despite early attempts to sever the link between Swahili and Islam (for example with the German decision to abolish the use of Arabic script for Swahili [Topan 1992: 339]), the view of Swahili as being historically associated with Muslim societies is quite persistent. We will see shortly how these conflicting views on the history of Swahili and its speakers influenced scholarly debates on the status and the future of the language.

4.3 CONTINUITY IN LINGUISTIC RESEARCH: THE COLONIAL LEGACY

It is not uncommon to see Tanzanian Swahili scholars give credit to pre-independence efforts in the field of Swahili standardisation. Massamba (1989), for instance, states that: '[t]he development of Kiswahili in Tanzania has a long history, beginning before independence when a number of steps were taken for its promotion and development. After independence the government of Tanzania actively promoted the development of the language' (Massamba 1989: 61). He then presents a survey of the pre-independence activities of various church denominations and of the Inter-Territorial Language Committee. Although clearly the product of colonial motives, Massamba praises the work of the Inter-Territorial Language Committee, because:

> [i]ts involvement in the promotion of Kiswahili was tremendous and remains unparalleled. Whether or not the colonialists' endeavor to develop the language was in their own best interest need not concern us here; rather, what is important to note is the seriousness with which the colonialists attended to the development of Kiswahili . . . it can be said that the work of the Committee laid the foundations for the development of Kiswahili as a modern language. (Ibid.: 62.)

The importance of the Committee's work is further stressed by the fact that its original agenda for the standardisation and development of Swahili was almost entirely adopted by its successor in post-independence Tanzania: the Institute of Kiswahili Research, TUKI (ibid.: 62 and 63–4). Thus there seems to be an unquestioned (and apparently unquestionable) coherence between pre-independence language efforts and post-independence efforts; the latter are seen to be a continuation of the splendid work performed by the colonial Committee, albeit in a changed socio-political environment (see also Topan 2008). It is acknowledged, both in Massamba's statements and in the comparison of the agendas of the Inter-Territorial Language Committee and the Institute of Kiswahili Research, that the colonial approach to Swahili resulted in genuine promotion and development of the language; in other words, that it was a *good* approach, the quality of which should override considerations about the ideological and political motives it served.

It may well be the case, of course, that the actual quality of the scientific output of the Inter-Territorial Language Committee was good, and that the members of the Committee were relatively mild colonialists. Still, the perception of continuity between the colonial and the postcolonial ways of treating language for the purpose of what is called promotion and development is remarkable, especially in light of the radical anticolonialism that pervaded Tanzanian public culture in the decades after independence. It detaches the scientific activities from their ideological underpinnings, invoking a level of objective detachment that is supposed to allow neutral, Archimedean assessments of the results and only the results. This, however, bumps into the deconstructivist argument that 'knowledge of other cultures and eras depends on the cultures and eras doing the knowing' (Boon 1982: 45). In other words, the adoption of the *linguistic apparatus* developed by colonial institutions may involve the adoption of an *ideological grid* on language and about language as well. In that case, postcolonial language activities in Tanzania may display features derived from the colonial outlook on language.

A detailed analysis of this *regard colonial* on African languages is beyond the scope of this book; furthermore, it has been attempted in more authoritative ways by scholars such as Fabian (1983a, 1983b, 1986) and Samarin (1982, 1984). I will therefore restrict myself to a brief examination of linguistic colonialism in which I will formulate a number of general observations on what constitutes linguistic knowledge in the colonial outlook on African (more specifically, Bantu) languages.

Bantu linguistics – a scientific venture closely related to the development of the colonial system, as Fabian (1986) demonstrated – has yielded a remarkable body of linguistic knowledge, enough to fill libraries. The development of Bantu linguistics paralleled that of the colonial system. But, also, the development of the colonial system itself reflects on who could qualify as Bantu *linguists*. Three rough historical phases can be distinguished, in which the structure of the colonial enterprise seems to entail shifts in the profiles of Bantu linguists. The first period, that of early discovery and colonisation, yields linguistic descriptions mainly carried out by non-professional linguists (military or administrative personnel, or missionaries), while professional linguists are in the minority. The second period, that of the consolidation of the colonial system, is characterised by a more or less equal ratio of professionals (members of academic institutions) and non-professionals (administrators and missionaries). The third period, that of the decline of the colonial empires and of decolonisation (post-World War II), shows an increasing professionalisation of Bantu linguistics.

The second period of this chronology is particularly interesting. In the enormous pile of published material on this period, academics, missionaries, administrators and settlers sit side by side in what seems to be an *ad hoc* scientific community very often embodied in national Academies for Colonial or Overseas Studies or other scientific organisations. Each sub-group's works were apparently recognised as scientific, though it is needless to say that they display enormous differences in quality and degree of sophistication. Massive state-of-the-art grammars and dictionaries stand next to small *esquisses de grammaire* ('grammatical sketches') and practical manuals containing a rough grammatical outline, a short lexicon and a set of 'common useful phrases' (the kind of material so lovingly analysed by Fabian; see also Blommaert 2008a). How could this happen? How could sketchy, hardly reliable publications on Bantu language be granted the status of scientific material or linguistic knowledge? The answer, I believe, must be sought in two attitudinal complexes which both touch the core of colonialism as a historical ideology, and which at the same time serve as the epistemological justification for this type of linguistic knowledge.

The first attitudinal complex could be called the *discovery attitude*. Africa, prior to the arrival of the Europeans, was a blank spot on the maps. Everything had to be discovered, created and formulated in the discourse(s) of the colonial enterprise. Consequently, anyone who could justifiably claim to have some knowledge of some facts, could present them as 'findings' or 'discoveries'. The second complex can be captured under the term *'Being There'* (see also Said [1978] 1985: 156–7). A sufficiently long personal presence among Africans (as a missionary, trader, police officer or administrator) was enough justification for claiming knowledge of the Bantu languages, societies and cultures. This can be seen from the front pages of many publications from that period: the subscript of the author's name often mentioned or suggested the duration of the author's overseas experience. Whitehead and Whitehead's *Manuel de Kingwana* (1928), for example, thus qualifies the authors as: *qui furent missionaires de la B.M.S. pendant 35 ans* ('who were B.M.S. missionaries for 35 years'). This long stay in the field automatically suggested success in communication and, by implication, of competence and fluency in the local language(s). Authors motivate their endeavour in writing a grammar book or a course book by appraising their own success in intercultural communication with the natives. This also is one of the standard features of introductions to booklets from those days. It means, however, that the author not so much describes the language he or she observes in the practical use of the native speakers, but rather describes the variant he or she uses in interaction with the Africans. Not surprisingly, therefore, some authors (for example D'hondt n.d.) state bluntly that their own competence serves as the basis for description, and not a native informant's utterances.

The picture which emerges is one in which European colonists after some period of time claim enough competence in a Bantu language to be able to write a grammar or a course book of the language. This grammar, then, is often explicitly presented as reflecting the 'real' language in subtitles referring to the 'naturalness' or 'nativeness' of the described language (*tel qu'on le parle, tel qu'il sort de la bouche des noirs'* – 'as it is spoken', 'as it comes out of the mouths of the blacks'). Many authors go even further. They state that their effort of describing the language has had a beneficiary effect on the language and its speakers. The language they describe and publish is purified, improved and therefore better and nobler than that previously spoken by the natives. Whitehead and Whitehead (1928), for instance, describe the purpose of their linguistic activities as follows:

[The authors] proposed to discover the agreements and the disagreements of the parent Swahili and its daughter Kingwana, and to harmonize all that they found

agreeable to the known Bantu laws of speech, transforming the disagreeable
foreign elements into the indicated agreeable forms, eradicating the DOUBLE
and TRIPLE ENTENTES in many Swahili words or phrases, and so making
Kingwana a worthy medium for all forms of instruction and translation. They
believe that the way to literary success has thus been opened to Kingwana . . .
Many grammatical divergences have been turned into grammatical convergences,
and many anomalies have been turned into relative conformity. (Whitehead and
Whitehead 1928: iii–iv; emphasis in the original)

This fragment reveals many of the underlying assumptions of colonial linguists.
First, they 'discover' things. Next, they 'harmonise' and 'transform', they 'con-
verge' and 'make conform'. They 'eradicate disagreeable elements' and make
Kingwana into a worthy medium. They do all this in a scientific manner, according
to the 'known Bantu laws of speech'. Finally, the target functions of Kingwana as
described by Whitehead and Whitehead are unilateral forms of communication:
'instruction and translation'. In sum, the authors seem to perform a surgical operation on the language, backed by science, in order to make the language 'worthy' of
serving the missionary functions for which Whitehead and Whiteheaded needed
it.

This statement is also a definition of prescriptive linguistics. Whitehead and
Whitehead have a precise goal: 'improving' the language so as to cope with sophisticated tasks ('translating, both prose and poetry, scientific definition and math-
ematical precision, clear thinking and its true expression' [ibid.: iv]). This target
cannot be reached by the natives themselves because they lack the knowledge of the
'known Bantu laws of speech'. Whitehead and Whitehead thus combine their own
competence of Kingwana gathered during thirty-five years of missionary work, with
Western science (or, at least, with a Western scientific attitude): 'Being There' was
complemented by 'the European way', that is using ratio, science, structure, and
the noble intention of instructing the natives and translating the gospel into their
language.

In summary, the legitimation of all kinds of published material as linguistic
knowledge was found in the spirit of discovery coupled with the assumption that the
prolonged presence of a well-educated, rational European would be a sound basis
for producing linguistic knowledge about the Bantu language in which he or she was
competent. Knowledge was associated with prolonged presence and the structuring
of the communicative experience thus gathered by means of scientific methods.
Both criteria make knowledge of a Bantu language inaccessible to its native speakers.
Since competence is not enough, and since Europeans have the monopoly on scientific thought, natives at most can be equally good linguists in their own language,
but never better linguists. Their knowledge of the language is necessarily inferior to
that of the whites because they have no direct access to the scientific complex that
structures the experience into real linguistic knowledge. It is therefore no surprise
that many course books were based on the author's own competence in the language
(the level of which often left much to be desired [Samarin 1982]), even dispelling

the role of Africans as informants, and that only very few Africans rose to the status of 'linguists' during that period.

An additional dimension to these assumptions is the suggestion that producing scientific knowledge about a Bantu language automatically *improves* that language. It raises its status from an inferior level to that of an instrument capable of expressing thoughts and ideas that were sensed to be far beyond the natural level of development of the African societies. This is reflected in the interesting ways in which languages were labelled by their discoverers. Some were qualified as 'languages', others as 'dialects', still others as 'vernaculars', 'sabirs', or other weird categories of human languages. A particularly explicit example can be found in D'hondt (n.d.: 15), a Belgian colonial officer who published a practical Lingala course book in the 1950s. In his introduction, he provides a list of possible linguistic varieties of Lingala, and defines them as follows:

(1) *LANGUE: ensemble des termes d'un IDIOME et des règles de sa grammaire* ('LANGUAGE: sum of the terms of an IDIOME and of the rules of its grammar')

(2) *IDIOME: parler propre à une région plus ou moins étendue. Langue dont l'usage est peu répandue. Est également la langue considérée dans ce qu'elle a de particulier dans ses tournures et sa syntaxe* ('IDIOME: the speech characteristic for a more or less vast region. A language of which the usage is not widespread. Is also language considered in terms of the peculiarities of its application and its syntax')

(3) *DIALECTE: nom donné aux formes particulières qu'a prise une langue dans une ville ou contrée* ('DIALECTE: name given to the particular shapes a language has taken in a town or an area')

(4) *PATOIS: dialecte qui ne possède pas de littérature écrite* ('PATOIS: a dialect that does not possess a written literature')

(5) *LANGUE VEHICULAIRE: les composantes d'une langue véhiculaire sont divers dialectes qui, parfois légèrement transformés et fusionnés, donnent une nouvelle langue comprise par les peuplades dont elle a emprunté ses mots ou expressions* ('LANGUE VEHICULAIRE: the components of a 'langue véhiculaire' are various dialects which, sometimes slightly transformed or blended, yield a new language understood by the peoples from which it has borrowed its words or expressions')

The definitions are rather awkward. An *idiome* is three things: a regional *parler*, a rarely used *langue*, and the set of *idiomatic features* of a *langue*. A *langue* is the grammaticalised, abstract version of the *idiome*. A *dialecte* is identical to the first definition of *idiome*: a regional variant. A *patois* is a *dialecte* without alphabetical orthography; consequently, almost all Bantu languages were *patois* prior to colonisation. A *langue véhiculaire* is a mixture of *dialectes* that make a new *langue* (*langue* has an inconsistent meaning here). Its main characteristic is the fact that it is being 'understood' by the speakers of the dialects. To put it mildly, D'hondt is unclear with regard to what *idiome, dialecte* and *langue véhiculaire* actually are. But he is remarkably accurate in his definition of *langue* and *patois*. They form the extremes of a scale which can be sketched as follows:

idiome

patois > *dialecte* *> langue*

langue véhiculaire

This scale places *patois* at the bottom and *langue* at the top of a hierarchy of observable linguistic phenomena. A *patois* is the lowest, least developed kind of human speech; while a *langue* is a full-blown, sophisticated medium of human communication. The intermediate categories have characteristics of both extremes, and in the definition of *idiome*, *dialecte* and *langue véhiculaire*, for instance, reference is made to *langue*. But they are no longer *patois*, and not yet *langue*. This hierarchical scale also represents degrees of knowledge of linguistic phenomena by Europeans, and by extension, degrees of existential status. *Patois* are non-existent, invisible *idiomes*, *dialects*, and so on. They are not yet controlled by the colonisers, and they represent African speech in its precolonial shape. *Dialectes*, *idiomes* and *langues véhiculaires* are put on the map, they exist, they have a shape and a structure about which something is known to the colonisers. But all these phenomena become *langues* only when their lexicon and their grammatical structure have been determined, and when they have been given an orthography. In practical reality, these languages become *langues* when they have been placed under colonial authority and control. The existential status of the various linguistic phenomena encountered in the field depends on the degree of European colonial control over these phenomena, on the possibility to alter them so as to fit into a 'white' model of a 'good' language: a language in which one writes creative literature, in which one expresses philosophical, religious and scientific ideas.

For the purpose of the discussion here, what should be remembered from these admittedly sweeping remarks is this: the continuity of colonial and postcolonial ways of working on and thinking about Swahili, seen by African scholars such as Massamba, is based upon an assumption of scientific autonomy and objectivity that demands some caution when one looks at colonial linguistics as a discursive domain embedded in time- and culture-specific ideological complexes. I confess to having focused on very bad work in this discussion, but the fact remains that even this kind of work was accepted as *scientific knowledge of languages*, as knowledge that was either scientific in structure or that could be used as data for scientific purposes such as comparative Bantu studies (for comments on 'good' and 'prominent' work, see for example Irvine 1995; Blommaert 2008a).

The distance between the bare collection of facts and impressions on the one hand, and science on the other hand, was bridged by a complex of rationalisations and justifications that are part of the ideology of colonialism. Therefore, it is not unreasonable to suspect that some of the ways of looking at Swahili, characteristic of the colonial enterprise, have been adopted by postcolonial African Swahili scholars as part of a misconstrued notion of linguistic technique. In the eyes of Massamba and others, linguistic *métier* appears to be immune to ideological influences. It stands on itself and can be integrated into any kind of political and ideological context. This is why the approaches of the Inter-Territorial Language Committee are so highly praised: stripped of their colonial ideological context, they can be reintegrated into the Ujamaa project, because they are perceived as *good* methods.

Another element of the colonial legacy which penetrated Tanzanian linguistic-scientific thinking was a colonial language ideology revolving around a basic perception of 'language' as hierarchically related to other forms of speech. 'Language', as we noted above, was an exclusive category strongly connected to colonial control. Only those forms of speech that had been modelled, transformed, appropriated and structured by Western experts, or by African experts using Western expertise, were labelled as 'languages'. Linguistic forms only became 'language' once they were moulded in an 'artefactual' ideological shell, the format of modern advanced linguistics. Hence, the need to 'modernise' and 'develop' Swahili through the production of standard grammars and dictionaries (Blommaert 2008a). Hence, also, the emphasis on Swahili as a 'great' language, connected to a rich cultural heritage, and, most of all, connected to a long and impressive history. The fact that throughout the history of Swahili language planning, English was used as the model of a 'developed' language, testifies to the penetration of these pre-theoretical language ideological grids. Only those forms of speech that were rooted in a long tradition of cultural performance, expressed in written literature and embedded in a politically powerful and prosperous community could be labelled as a 'language'. To some extent, this emphasis on what could be called the Western-civilised model of a language obscured the African predicament of extreme societal multilingualism and functionally determined multilingual language repertoires, and the monofocal bias of most language planning efforts in postcolonial Tanzania can be seen in that light as one of the main factors of failure. The root of this failure lies in the adoption of language-ideological categories and concepts that may have seemed compatible with the homogenising dimension of Ujamaa, but could hardly account for the sociolinguistic reality of Tanzania.

4.4 THE GUIDING METAPHORS: DEVELOPMENT AND MODERNISATION

Almost all efforts in the domain of language planning and research during the colonial period, and even more so after independence, were labelled as efforts aimed at the development and/or modernisation of Swahili. We have already seen that the use of the notion of 'development' in contexts such as these presupposes that Swahili, prior to and during the 'development' efforts, is an underdeveloped language. We have also seen that the notion of 'development' introduces a scale according to which the degree of 'development' of Swahili is measured against that of other languages, notably English.

The metaphorical frame of thinking about Swahili in terms of development and modernisation is part of the colonial legacy in which an African language was evaluated against the standards of the 'civilisation' of its speakers. Williams (1992) associates the drive for modernisation in the domain of language with 'the search for a form of communication which can transcend impure thought and reasoning'. Thus:

a 'developed' language can be adopted as a language of wider communication in place of the impure 'native' form! Evidently these views on society, world development and language carry in them the ethnocentrism that was so evident in nineteenth-century thought on the same issues. (Ibid.: 125)

In that context, there is little doubt that when the Inter-Territorial Language Committee expressed its predilection for Arabic-sounding Swahili by adopting the Zanzibar variant as the basis for standardisation, the Committee's members were inspired by a perception of Arab culture – and language – as being 'nobler' and more civilised than that of the black Africans.

But there is more to the collocation of 'development' and 'modernisation' than just the colonial legacy. The ideological frame it imposes is in itself an obstacle for certain forms of thinking about language. As the frame guiding the Tanzanian government and research institutes in their efforts with regard to Swahili, it is one of the deep influences of Ujamaa on the emerging linguistic tradition in Tanzania. A look at some of the published work of Tanzanian linguists, and mainly at the authoritative journal *Kiswahili* (formerly *Swahili*), published by TUKI, can testify to this influence.

Kiswahili was an official journal, published by an institution that had been assigned an important nation-building task. As a consequence, it can be taken as a good source for scrutinising the types of research carried out on Swahili within the official Tanzanian linguistic circles, the ways in which this research was carried out (namely, by whom, by means of which theoretical and methodological instruments, in which domains, and for what purpose) and the general attitudes and ideology underlying linguistic research. When taken together with some other publications by TUKI researchers, a fairly precise picture can be drawn of the way in which an official tradition of linguistics emerges in Tanzania. This emerging tradition can best be described as a conglomerate of legitimate ways of speaking about Swahili, correspondences between reality and theory (which create the basis for assessments of scientific 'truth' and knowledgeability) and a series of action procedures (specific forms of research) considered to be in line with the general idea. For this new tradition, there must be a model or archetype of Swahili linguistics. This model provides the sources for constructing the tradition. More concretely, there must be a specific model of linguistic research reflected in the emergence of a local linguistic tradition.

Let us first take a look at a definition of 'language development' given by the then Director of TUKI, David Massamba (1987a: 180):

We might say that language development is a deliberate move by a social group (e.g. a nation) to adopt, choose from available dialects or languages, or even invent a language for the sole purpose of equipping it with the capability of being used as a medium of either instruction or communication. In order for this end to be realized a number of factors have to be considered seriously. These are factors such as Language Policy, Language Planning and Language Modernization.

In elaborating this definition,[2] Massamba sketches the following procedural model. Language development is the overall term denoting a three-step programme consisting of: (1) language policy, that is, an elaborate statement of priorities formulated by the nation; (2) language planning, that is, the scientific translation of language policy into a plan for scientific research; and (3) language modernisation, that is, concrete steps undertaken by scholars within the frame of language planning (cf. ibid.: 181ff.).

Massamba strongly emphasises the technocratic nature of the language development work, and complains about the political interference in the process. He then spells out three exemplary domains in which language planning could and should be elaborated (ibid.: 183–4): (1) language planning for pedagogical purposes, that is, the production of adequate textbooks and didactic materials for formal education in the target language Swahili; (2) language planning for normative purposes, aimed at producing descriptive/prescriptive grammars, dictionaries and orthography; and (3) language planning for modernisation, that is, designed to 'enable the language to cope with modern technological advancement'. This last domain is further defined in these terms:

> Language modernization may be defined as the development of a language in a way that will enable it to express both new and technological concepts. The most crucial aspect of language modernization is the development of scientific and/ or technical neologisms. With new scientific and technological innovations and inventions new concepts are bound to emerge. Hence the need for terminology. (Ibid.: 184)

From these fragments, it appears that language development is directed at three target areas: teaching materials, language standardisation and lexicological updating. Moreover, all this is a technocratic undertaking, carried out by trained linguists (even if reluctantly) in line with political directives. We see the artefactual ideology of language in full force here (Blommaert 2008a). Modernisation, then, is a specific part of this programme, defined as the creation of a new Swahili vocabulary for innovations in the field of science and technology. Consequently, colonial efforts can also count as efforts resulting in development or modernisation. All activities past and present that resulted in a larger spread, an increase of grammatical description or standardisation, or literary production, are captured under the term 'development'.

Modernisation, however, is historically contingent. The Inter-Territorial Language Committee did not mention it in its original agenda. Modernisation evolved later, after independence, and as a by-product of Swahilisation in the education system. As early as the early 1970s, it was realised that in order to be able to teach in Swahili at a high level of scientific sophistication, adequate equivalent Swahili terminology would be required. Optimism was great in that period – the heyday of Swahilisation – and researchers at TUKI started to coin terms in domains such as politics, the social sciences, engineering, medicine, mathematics, biology, physics, and so on. Various procedures and techniques were used (see Temu 1971, 1984; Mac-William 1985; Mdee 1986; Mutahi 1986; Berwouts 1989), ranging from borrowings (Arabic and English), through phonological adaptation of internationally standardised terms, to outright *assemblage* on the basis of existing terminology.

But word-coining is a very problematic activity, especially when it is associated with a concept such as modernisation. Basically, word-coining is translating already existing (mainly English) terminology. Thus, modernisation, in its word-coining reality, has a clear implication of deficit: nothing is really invented, inventions from elsewhere are simply translated. If Swahili, in Massamba's terms, was to be equipped with the capacity to function as a medium of scientific communication, but if, on the other hand, it had to rely on the translation of previously introduced English or international terms, then Swahili would obviously never become entirely equivalent to English. English would always be the source language, in which new terms are introduced first. It would therefore always seem superior, and the modernisation of Swahili would seem a never-ending and hardly gratifying process.

Similarly, the idea of developing Swahili – which is consistently defined as a 'developing' language as opposed to a 'developed' language like English, French or German (see Massamba 1987a and 1989, *passim*) – is bound to be frustrating in the long run. The reason for this is the assumption of a model or a target inherent to the metaphor of development. Apart from the relative absurdity of a distinction such as 'developed-underdeveloped' for natural and widely used languages, there is the simple observation that a developed language is not a steady-state object, but something dynamic. An underdeveloped language can therefore never become developed, since the developed languages themselves develop further. Swahili, therefore, on the basis of this metaphorical scheme, will never be able to close the gap between its state of underdevelopment and the state of development of languages such as English.

The view of Swahili as an underdeveloped language in need of modernisation is related to more general development attitudes in Tanzania. The gradual shift from optimism to pessimism among Tanzanian linguists (witnessed by, for example, Massamba 1989; Mulokozi 1991) runs parallel to the evolution of the country's economic and social problems, and the chronology of these developments can be neatly followed in the papers published in *Kiswahili*. The optimism of the early Ujamaa period is reflected in highly euphoric papers by Tanzanian scholars and politicians.[3] Swahili had become more and more 'Africanised' as a 'chtonic' scientific object. African authors largely outnumbered Westerners in the post-Arusha volumes of *Kiswahili*; an increase of papers on Swahili in education was triggered by Nyerere's *Elimu ya Kujitegemea* policy paper; language planning as a general topic was the most prominent feature of *Kiswahili* between 1969 and 1973. At around the same time, literary criticism of Swahili literature had taken off, and the first papers began to appear in *Kiswahili*.

From 1975 onwards, when the failure of Ujamaa began to dawn upon the people and when the oil crisis had crippled the Tanzanian economy, the tone and type of papers in *Kiswahili* changed significantly. First, the volume of published material decreased. Far fewer papers were published. Second, language planning papers virtually disappeared, except for strongly apologetic papers on the education problem. Papers on less ideologically biased subjects such as (descriptive) ethnolinguistics, hardcore linguistics and literary analysis featured more prominently.

When in 1982, at the apex of the economic crisis, Nyerere declared that the Swahilisation of higher education would be postponed indefinitely, researchers reacted as could be expected. 'Neutral' papers on linguistics, literature and lexicography and apologetic papers on the education problem continued to dominate *Kiswahili*'s tables of content. *Isimujamii* ('sociolinguistics') disappeared altogether as a separate section of the journal. The only sociolinguistic papers were assessments of language planning measures undertaken earlier (see, for example, Ohly 1982; Massamba 1987b). Whereas in the early days of independence and after the Arusha Declaration of 1967 Swahili was conceived of as an engine for national development and as the language of liberation and Africanhood, attitudes towards its fiercest enemy, English, changed from 1974–5 onwards. In line with the increased need for foreign economic support, English regained respectability in the eyes of Tanzanian policy makers.

The association between economic evolutions and attitudes towards Swahili is not only present in the similarity of historical facts. The linguistic ideology governing Tanzanian linguistics after 1967 dictated a close connection between language and socio-economic structures. The growing impact of radical socialists on the University of Dar es Salaam from the mid-1960s certainly contributed to the growth and elaboration of this trend. This is most prominently articulated in Rajmund Ohly's works (especially 1978, but see also 1982). Ohly views language as an artefact, a material thing that can be manipulated, influenced and planned very much like other material sectors of society (for example, industrial production or agriculture). Linguistics, for Ohly, is a matter of assessing the market demand, of producing and marketing the product. Traces of this attitude can still be found in Massamba's ideas, as quoted above.

The pervasiveness of this attitude is such that it gives rise to the impression that Swahili is a correlate of general socio-economic development. The same model is used in both instances: especially since the end of the Nyerere era, the West (the English-speaking world in particular) is the model for development, just like English is the model for Swahili language development. The refutation of Western recipes for development, contained in the Arusha Declaration, caused a strong commitment to Swahili as a medium of education and boosted Swahili research. The decline of this self-reliance ideology during the second half of the 1970s triggered a decline in Swahili research and an accentuation of the role of English as a model for language development. The turn to the West in the early 1980s was reflected in a radicalisation of the Swahili-in-education debate (see, for example, Mulokozi 1986 and 1991; Massamba 1989) and a continued decline of (especially socio-) linguistic research.

Thus the attitudes towards Swahili seem to be governed by more general attitudes about the way out of underdevelopment. In the aftermath of Arusha, papers expressing linguistic and cultural self-confidence were abundant (see, for example, Mwangomango 1970; Abdulaziz 1971; Mkelle 1971; Besha 1972; Kombo

1972; Mhina 1972, 1977; Akida 1974; Lodhi 1974; Ansre 1977). Papers such as Mwangomango (1970) emphatically stressed the relationship between the teaching and correct usage of Swahili, and the development of a truly independent unified nation in which the vestiges of British colonialism have been eradicated. Papers by Western scholars who pointed out some difficulties in Tanzanian language planning (for example, Harries 1968) were fiercely attacked by local scholars. This euphoria and radicalism vanishes from 1974 onwards, to be replaced by more conservative and neutral papers. The second half of the 1980s, when the Swahilisation project faded together with the Ujamaa policy, generated papers such as Mulokozi's (1986, 1991) and Massamba's (1987a and 1989), in which disappointment about the development of language policy is expressed. This period also generated an increased importance of lexicography, the type of linguistic work in which the frustrating modernisation metaphor and the role of English as a model are most prominent.

The connection between linguistic thinking and more general socio-political developments can also be witnessed from the tone and style of papers in *Kiswahili*. The discourse on Swahili is somewhat hybrid. On the one hand, there are lots of papers written in a curiously non-academic key, from a linguist's point of view. In these papers, mostly dealing with sociolinguistics (language planning) and literary criticism, the authors blend linguistic and ethnographic observations with outspoken political-ideological statements. Language planning measures are motivated by means of state-ideological principles, as in this rather typical statement:

> Therefore, in teaching Kiswahili, we should realize that we are waging war against the colonial ideas. It is necessary that we teach Kiswahili in order to 'build' young people who adhere to the ideas of Ujamaa. (Mwangomango 1970: 33)

To Mwangomango, and to many others, the rationale for introducing Swahili in education is its nationalist potential, as opposed to the connotations of colonial oppression attached to English. Also prominent as an argument for the introduction of Swahili in educatio is the (hotly debated, see above) assumption that it is a truly African language. Papers on Swahili literature very often adopt a kind of Négritude attitude. Literature is seen as evidence of the cultural and intellectual equivalence of Africans with Europeans (see, for example, Balisidya 1987).

On the other hand, *Kiswahili* contains core-grammatical or phonological papers, mostly applications of existing grammatical/phonological theories to Swahili or other Tanzanian languages (see Mukama 1978; Mazrui 1983; Batibo 1987). Theories such as systemic grammar, lexicase grammar and transformational grammar are adopted in their standard versions, aspects of which are then applied to fragments of Swahili grammar. Lexicography – a prominent section – is characterised by a pragmatic approach that keeps in touch with recent developments in the field of lexicography and dictionary making (see, for example, Mac-William 1985). But there again an ideological undercurrent can be distinguished (see Temu 1984): detached, objective expertise is still framed in the wider context of nation-building targets, and word-coining, for instance, is guided by preferences expressing a desire to Africanise (or, rather, de-Europeanise) Swahili as a medium of scientific discourse.

On the whole, *Kiswahili* oscillates between two extremes. On the one hand there is politically committed science, in which scientific research is granted the status of political action. On the other hand, there is uncommitted science, in which theoretical elegance, detachment and, ultimately, a low degree of applicability seem to figure. So at one end of the scale there seems to be a scientific credo which dictates that Swahili research is part of politics, while at the other end there is a credo which seems to deny this connection and which places high hopes in empiricism, objectivism and the most central approaches of Western linguistic science. Whereas the first end of the scale could be seen as maximally socioculturally embedded, the other end is maximally decontextualised in nature. There is little between the extremes; peripheral linguistics such as the ethnography of speaking, interactional sociolinguistics, psycholinguistics, pragmatics or discourse analysis, are virtually absent.

Two sources can be connected to these features of Tanzanian linguistic discourse. On the one hand, Swahili linguistic discourse blends with political discourse, particularly with Ujamaa discourse; on the other hand, it seeks a connection with formalist linguistic discourse in the structuralist-generativist tradition. Again, we can detect an allegory of the overall ideology of development and modernisation. Swahili linguistics is part of a general development strategy outlined by Ujamaa policy, and closely following its historical track (first source). This development strategy is geared at modernisation or, more precisely, technologisation. High-tech is here associated with 'modern' linguistic theories within the formal paradigm, provided that these theories have demonstrated their usefulness (second source). Hence the interest in widespread, successful theoretical models such as transformational grammar, and the absence of more peripheral and interdisciplinary types of linguistic research. As predicted by the contextual semantics of 'modernisation', Swahili linguists scrupulously adopt successful Western methods, since these methods represent progress or development in linguistics and thereby fit into the development frame governing linguistic research. Hardly any local solutions are tried or tested; Swahili and the other local languages are brought into existing, borrowed frameworks of Western origin. The sources of Swahili linguistic discourse prevent innovation in more than one way, because the idea of development implies a foreign model, to be copied as accurately as possible.

The paradox is clear: in their attempt to re-appropriate Swahili, Tanzanian linguists adopted some of the basic scientific assumptions that had been a source of oppression to them before. They adopted a frame of thinking about language and levels of efficiency, levels of civilisation and functionality that had been used before, in colonial linguistics. This frame of thinking had defined Swahili, as it had other Bantu languages, as an inferior language, not as modern and not as developed as, for instance, English or French. By adopting this basic frame – a colonial language ideology – the linguists almost necessarily reproduced it, and so found themselves in an intellectual deadlock in which every effort to demonstrate the equivalence of Swahili to English in effect demonstrated the opposite. But this frame, in which the language had to be modernised and developed, was strangely coherent with and supportive of the general development philosophy of Ujamaa, because its object –

Swahili – was an African element that could now be lifted to a status equal to that of English. As a humanistic development ideology, Ujamaa could be easily mirrored in a humanistic development endeavour: the development of the people's language. But language proved to be a rather more elusive object than other areas of social and economic life.

4.5 THE PROBLEM OF IDENTITY: THE CREATION OF THE NEW WASWAHILI

Given that Swahili was the national language, a number of linguists and anthropologists found that Swahili had to be connected to some kind of 'Swahili-ness', to some deeper sense of national belonging. Seemingly clear and simple as it sounds, this proposition hides a complex of conceptual and theoretical problems, some of which prompted huge debates in Tanzania. Here also, political ideology has deeply penetrated the realm of thinking about language. And here also, this resulted in lines of thought that are as unproductive and paralysing as those that developed within the frame of development and modernisation. A closer look at the way in which linguists dealt with the question of Swahili identity should demonstrate some of these conceptual and theoretical problems.

The discourse of language and identity relies on two main rhetorical strategies: (1) *naturalising* new concepts by means of historical evidence; and (2) *legitimising* them by means of authoritative discourse such as science. Together they create a diversified concept of the Swahili person, the *Mswahili*, a complex of definitions, some of which refer to 'ethnic' – or 'objective' – identities, while others refer to 'subjective' or political identities.

Let us turn to the strategy of *naturalisation*. Although the choice and promotion of Swahili – first by the colonial authorities and later by TANU and the independent Tanzanian government – may have meant a relative preponderance of the coastal Waswahili societies over inland peoples (cf. Khamisi 1974: 290), the language was not perceived as outspokenly ethnic. This de-ethnicised connotation of Swahili, as we have seen, became even more important when TANU made Swahili the medium and emblem of the nationalist struggle against the British, and it became the official dogma of Swahili: Swahili was an egalitarian medium enabling national unity among all Tanganyikans.

As noted earlier, Nyerere, one of the first African leaders to develop intensive and productive relationships with Mao Zedong's China in the second-half of the 1960s, was exposed to the procedures and effects of the Great Proletarian Cultural Revolution there. It is not unreasonable to expect that he was influenced by it and believed in the possibility of radical, revolutionary ideological and political change in sociocultural systems. In any event, the gradualism that characterised TANU's policies in the early years of independence ended in 1967 with the brusque and radical acceleration of the Arusha Declaration. I observed that the main vehicle for change in this new and revolutionary stage of socialist transformation was education; hence the enormous attention given to Swahilisation and curriculum reform in primary and secondary education, and to adult education: 'For Tanzania, independence basically implies development through education' (Hall 1975: 60). And of course: 'The greater the amount of schooling an individual has had in Tanzania the greater would his proficiency in Swahili be likely to be' (Abdulaziz 1971: 172). The new education policy also contained a belief that Tanzanians could be gradually transformed from 'traditional' (that is, ethnically-based) Africans to oppressed colonial subjects, and finally to free citizens whose way of life would have absorbed elements from the two previous historical phases: they would live like Africans, but in a modern and deeply changed environment. That environment would be the socialist state, Tanzania, a new social system replacing the ethnic group. Life in that environment, however, should be based upon similar principles as those organising life in a rural village: solidarity and dialogue among the members of the group, group participation in decision making, common ownership of the means of production, and so on. As noted repeatedly in Chapter 3, this is of crucial importance, because the last feature was undoubtedly intended as a means to naturalise the process of nation building. The revolutionary change was supposed to develop along the natural characteristics of the Tanzanians, namely the traditional principles of African village organisation, but projected onto and converted into a modern state.

The new Tanzanian, the product of the Ujamaa revolution, was constructed around a feature cluster, a rather intuitive conglomerate of qualities that was supposed to make up a human being as a member of this new society. These characteristics were spelt out in documents such as the Arusha Declaration and were reiterated in a wide variety of post-Arusha speeches and policy papers. The feature cluster comprises, among other things, elements such as:

- *occupation*: the ideal Tanzanian is a villager involved in agricultural production;
- *faith*: the Tanzanian believes in Ujamaa, very much in the way of a religious belief;
- *character and ethics*: a Tanzanian is diligent, inclined to help his fellow man, and opposed to injustice and exploitation;
- *common background*: all Tanzanians have joint experiences with colonial oppression and liberation; they all live in a poor country in which the traces of colonial injustice are still visible; and
- *language*: all Tanzanians are educated in Swahili; Tanzania is a Swahili-speaking country.

Notably absent from this feature cluster are things like *race* or ethnic descent, and *religion*. Further, both the multi-ethnic and the secular (or, rather, multi-religious) nature of the new society are repeatedly emphasised. Religion belongs to the domain of the Tanzanian's free individual choice, and the state should not interfere with it. But the state itself was typically seen as a secular unit (cf. Young 1993: 13). To Nyerere, socialism appears to be a return to the roots, to be the natural state of the African man. Also typical in this respect is that the economic programme of Ujamaa takes a very 'African' shape, with its connotations of naturalness: rural, agriculture-based self-reliance.

Let us take a look at language now. Swahili is seen as one of the natural features of a Tanzanian, it appears as an indisputable, unquestionable element of Tanzanian identity. It is one expression of, as well as a medium of reproduction for, the fundamental equality of man. As noted earlier, this connotation of Swahili stands in contrast to the pragmatic nature of the spread of Swahili throughout the country. Swahili was never a characteristic of the people who became Tanzanians; it was (one of) their language(s) because of conscious language planning and linguistic engineering. The TANU ideologues minimised the fact that the spread of Swahili was basically a historical accident (as well as that it was not the mother tongue for the majority of their countrymen) and attributed fundamental identity-constitutive values to the language. However, Swahili is not the marker of a traditional identity, but of a *new* identity: that of the national culture of the Tanzanian.

This is where the ambiguity of the cultural philosophy of Ujamaa becomes very clear. Although the target of Ujamaa is a *modern* society, all the building blocks explicitly associated with its construction are *traditional* elements that would be *modernised* in the construction process. It is a peculiar and somewhat paradoxical construct. The road to modernity looks longer when one starts with 'traditional' things than when one starts with adopted 'modern' things; we have seen this before. This, for one, accounts for the frustration experienced in later years by Swahili scholars who attempted to 'modernise' Swahili. The irrational element causing the ambiguity is the concept of *naturalness*, which appears to have been a major preoccupation for the architects of Ujamaa. The development process should move along natural lines, the natural characteristics of humans and their societies. It should, first and foremost, be an African kind of development towards modernity; hence the adoption of an African ('natural', 'organic') language, as constitutive of the identity of the modern Tanzanian.

We have arrived at a critical point here. In this association of language and 'natural' identity, Nyerere and his associates followed a deep-rooted and widespread linguistic ideology – in fact, it is the language ideology that defines modernity (Bauman and Briggs 2003). This linguistic ideology, which can be traced back to Herder and the Brothers Grimm, is that of the inseparable link between language, society and culture: the ideal society consists of a sovereign people, living in an independent state and sharing a common culture which finds its expression in a common language. Their language is the mirror of their *Volksgeist*, of the set of values, customs and knowledge they share with one another. Language is the inalienable marker of membership in the community. It is basically a romantic vision, which is (certainly in the case of Swahili) hardly ever realistic. But, just like everything else, it is more an object of change than a fact of reality: the ideology of language is part of the general transformation of attitudes and ways of life that make up the Ujamaa programme. The fact that it is rhetorically presented as an achievement rather than as a project may be attributed to its instrumental role in the process of diffusion and implementation of Ujamaa. Thus, eventually, the Tanzanians would all become free Africans, *wananchi* ('countrymen', 'citizens') and *wajamaa* ('supporters of Ujamaa'), and in the process would have become *new Waswahili*.

This romantic vision is eloquently expressed in S. S. Mushi's speech, 'The role of Swahili books in nation building endeavours' (Mushi 1968). Mushi, who was the governmental Promotor of Swahili Language and Literature, delivered this speech shortly after the Arusha Declaration in 1967; the following extracts illustrate the ideological pattern I have just outlined:

> . . . if we are really determined to evolve a national culture and to disseminate that culture to the nation as a whole, we ought to write books in a language which is understood by the people to whom we address the books we write. It is very difficult to promote a culture using a foreign language . . . Our reliance on school books written by foreigners has, on the whole, been responsible for inculcating unrealistic ideas about our society to most of our educated men and women . . . What we now need are Swahili books written by nationals who can best depict our cultural past and reflect our national ethic as well as the current policy of 'Socialism and Self-Reliance'. (Mushi 1968: 5)

We notice a direct association between language, culture and ideology, together with an emphasis on the 'naturalness' of being a speaker of the language. Only a Tanzanian writing in Swahili can produce appropriate books for Tanzanians and thus disseminate the national culture and its values. A European writing in Swahili is likely to produce unrealistic ideas; similarly, a Tanzanian writing in English would not make the point, so it is implicitly argued. The statement is, in sum, vintage Herderianism.

Let us now turn to the strategy of *legitimation*. Opinions such as Mushi's above were soon echoed by many academics. Kujitegemea ('self-reliance') was also thought to apply to intellectual performance and production, as Nyerere had repeatedly stressed. Tanzania should produce its own particularised and chtonic form of science adapted to the characteristics of its cultural and political system. Especially in the social sciences dealing with aspects of local culture and society, academic realism was very often outmanoeuvred by a programmatic stance more or less in line with Ujamaa. Swahili would (or should) become the instrument of a cultural transformation in the sense outlined above, and scientific efforts had to be geared to that end. The Herderian concept of language should be converted into nationwide, conscious engineering efforts. Herderianism is here, thus, converted into pure modernism (cf. Bauman and Briggs 2003).

The type of rationalisations used for the purpose can best be illustrated by this extract from a speech by the well-known Swahili scholar and writer, Abdulaziz Lodhi (1974: 11 and 13):

> The Tanzanian Culture therefore is the sum-total of all the good customs and tra- ditions of the different language groups in Tanzania. All these regional cultures using local languages, or dialects, are now being transformed into a National Culture using Swahili, which is increasingly commanding the loyalty, affection and respect of Tanzanians.
>
> Swahili is borrowing from other Bantu languages and vice versa which makes

Swahili an instrument of cultural infusion. Tribal words and their cultural signi-fications are blending to develop a way of life that will soon come to be known as typically Tanzanian, since any process of cultural homogenisation must lead ulti-mately to the acquisition of common values, modes of expression and elements of life-style.

After a few generations, the so called tribes, their cultures and languages as we know them today disappear to give way to a unified culture expressed in a rejuvenated Swahili.

In this fragment, the function of the language as a carrier of cultural values is strongly emphasised. The 'nation' is clearly seen as a *cultural* complex. Second, this cultural complex is changing in a politically well-determined and properly planned way: together with Ujamaa, a national culture will develop and replace (or absorb) the local cultures. Naturally, this is one of the reasons why so little attention was given to the 'ethnic' or 'tribal' languages: they could at best be simply *building blocks* for the new culture and language. Third, this process of change is a natural process assisted or facilitated by policy and planning. Nature will get a helping hand from the state and its experts.

All the ideological dogmata have been absorbed in this statement, and science is politicised: linguistic research is part of the overall modernisation policy which will steer the country into a bright new future, centred around a new human being. Swahili is the metaphorical correlate of overall independence, freedom and develop-ment. The independent Tanzanians had been taught to 'think of themselves and behave *as Waswahili, an erstwhile accursed label*' (Mbuguni and Ruhumbika 1974: 275; my emphasis). These ideological components dominate the overwhelming majority of published linguistic research on Swahili in the years between 1966 and 1978, and also appear sporadically in later publications.

In the meantime, other scholars went to search for a national history in Tanzania (see Denoon and Kuper 1970). In this search, the geographical space now taken by Tanzania was treated as a legitimate historical spatial unit, with a history different from that of neighbouring areas. Also, much emphasis was given to the emergence of anticolonial resistance or nationalist movements. In the eyes of Denoon and Kuper 'this is ideological history' because:

> the new historiography has adopted the political ideology of current African nationalism, and has used it to inform the study of African history. That commit-ment inclines the school towards rhetoric in defence of narrowly selected themes and interpretations, and the stereotyping and total rejection of alternative views. We suggest also that the basic assumption regarding the continuity and impact of national movements is questionable, and is asserted rather than demonstrated. (Ibid.: 348)

In the eyes of the Tanzanian scholars themselves, the construction of a national history was part of the process of the re-appropriation, or decolonisation, of their own culture. Similar national histories were written about Swahili, the most notable being Chiraghdin and Mnyampala (1977), and in these fields we witness the growth of a chtonic national science (cf. Arnaut and Blommaert 2009).

In the late 1980s, after years of relative peace, the debate was reopened by the senior TUKI scholar, T. S. Sengo. In a polemical article in *Kiswahili*, Sengo advocated a more 'honest' (that is, a coastal and Islamised) perspective on Swahili in Swahili scholarship (Sengo 1987). An animated in-house debate ensued, and Sengo was tackled by his colleague, Madumulla, who reiterated the socialist, secular and Tanzanian perspective on Swahili (Madumulla 1989). It was a fine example of a clash between those who emphasised historical cultural continuity in Swahili and those who wanted to emphasise the revolutionary break between the past and the present in Tanzania. At the same time, the identity debate is an accurate demonstration of the diversification of the concept of Mswahili (Swahili Man). Sengo advocates the 'objective' ethno-cultural approach to identity, while Madumulla emphasises the 'subjective' or political approach. None of the parties involved, however, challenges the Herderian, romantic view on Swahili as a container of culture. Rather, the debate is about *which* set of values should be contained in and transmitted through Swahili (see Madumulla et al. 1999 for a discussion).

Note, in passing, that when we apply Neustupny's (1974) dichotomy between a 'policy approach' and a 'cultivation approach', the Tanzanian debate about Swahili identity clearly should be typified as belonging to the 'cultivation approach'. The debate between purists from both sides was not about policy matters, but it was surely political in the sense of a matching between styles and genres of using language and the socio-political structures they were sensed to reflect. Neustupny's forecasting that developing countries would focus on policy approaches, while cultivation approaches would be more typical for developed countries, should therefore be amended: in as far as policy matters involved issues of identity and culture, the cultivation approach was never far away. In fact, in Tanzania it became the content side of the policy approach.

The main problem encountered by scientists involved in Ujamaa-inspired research was that of *history and tradition*, of continuity and discontinuity. In their search for a chtonic scientific legitimation of Tanzanian national culture (the Tanzanian *nation*), scientists tried to incorporate politically acceptable views on the history of Swahili, the clearest mark of this national culture, into their work. But in the theoretical direction imposed by the 'naturalness'-connotation of Ujamaa, culture is of course associated with continuity: people (naturally) are what they have always (naturally) been. This, then, resulted in ambiguous conclusions, because Ujamaa was only partially based on cultural continuity ('African' socialism), while it stressed the revolutionary (that is, discontinuous) character of Tanzanian history. The resulting Gordian Knot is that the *new* culture contained in the Ujamaa programme is fundamentally a contradiction in terms. Thinking about culture as tradition has little to offer when this thinking has to be applied to a synchronic process of sociocultural transformation.

In a similar vein, the *nation*, which in Ujamaa theory carries the national culture transmitted through Swahili, is in fact the *state*. Thus state ideology and national culture become synonymous – a synonymy which has triggered the confusion between 'objective' Swahili culture (the historical culture of the coastal societies) and 'subjective', political Swahili culture (that of the contemporary Tanzanian state), resulting in huge intellectual and political paradoxes.

For instance, it is not uncommon to read an essentialist statement about the close association between language and culture, illustrated by means of references to (coastal) Swahili greetings and accompanied by a jab about 'how Swahili culture is murdered in what is supposed to be Swahili literature' (Mhina 1972: 45), and another, political, statement by the same author a few pages later about how usefully and easily Swahili could be introduced in other African countries to solve their nation building problems. Two levels of factuality and argumentation are juxtaposed here. On the one hand, there appears to be a need to justify the adoption of Swahili as a national language in terms of its historical cultural embeddedness in coastal Swahili societies; on the other hand, exactly the opposite has to be argued (the de-ethnicised and egalitarian qualifications of Swahili) in order to sustain the political (socialist) usefulness of Swahili. Both levels of argumentation use the same central term – culture – but in an incompatible way: one refers to a diachronic and continuous entity (the traditional society), the other one to a synchronic and discontinuous entity (the state). This is more than just heteroglossia: it is a paradox. The scholar encounters the paradox between historical culture and the synchronic process it is supposed to justify.

I believe that much of the scholarly work on Swahili, national culture and education in Tanzania must be interpreted in the light of this paradox. A romantic-modernist and essentialist view on language in relation to culture, so it appears, is particularly ill-suited for a political programme such as Ujamaa. As soon as the connection between a language and a cultural tradition has been established, the basic rationale for the adoption of Swahili collapses: the assumption that it was nobody's language, which was needed to make it everybody's language. In the postcolonial history of Swahili, scientists, in their attempt to legitimise the naturalness of Swahili as a central component of Tanzanian cultural identity, have in fact falsified the very argument they were trying to build.

4.6 DISCUSSION: POLITICS AND LINGUISTICS

A close reading of products of Ujamaa linguistics shows that linguists and language planners worked within a theoretical and ideological frame which in part had been handed down to them by the political establishment, and in part had been adopted from earlier, colonial work on Swahili, including perceptions of 'good' linguistics. Thus, linguists worked on theoretical assumptions that were repeatedly challenged by their own findings. The political assumptions can be summarised in one proposition: Swahili was a metonymic, emblematic extension of the newly-independent state of Tanzania; therefore it was underdeveloped, and therefore it had to be reconstructed so as to fit the nature and the needs of the modern Tanzanian society. It was neatly paralleled by assumptions borrowed from previous

Swahili research, in which 'language' was associated with concepts of modernisation and Westernisation.

This proposition contains a theoretical hurdle: language and society are seen in a one-to-one situation, and both components of the equation are heavily idealised. It was taken for granted that Swahili would and could be distributed in an egalitarian way, assuming that society was egalitarian simply because it was socialist. When this did not seem to happen, as Ohly's rather naive survey on the absorption of new Swahili terminology in the peripheral area of Bukoba demonstrated (Ohly 1982), the causes of this failure were sought not in the political assumptions guiding the linguistic engineering, but in the engineering processes themselves. The method was questioned, not the theory.

Linguists must have been aware of the oversimplification of the socio-political theory on which they were supposed to operate. Khamisi's (1974) overview paper – though it appeared in a volume published to celebrate TANU's twentieth anniversary and therefore pays enough lip service to the official dogmas – already contains seeds of discontent. He calls for more intensive research in areas of language diversity: the pre-school linguistic conditions of children in areas where Swahili is not (yet) the mother tongue, dialects and sociolects, the socio-economic conditions of the use of Swahili, and so on. Apparently, some linguists must have noticed at that time that, basically, Swahili took on a role similar to that of English in rural peripheral areas. It was for many Tanzanians a foreign language associated with control and hierarchy, not replacing or absorbing local languages and cultures but rather superposing them in a stratified, vertical way rather than a horizontal way. It took many more years before such issues were effectively researched (Msanjila 1990; Mekacha 1993; Yahya-Othman 1997). Linguistic logic also clashed with political logic in the domain of language and education. Although Swahili was by all standards 'ready' to be introduced in post-secondary education at any time after independence, political arguments prevented the implementation of Swahilisation in secondary and higher education, and this was a source of great frustration to many Swahilists (see for example the papers in Rubagumya 1990).

Part of the political influence on linguistic work was unavoidable: postcolonial Tanzanian society was heavily politicised, certainly after 1967; Ujamaa politics enjoyed a significant degree of popularity, also among intellectuals; and intellectuals functioned as a vanguard group in society as we have seen in Chapter 3. On a more speculative plane, the attention and relevance given to linguistic and culture-theoretical work must have boosted the morale and self-confidence of the scientific community, as well as boosting their energy and commitment. Scientific advancement was part of the general progress of Tanzania, and the closer scientific products were associated with the explicit goals of Ujamaa politics, the more relevant they were judged to be.

This led to the sort of paradoxes and imbroglios I have outlined in the preceding sections. Most linguists had received (at least part of) their training abroad in European or American universities. This background was seen as merely instrumental, it was neutralised as an ideological factor. As soon as these linguists started working on Swahili in Tanzania their skills were integrated into the social theory of Ujamaa, which gave perspective and purpose to their work. However, the skills they had received were not neutral in themselves. In as far as they had received training in sociolinguistics they had been educated in the dominant Parsonian structural-functionalist paradigm criticised by Williams (1992). They had also learned to work on the two assumptions I outlined at the beginning of this chapter: the efficiency assumption and the integration assumption, both of which operated within the ideological framework of homogeneism and started from the premise that linguistic diversity meant social complexity and political inefficiency. Finally, they had also absorbed the hierarchical stratification of language varieties, in which a 'pure' (written) and codified language 'owned' by a historical speech community boasting a rich cultural heritage ranked highest. Thus, as became clear from the use of the metaphors of development and modernisation, they had assumed an implicitly pejorative attitude towards Swahili as a language which was not (yet) as flexible, functional and modern as English. Yet they took their linguistic training as an unproblematic given, dissociated from the culture-philosophical and ideological climate in which it had originated, and then transferred it to the progressive and nationalist ideological universe of Ujamaa.

Ujamaa seemed to offer a number of theoretical possibilities and challenges for linguists. First, in its emphasis on nation building, it was a homogeneistic theory of society and could be neatly integrated in the dominating paradigm of language planning as aimed at reducing language diversity to a workable degree. In Ujamaa theory, diversity (defined not only in terms of social classes but also in terms of ethnic and linguistic groups) was perceived as centrifugal. Furthermore, ethnicity and its linguistic correlate were seen as remnants of the pre-independence and pre-revolutionary situation. Now that Tanzania had entered the modern world, 'tribes' were no longer a legitimate basis for mobilisation and group formation. This fragment from Khamisi (1974: 294) summarises the whole argument:

> We know that we may be having different cultural backgrounds, supported by our tribal languages, but that we already belong to a modern nation which does not allow the moving back to the tribe. Our economic and social reality is already forcing us to subordinate our cultural differences to a national culture in formation. Swahili represents this culture.

Swahili was consistently defined as a 'binding force' that appealed to its users, 'many of whom have been for a too long time victims of too many dividing forces' (ibid.: 295). This view heavily symbolises Swahili as the vehicle for the new values of the egalitarian Ujamaa society. On the other hand (and strange though it may sound), it *depoliticises* Swahili. The language is stripped of the power by means of which it was introduced, promoted and enforced throughout the country, and of the power and status hierarchy in which it became integrated in the life-world of the Tanzanians. After all, it was the language of government, of control, of decision making; in short, of social and political power (cf. Williams 1992: 127).

A second challenge for linguists was the fact that they became involved in a massive programme of social engineering, in which they were given a very prominent position. This increased their social status and created relatively prodigious research circumstances. If research targets can be at all clear, here was one: full Swahilisation, most importantly in education but also in all other domains of social, cultural and political life in Tanzania. Given their definition of the notion of 'language modernisation' this could be achieved through language engineering, especially in the field of lexicology. And indeed, the accomplishments in this field were substantial. Many thousands of new Swahili terms were constructed, discussed, submitted for approval and disseminated.

But the setbacks in this enterprise are equally clear. Apart from the theoretical problems discussed earlier, it should be clear that a great deal of effort had been spent on just one aspect of language planning: the expansion of the lexicon. Metonymically, however, vocabulary expansion came to stand for the total state of the Swahili language: the lack of terminology and the need for further lexical expansion appeared time and again whenever the degree of 'development' of Swahili was discussed. Thus, the availability of, for example, terms for scientific concepts would determine whether or not Swahili could be called 'a scientific language'. This, as shown in the section on development and modernisation, paralyses part of the discussion. The process of terminological innovation depends on the evolution of an outside model (English, or internationally standardised terminology); therefore there is no point at which the process of terminological innovation can be said to be completed nor even to have reached a sufficient degree of development to start writing textbooks or other teaching materials. Also, the process of language development is made a laboratory business. It depends on the activities of specialised academics – when they have done their work their product can be transferred to the world of praxis. Teachers are then supposed to neatly implement the prescribed measures; if they don't, something in the language planning process has gone wrong (see, for example, Msanjila 1990). Reducing the scope of language development to the narrow domain of terminology development thus affects the way in which sociolinguistic problems are diagnosed and remedied.

The truly fascinating thing about Tanzanian linguistics in the postcolonial era is the fact that there was an explicit attempt towards particularising science and adapting it to local socio-political circumstances. Ujamaa linguistics is a *local tradition* of chtonic linguistics, of course based on international models for linguistics and sociolinguistics, but at the same time working on the basis of premises and social models that are not shared by the rest of the international academic community but are explicitly anchored in local political, social and cultural strategies. These premises and models are not just 'context'; it is not just so that Tanzanian work refers to Tanzanian situations, which would be a truism. The premises and models are the chtonic *substance* of Ujamaa linguistics, not just the kind of particular circumstances under which any linguist works worldwide. The relevance of this phenomenon should be clear: those who still believe in the existence of an abstract, coherent scientific discipline such as linguistics, characterised by an open exchange of ideas, maximum communicability among colleagues and a gradual internationalisation of methods and insights, should realise that parts of the linguistic world are a universe in themselves, separated from 'mainstream' scientific development (an abstraction itself, of course) by what could rightly be called an intercultural barrier. Ujamaa linguistics operated with local criteria for the quality and relevance of work – the product of a local emerging scientific tradition the characteristics of which have been described in the previous sections.

Two more general remarks should be made. The first one pertains to the role of language in nationalist ideologies. The pattern we found with regard to Swahili in Tanzania fits the more general picture developed in Blommaert and Verschueren (1992). In that paper, based on an analysis of European newspaper reporting on inter-ethnic conflicts and nationalist movements, we found that language is consistently seen as a marker of identity related to 'nations' or 'peoples'. 'Nations' or 'peoples', in turn, are seen as natural discontinuities comparable to zoological species. A particular language is thus seen as predictive of a certain group iden-tity; although preferably combined with other features (physical characteristics, religion, 'values', a common history, and so on), it may sometimes be sufficient to grant the language's speakers the status of a 'real' ethnic group or nation. This folk theory (an aspect of what we called homogeneism) is quite pervasive, and does not seem to be affected by more soundly grounded anthropological, linguistic or sociological counter-evidence. Its validity is claimed to be universal, although it is abundantly clear that, since it is based on the one language-one culture assump-tion, it can only be said to provide an approximate representation of the state of affairs in a very limited number of cases. It is an ideological 'monoglot' imagination (Silverstein 1996).

With regard to Swahili, the Tanzanian 'nation' seems indeed to be built around a common language, Swahili, and a common state ideology, Ujamaa. Both are, of course, narrowly intertwined, as the discussion in this chapter should have made clear. In the last few decades Ujamaa has lost much of its value as a distinctive feature of Tanzanian national identity, while Swahili has retained much of that status. But it should be kept in mind that Swahili is not the mother tongue of the majority of Tanzanians. Hence, it cannot even be considered a 'natural' marker of Tanzanian national identity. The fact that it is consistently presented as the common language of all Tanzanians (which would in other situations count as a decisive empirical argument legitimising the 'nation') is already part of a nationalist rhetorical strategy. It is not, as in so many other cases, the point of departure for the ideological con-struction of a 'nation'; instead, it is part of that construction itself. In fact, it only became a widespread national language through other emancipatory measures taken by the postcolonial government, most prominently the spread of mass literacy and other forms of basic education. As Hobsbawm (1990: 52) observes:

in the era before general primary education there was not and could not be a spoken 'national' language except such literary or administrative idioms as were written, or devised or adapted for oral use . . . to address popular audiences across dialectal boundaries . . .

The linguists' efforts contributed significantly to the a posteriori legitimation of Swahili as a marker of national identity: they were the ones who designed the standard language and plied it into an instrument flexible enough to reach large portions of the population.

This brings us to the second point. In studying ideologies and the way they work through processes of hegemony, the Tanzanian situation indicates that an analysis of the role of specific *actors* may yield significant insights into the often somewhat transcendentally presented processes of hegemony (cf. Blommaert 1999). Sometimes, hegemony may have a face, a name, a well-known identity. This is because certain forms of communication simply have more impact than others, they have a particularly authoritative status. Scientific discourse is undoubtedly one of these authoritative forms of communication. In Tanzania, politics and science stood in an alliance, and together they created – though sometimes grudgingly – a dominant pattern of thinking and speaking about the Tanzanian nation and its attributes (beliefs, values, culture, language).

Part of the power of this discourse can be explained by the particularly high status both actors held in the newly independent, economically underdeveloped country in which scholarship, academic degrees and even literacy were such rare commodities, and in which the politicians had secured freedom and independence for their countrymen. Another part of it, however, seems to be related to a more general pattern of perception of modes of communication such as scientific discourse. Everywhere, and at all times, politicians have drawn on scientific arguments to legitimate their programmes, because, apparently, the scientific word is more reliable than that of the common man or even that of the politician alone. In many ways, scientific discourse depoliticises the issue it represents, makes it more 'neutral' and less open to rough political contestation. It can therefore become a very useful political instrument capable of persuading people who otherwise would be hard to persuade. Its discourse can hardly be called 'normalising' – it emerges from a very 'abnormal' sphere of society – but still it makes more 'normal', less marked and less controversial certain opinions or political decisions. Other intellectual and artistic voices can have this impact too, and in the next chapter we will look at writers, poets and literary scholars who engaged in their language-ideological debate.

4.7 NOTES

1. The claim that English and French are African languages is remarkably similar to Léopold Sédar Senghor's assimilationist view on French in Africa, a view otherwise totally alien to Ujamaa thinking.
2. The first part of the definition is intriguing from a sociolinguistic or pragmatic point of view. First, there is the either/or construction: either a language serves as a medium of instruction – meaning, presumably, that it is used in formal education – or it is used as a medium of communication – which would entail that 'instruction' is not communication, and that there are languages which do not serve as means of communication. Second, there is the 'equipping it with the capability . . .' phrase, which begs the question as to how a language could *not* be equipped with the capability to be used as a medium of

communication, and, if so, how such a language could consciously be equipped with that capability.

3. Part of the data and the sample analyses in this section are taken from An Stans' unpublished MA thesis (Stans 1989). I am grateful to her for letting me use this material.

Chapter 5

Ujamaa literature: the politics of shape, style and topic

5.1 INTRODUCTION

The target of the analysis in this chapter is postcolonial Swahili literature, seen here as a 'way of speaking', a particular way of using language. Literature, in its written contemporary form, is an innovation in Africa which has come as a companion of colonisation. Yet written artistic literature, like modern, state-based politics or institutionalised scientific research, has become an ingredient of modern African culture. It has acquired a place in the generic repertoire of every contemporary African society, be it in ways that may be fundamentally different from those that prevail in the West. In a society in which literacy is an unequally distributed resource, it is only to be expected that books, both as material products of literacy and as the 'food' for sustained literary practice, may have a different semiotics than in societies where an overwhelming majority of the population are skilled readers. In the former type of societies, books may be more important, they may be more remarkable, their impact may be greater, and people may want to find more than just one message in the book. Furthermore, the literate audience may be heavily concentrated in urban areas and/or in the higher social strata, making literary consumption almost automatically into a communication type which develops among urban elites. This, in turn, may structure literary practice itself: authors may be aware of the social significance of the act of publishing a book – a product which is almost by definition a rare commodity – and they may adapt their style and content accordingly.

Thus, due to this peculiar sociology of communication, literature may be a highly sensitive index of socio-political developments and may assume a far more important place in the political debate than what we are used to in the West. It may become a vehicle for the reproduction of dominant political values as well as for dissenting opinions and ideas, and it may become such a vehicle *intentionally*. The question of what one should write about, and for whom, has in fact been a lively topic of debate among African writers (for example, see for East Africa: Gurr and Calder 1974; Nazareth 1978; Wanjala 1978; Ngugi wa Thiong'o 1981a; Okot p'Bitek 1986).

According to Mazrui, 'African literature has, in fact, been a meeting point between African creativity and African political activity at large'. Writers either use literature as a vehicle for political protest, or as 'an exercise in political observation and recording' (Mazrui 1978: 9). Writers have always taken a particular position in contemporary African societies, as the vanguard of the literary elites on the one hand, and as the utilisers of an important intellectual and ideological instrument on the other. The latter role, of course, is ambiguous: writers can either use their instrument to support the ideas and plans of those in power or they can use it to attack them. Either way, the literary discussions in Africa teach us that writers are very much aware of the impact of their writings, and that they want to complement their literary-artistic credo with an ethical and political one.

Writers are not always, and not even very often, the creators of political ideologies. They take the role of mediators, consuming ideas that are being handed down to them, but at the same time transforming them into a powerful new type of indirectly political discourse. The next sections will elaborate on the process of penetration of political ideology into literature, both in a general sense (the politisation of the literary field and of literary practice at large) as well as at the level of the structure of the literary message itself. I hope to show how and to what extent Ujamaa provided an overall orientation for literary practice in Tanzania, how it structured this field by determining the relevant topics of literary discussion and debate, how it influenced criteria of quality in assessing literary products, and how it came to be used as a default mode for discussing social themes in literature.

5.2 UJAMAA AND SWAHILI LITERATURE

The politisation of writers can be the product of their own preferences or their own responses to political developments, or of an old tradition of concern for society rather than for the individual (as suggested by Mazrui). But it may also come from above, it may be part of the hegemonic alignment of various discourses, instigated and promoted by the authorities. In the propaganda campaign which followed the initiation of Ujamaa politics, creative writing in Swahili acquired a particular place. Harries mentions a meeting at the State House in Dar es Salaam on 6 June 1968, during which Nyerere invited a group of poets 'to use their talents in order to promote a better understanding by the people of the land . . . of national politics, and particularly of the responsibilities of the citizen resulting from the implementation of the Arusha Declaration' (Harries 1972: 52). The poets, led by Mathias Mnyampala, formed a literary-political association, the Society for Swahili Composition and Poetry in Tanzania (*UKUTA: Chama cha Usanifu wa Kiswahili na Ushairi Tanzania*). UKUTA became the leading literary association in Tanzania, and its professed aim was to develop an Ujamaa literature. Just like the linguists and other influential groups in society, writers were drawn into politics and literature became a form of political activity.

But why was literature seen as a relevant object of nation building? Probably because of a combination of ideological reasons (literature is commonly seen as an important activity in the socialist tradition), cultural reasons (Nyerere repeatedly emphasised the importance of culture as part of genuine independence) and educational reasons (literature being one field in which education could be explicitly 'Ujamaa-ised'). In the early years after independence, the literature syllabus of secondary schools was still largely a British syllabus, containing literature which, in the eyes of Tanzanian intellectuals and politicians, was entirely irrelevant for Tanzanian children. This begged the question formulated by Mbuguni and Ruhumbika (1974: 283): 'How can we possibly bring up a young Tanzanian *mjamaa* on that kind of stuff, some of which is long dead even in Britain?' Creative writing in Swahili had to be stimulated because Tanzanian children should be supplied with books that were Tanzanian in style, content and atmosphere.

The development of an Ujamaa literature, however, was not unproblematic at all, and the story of the development of Ujamaa literature is merely the story of an *attempt* to gain political control over literature. To some extent, this attempt was a success; to some extent, however, it failed. The next section will discuss the way in which Ujamaa spurred writers and literary scholars into developing a new literary tradition. It will be shown that Ujamaa was indeed an important impetus for writers, but also that it created a literature of dissent. The development of post-Arusha literature was marked by heated debates on literary form and content. Apparently, the tight control that was acquired in linguistic research and language planning could not be acquired in literature, for literature is still a more personal, by definition less doctrinaire and less rigorously structured medium than scientific discourse, and less embedded in institutional power structures. However, Section 5.4 will show that the pervasiveness of Ujamaa should not be underestimated. When we move away from elite forms of literature and into the field of popular literature, the impact of the topical and semantic tradition created by Ujamaa will become clear.

5.3 UJAMAA LITERATURE

The introduction of Ujamaa was a momentous decision with great social and cultural impact. In the field of literature, it gave rise to at least three meaningful new developments in Swahili literature.[1]

1. It stimulated a *quantitative boom* of all kinds of creative writing in Swahili, as part of the general emphasis on culture and mass education. Mass literacy schemes contributed significantly to the enlargement of the literary scene in Tanzania. Of course, Ujamaa politics was not the only factor contributing to the growth of Swahili literature after independence. One important precondition for the boom was the shift in power provoked by decolonisation. Africans now became heads of their own publishing firms, and could thus select, produce, distribute and promote their own preferred literature. The local publishing industry, spearheaded by the Tanzania Publishing House, now became part of the nation building infrastructure. A second important factor contributing to the growth of Swahili literature was the literary tradition in Swahili, a centuries-old phenomenon and quite exceptional in Africa. Its influence was, however, largely mythical and symbolic: it allowed for a

perception of continuity in literary production and for an extra argument to lift Swahili to the status of an additional language with a great cultural and artistic heritage. More important, in real terms, was the groundwork laid by pre-independence Swahili writers such as Shaaban Robert, Mohamed Said Abdullah and Sheikh Amri Abedi who had already initiated a tradition of high-quality, modern and innovative written literature. Yet still more important was the fact that Tanzanian authors got involved with the emerging African literary scene. They participated in African literary congresses where they met authors such as Achebe, Ousmane and Soyinka, and this at a time when fundamental questions on literature in Africa were being hotly debated.

These questions were also tackled by East-African writers, and in a way that sets them apart somewhat from their colleagues in other parts of Africa. There was a distinct East-African literary scene, of which the Tanzanian writers became part and to which they contributed. Intellectuals moved freely between Nairobi, Makerere and Dar es Salaam in the context of the East-African Federation, and the University of Dar es Salaam especially 'was a major cooking place of ideas, and provided a splendid platform for debates and discussion' in the years following the Arusha Declaration (Othman 1994: 10). Authors such as the Ugandan Okot p'Bitek and the Kenyans Taban Lo Liyong and Ngugi wa Thiong'o (who was an external examiner at Dar es Salaam University) had some influence on the upcoming generation of Tanzanian intellectuals. Their message was substantially more revolutionary than that of their West African colleagues and fitted well into the socialist radicalism developing in Dar es Salaam. To varying degrees they all adhered to the view that African literature should not be just a copy of Western literature, and that the aesthetic and thematic criteria of literary evaluation should be adapted to the local – African – contexts.[2] Of particular importance was the fact that they all struggled with the question of who they were writing for: were they writing for an international audience or for the local people who were just starting to acquire literacy? (See Kezilahabi 1980.) This question obviously had a bearing on the language in which they would write. If they chose English as their literary medium, that would mean that the overwhelming majority of their countrymen would be unable to read their books; if they were to write in local languages, this would mean that they reached the local masses (assuming, that is, a dramatic increase in literacy) but missed the international literary market with its commercial bounty. If they chose to write in a local language, could they just impose Western styles and genres on that language? Or rather should they try to adopt local literary genres and create modern literature in them? Taban Lo Liyong opted for a combination of English with local genres, a 'genre synthesis' as he called it. Okot p'Bitek (who had carried out anthropological fieldwork among his ethnic group, the Acholi) selected the Acholi 'song' as his preferred literary medium, challenging Western conceptions of literature as being inappropriate to cover the African view on literature (see especially Okot p'Bitek 1973 and 1986).

All of these questions also penetrated the emerging Tanzanian literary scene, and they found a fertile ground in the general intellectual climate in Dar es Salaam.

The product of these developments was a truly impressive literary production with an identity of its own. Ohly (1981) identifies the literary development of the 1970s in Tanzania as 'aggressive prose': authors designed their stories around the tensions between an often antisocial lead character and the new norms of society, and did this with a didactic purpose. In doing so, authors sometimes attacked some of the fundamentals of Ujamaa. The novel *Dunia Uwanja wa Fujo* (*The World is a Chaotic Place*), the masterpiece of the leader of the new generation of creative writers Euphrase Kezilahabi (1975), depicts the struggle of an individual entrepreneur against the imposed land reform that was part of the villagisation project. In *Gamba la Nyoka* (*The Snake's Skin*), Kezilahabi (1979) criticised corruption and inefficiency in the sphere of the implementation of Ujamaa policies. Finally, his never-published play, *Kaputula la Marx* (*Marx's Baggy Shorts*) (1978), openly criticised socialism as an inadequate political framework which allowed exploitation and imperialism to re-enter Tanzanian society. Thus, although these works are all framed within the thematic context of a society on its way to Ujamaa, works such as Kezilahabi's clearly expressed discontent and criticism about the way in which this process affected individuals' lives. His books are about Ujamaa, but not necessarily in support of the practice of Ujamaa as performed by the government.

2. Ujamaa directly or indirectly provoked the *development of new genres* in Swahili literature (cf. Bulcaen 1994: 76ff). Classical verse forms such as the *Utendi* (long, epic poems) were being revitalised by poets who started writing eulogies of Ujamaa and its leaders, or narratives on the liberation struggle in Tanzania and elsewhere in Africa. The traditional shorter *Mashairi* genre became one of the preferred vehicles for political debates in the opinion columns of newspapers. Government-supporting poets such as Mnyampala and his UKUTA members even expanded the realm of what was perceived as traditional Swahili poetry with a new (but classical-looking) form of poetical expression, the *Ngonjera* (see Harries 1972; Bulcaen 1994).[3] The Ngonjera was an explicitly political genre, to fulfil three functions according to the then Prime Minister Rashidi Kawawa (cf. Harries 1972: 52–3):

> First, to give the people a new fluency in Swahili so that they would be able to explain in public and with ease the politics of the nation. Second, by learning the words by heart the people would be familiarizing themselves with national aims as envisaged in the Arusha Declaration, the Ujamaa villages project, the concept of Self-reliance, etc., and they would come to know just who their national leaders in the various segments of the political organization were. Third, the people would achieve a consciousness of their national culture and would learn to reject foreign culture.

Although Mnyampala's own Ngonjera poems (which carried titles such as *Sielewi Azimio*, [*I don't Understand the Declaration*] and *Viongozi Wetu* [*Our Leaders*]) were not all that successful, the genre itself became firmly established in contemporary Swahili literature. It became compulsory for high-school students to write a Ngonjera as part of their graduation-year exam requirements.

It is not only the directly Arusha-related Ngonjera verse form that should be mentioned here. In addition, the experimental poetry of the 'modernist' writers discussed below was a generic innovation that came about against the background of the development of a socialist political strategy. In general, every stylistic of generic innovation in Swahili literature after the Arusha Declaration and up to the early 1980s can be said to have been inspired by the political question as to what or whom one was writing for in the context of Ujamaa society.

3. The question of the author-audience relationship discussed above was anchored in the wider issues of class formation and socialist hegemonisation that were central to the intellectual debates at the University of Dar es Salaam in the period. Consequently, it provoked a unique and very relevant *debate on literary values and aesthetics* among writers, intellectuals and politicians in Tanzania. Government favourites such as Mnyampala had made a bid for literary and political hegemony with the (re-)invention of Ngonjera. Ngonjera verse would be the most appropriate vehicle for the poetic formulation of Ujamaa ideas. Ngonjera, however, also had a deeper, more implicit functional dimension, one that created a paradox with the political dogma that called for its invention, and one we have encountered before. As a verse form similar to other traditional Swahili forms of poetry, it imposed *traditional coastal culture* on the socialist national culture. It represented an essentialist view on the cultural identity of the new Swahili-speaking Tanzanians: since the new Tanzanians all spoke Swahili, they should also adopt the original Swahili culture exemplified by the traditional verse forms. This idea met with severe opposition from younger 'modernist' writers and literature scholars (led by Kezilahabi) at the University of Dar es Salaam. They spotted a degree of political incorrectness in Nyampala's 'traditionalist' approach to poetry. Ngonjera poetry referred to an old, pre-Ujamaa society and broke the rule of the secular state because of its Islamic connotations, whereas politically correct Swahili poetry should be reflecting the new social and cultural transformation. Swahili, for the modernists, was no longer associated with coastal culture; it had begun a second life when TANU adopted it as the language of anticolonial struggle (see for example the introduction to Mulokozi and Kahigi 1979). As opposed to the Ngonjera and other traditional verse forms, the modernists proposed free verse as the clearest expression of the new Swahili (Ujamaa) culture. By doing so, they proposed an *inland perspective* on Swahili literature to balance the coastal perspective promoted by Mnyampala and UKUTA: free verse, they claimed, was a characteristic of *Bantu* oral

literature. Thus, even the progressivists searched for traditional roots for the new socialist culture, not surprisingly given the emphasis on African values in Ujamaa. And rather than accept the rehabilitation of the coastal Swahili culture as the traditional basis for cultural expression in Swahili, they propagated the view that the cultural tradition underlying Swahili was that of the whole of Tanzania.

This controversy became known as the literary debate of the late 1960s and early 1970s. The battle was fought in speeches, newspaper columns, poems and essays. Its political dimension was never dissimulated. The progressive young poets claimed that the traditionalists displayed a reactionary attitude and formed an obstacle to the construction of a socialist society. The traditionalists claimed that socialism should not imply the destruction of 'natural' Swahili cultural features, and that a distinction should be made between (genuine) 'Swahili literature' and 'literature in Swahili' (Bertoncini 1994). In general, the modernists were associated to the political left, while traditionalists such as Mnyampala were moderate and orthodox Ujamaa supporters. At one point, the protagonists in the debate made an appeal to Nyerere to state his preference for one or other of the two positions.[4] Given the clear connection between literary arguments and political-ideological arguments, Nyerere prudently declined the offer, and the battle never reached a conclusion.

Other meaningful developments in Swahili literature can also, in one way or another, be connected to the socialist and emancipatory spirit of Ujamaa. There were works that adopted a Marxist and proletarian perspective, and attempted to write the story of the common, oppressed African (for example, Shafi Adam Shafi's *Kuli*). There was the development of a feminist trend of writing and literary critique, epitomised in the works of Penina Mlama and May Balisidya. Furthermore, the retrieval of Tanzanian national history, local cultures and traditions resulted in stories set in rural, precolonial Africa (for example, Kitereza's *Bwana Myombekere na Bibi Bugonoka*) or historical evocations of resistance against the colonisers (as in, for example, Mulokozi's *Mukwava wa Uhehe*). In each of these instances, writers put their medium and skills at the disposal of Ujamaa, by developing themes that were seen as politically crucial for a society that advocated social equality, humanism and the development of human capital. Note, however, that their efforts almost by definition remained marginal in terms of impact, because of the communicative sociology outlined in the beginning of this chapter. They all wrote for a very small literate audience, largely concentrated in urban areas (foremost in Dar es Salaam) and largely confined to the middle-class and educated strata. The successes of the literacy campaigns of the 1970s may have shaped new and large groups of literates, but they did not instantly shape new literary consumers. This explains why authors in Tanzania, just like their colleagues elsewhere in Africa, engaged in a search for new media and new communicative codes. Folk theatre was advanced as one of the potentially effective media for mass literary education, but drama performances were expensive and hence rare.

It is clear that Ujamaa – as a large-scale socio-political transformation of the country, and as a new opportunity to circulate ideas about that society, its past, its structure and its people – offered tremendous opportunities for creative writers. The Tanzanian writers grasped these opportunities and produced a remarkable corpus of new, modern literature, sometimes of very high quality. Their literature reflected attempts to construct a cultural dimension of Ujamaa: a local aesthetic tradition in Swahili, with its (real, assumed or disputed) roots in the past, but very much focused on the present needs and requirements of their society. In that sense they became active players in the political debate. In their work, politics was a topic or a trope; when published, their work was also read politically, and when it was controversial, the writers found themselves in a political argument with other people in society.

As the literary debate of the late 1960s and early 1970s demonstrated, literature was a forum for public debate, albeit among a small but ideologically influential elite. Writers such as Kezilahabi could publish views that were not at all supportive of the Ujamaa credo, at least not of the credo as it was being promoted by the authorities. Probably also because of its low degree of popular impact, literature was a field in which some ideological latitude was granted, and this latitude was exploited by the intellectuals whose ambivalent relationship with the authorities turned them almost inevitably into (often extreme left-wing) dissidents. But the limits of the debate were firmly under the control of the authorities. The publishing business was state controlled, and one can assume that some books were not published for ideological reasons.

One of the remarkable things about the Tanzanian literary scene, however, is that this state filtering system did not create a sterile, dogmatic literature. On the contrary, the spectrum of published opinions was broad and diverse, and it included extreme Marxist views alongside very moderate ones (including what critics called 'liberal-bourgeois' views). This also testifies to the space granted to creative artists and intellectuals to present their own readings of Ujamaa and the ideal society for which they were working. At the same time, the totality of literary production in Swahili was ideologically recuperated. The growth and expansion of new creative writing served as a Négritude argument, demonstrating the cultural equivalence, the versatility and the potential for cultural innovation of the new socialist society. It demonstrated at the same time the artistic and aesthetic potential of Swahili. In fact, the traditionalists in the literary debate complained about the lack of ornament and stylistic elaboration in the 'literature in Swahili' (a term opposed to 'Swahili literature') written by new up-country and non-Muslim writers (Bertoncini 1994). Thus, the very act of writing a book in Swahili was always an argument to demonstrate the maturity of Swahili (its level of 'development') and its intrinsic equivalence to languages such as French, English or Russian. In turn, this maturity of the language was seen as an index of political and sociocultural development and emancipation. In the perception and critique of Swahili literature, ideological arguments are omnipresent, and they demonstrate the political-ideological importance of creative writing in Swahili.

5.4 UJAMAA AS A MODEL FOR WRITING ABOUT SOCIETY: A CASE STUDY

The impact of Ujamaa has been arguably deeper than simply the points mentioned above. Ujamaa rhetoric has also provided a kind of rhetorical blueprint for speaking about Tanzanian society, and for framing the individual's experiences in it. This influence is, in its most visible form, thematic. A significant number of Swahili poems, novels and plays explicitly deal with episodes in the struggle for independence, aspects of Ujamaa theory and its implementation in the villages, or philosophical and political questions related to Ujamaa values and principles. At a less visible level, however, the influence of Ujamaa rhetoric sometimes appears to be surprisingly pervasive. This is at the level of plot structuring, character selection, motives, description of setting and scenery, and so on. The pervasiveness of the rhetorical complex is such that it even appears where one would least expect it: in commercially written popular novels. I will now discuss one such novel, *Dar Imenihadaa* (*Dar [es Salaam] Has Betrayed Me*) by Rashidi Akwilombe, in more detail.

Akwilombe's *Dar Imenihadaa* (published by a commercial publishing house called Akajase Enterprises, Dar es Salaam, in 1988) is a booklet of 78 pages in extent. It contains 12 chapters of unequal length, varying between 11 pages (Chapter 4) and two pages (Chapters 10 and 12). Seven pen drawings illustrate the book.

Each chapter has a title, which mostly summarises what is going to happen in that chapter. The story is rather simple and can be summarised as follows. A beautiful young girl, Devota, travels from her home town, Iringa, to the capital, Dar es Salaam, where she is going to work as a secretary. Devota is pretentious and prefers to socialise with wealthy, powerful men. One day, she insults a poor young man called Shomvi. Shomvi decides to take revenge. Together with some of his friends, he sets up a complex plot of deceit and impersonation. Consequently, Devota meets three *matapeli* ('imposters'): Dezo, Cheki Bobu and Sekulu. All three are involved in the plot. Dezo and Cheki Bobu seduce Devota by pretending to be rich and Westernised, and then leave her alone in distress. Finally, Sekulu (a simple farmer) promises to marry her provided she abandons her snobbish ways. During a trip back home, Devota finds letters written by the matapeli, in which they explain their plot to her and urge her to adapt to the simple values of Tanzanian society: simplicity and modesty, hard labour, and equality among people. She realises that she was wrong, she marries Sekulu and they embark on a humble but rewarding life in Dar es Salaam.

Throughout the novel, Akwilombe puts great effort into making the narrative as realistic as possible. He uses a real geographical area, 'well known to the reader and associated with social standards of class prejudice of their fellow town dwellers' (Ohly 1981: 19), brand names, names and types of cars, planes, and so on. Although Devota's preferred lifestyle may correspond to the ambitions and aspirations of many of his readers in post-Ujamaa Tanzania (who would be found, after all, among the urban literate elite), Akwilombe sends out a negative message with regard to life in the fast lane. *Uzungu*, the way of the white man, is a powerful negative theme in the book. This theme is elaborated by means of the realistic depiction of the Westernised lifestyle: explicit information about places, things and activities commonly associated with Westernisation and wealth. Yet the most prominent characteristic of Uzungu is not Devota's pursuit of Western luxury goods, nor her delight in staying at the Kilimanjaro Hotel and in driving around in a Mercedes, but her usage of English.

Dar Imenihadaa contains a significant amount of English-Swahili code-switching. Devota and her friends are quoted having English conversations with each other. Yet the use of English in the book is a stylistic element, nothing more. English phrases are put in italics in the text, and they are followed by a literal Swahili translation introduced by phrases such as *akiwa na maana kama ifuatavyo* ('by which he meant the following')[5]. The English used by Akwilombe is often shaky. Lexical and grammatical errors are frequent, as in: 'Hello Darling D. Where are you going Honey? Can I call myself the luckiest person in the world to be with beautiful girl [sic] again?' Or: 'What do you want here, poor old stupid man? I do not know you and I do not give arms [sic] to the poor except on Friday. Go away at once.' In addition, the English orthography seems to be somewhat erratic, especially Akwilombe's peculiar use of capitals in expressions such as 'Do not mind about the House Rent because I will always be paying it for you', and 'Do you have the shape or Education to cope with me?' is also puzzling. I will return to this in greater detail in Chapter 6. The fact that Akwilombe includes literal Swahili translations after each English fragment seems to vindicate the suspicion of an imperfect knowledge of English, and it also indicates the degree of English literacy Akwilombe suspects of his readership.[6] The use of English is therefore clearly not a choice of medium with which to write parts of the book, but is largely metapragmatic and stylistic: it indexes an attitude towards English as an element of social identity, and it is part of the construction of the characters in the book.

This becomes clear when we look at which characters use English. Devota is the one who uses English the most. Not only does she speak English with her high-society boyfriends, but she also uses it in a face-threatening way against people who know hardly any English, as with an uncle from up-country and with Shomvi, the young man who later organises the deception plot. Furthermore, Devota is also quoted speaking English in situations that are perceived as disturbing by other people. During her bus ride to Dar es Salaam, she openly kisses Shuga Dedi, they have an obscene conversation in English, and Akwilombe summarises their behaviour as *[m]aongezi na matendo yao yote mle ndani ya Basi yalikuwa ya Uzungu mtupu* ('all their words and deeds in the bus were of an idle western type').

Shuga Dedi and Dezo are also depicted as frequent users of English. Shuga Dedi is a prominent government official and Dezo poses as a Tanzanian who has spent his youth in England. Shuga Dedi's preference for English is realistic, given his status as a high administrative officer, but Dezo's supposed command of English is quite unrealistic given that he is in fact a simple hired hand at the Kariakoo market. Cheki-Bobu is only quoted twice speaking English, but he is still depicted as an international businessman with a good command of English. Sekulu – the most 'common' character in the novel – uses no English at all but speaks Swahili. Sauda, Devota's cousin, is not quoted speaking English, but colloquial English expressions such as *aisee* ('I say') appear in conversations between the two girls. Devota's parents in Iringa apparently do not speak any English at all. Neither do the youngsters who organise the plot against Devota use any English, not even colloquial nor slang expressions, during their meetings.

The use of English is associated with Uzungu. It is a part and the expression of a lifestyle presented (mostly implicitly, but on occasions also explicitly) as amoral, asocial and, most of all, un-African. This association of English with Uzungu is a powerful theme, because it serves as a negative mirror image of Ujamaa with its emphasis on Africanhood epitomised in Swahili. Akwilombe identifies English with a lifestyle full of glitter and wealth, but also one full of deception and lost moral values.

But this negative depiction of English as the mark of Uzungu is somewhat anachronistic. When Akwilombe published his book in 1988, English had regained considerable status in Tanzania, and was no longer simplistically seen as the force of evil. Contemporary attitudes *vis-à-vis* English (or Western culture in general) were, in other words, much more tolerant than becomes apparent in the book. So Akwilombe adopted a set of ideological associations about Uzungu and Africanhood which were as good as defunct in Tanzanian society at the time he wrote his book. Furthermore, the type of society he proposes as the normative basis upon which Devota's behaviour is measured was largely a thing of the past at the time of writing. Akwilombe himself should know: as an independent, professional writer, he was the type of small entrepreneur who found a place in the post-Ujamaa liberalised economic system. Akwilombe himself, unlike most other well-known Tanzanian writers, is not an academic or an intellectual. He is a new kind of writer who emerged as a result of economic and ideological liberalisation. We are therefore confronted with a strange paradox here. The paradox lies in the discrepancy between the values promoted in the book through emblematic associations such as that of English with (negatively qualified) Uzungu, and the very act of writing and selling this book on a self-employed, capitalist basis. Here is a story that would fit perfectly in Ujamaa literature, and it is a commercial product of the post-Ujamaa era.

We now move to a second relevant theme in the book. The message of the book is that Uzungu is unacceptable in Tanzania. It leads to deception and disappointment, and someone who displays Uzungu – the *wazungu weusi*, 'black-skinned whites', as they are called – must be restored to fit into Tanzanian society. The instruments by means of which this restoration is carried out are the so-called *matapeli*, 'con men': youngsters with very little education, who prove to be very creative in deceiving people. Matapeli typically pretend to be someone else; they involve their victim in intricate schemes of deception invariably culminating in the loss of money or status to the matapeli (see Graebner 1991).[7] The characters of Dezo and Cheki-Bobu are prototypes of matapeli. Although matapeli are involved in small-time crime, their role in this novel is not destructive and they are not depicted in unfavourable terms by Akwilombe. On the contrary, it is the matapeli's scheme that causes Devota's catharsis and restoration to society. Furthermore, the matapeli's actions are qualified positively`: they display a high degree of solidarity and cooperativeness, they have a socially constructive purpose (teaching a lesson to somebody who violates the rules of society), and they don't speak any English among themselves. Their actions in the story are also anti-bourgeoisie, and a class-struggle reading of the plot is not unwarranted. They prove to be simple people who earn their living by working hard in modest jobs. So, strangely enough, the matapeli display many of the crucial features of an ideal Ujamaa-era Tanzanian citizen, and in terms of the moral economy of the book, they are the good ones.

Devota's restoration involves a series of confrontations. The first is that between herself (a *mzungu mweusi*, 'a black white person') and the matapeli; next, there is that between the city with all its deceptions, crimes and sufferings, and the rural countryside, where family bonds provide safety and warmth; and, finally, there is the confrontation between the values of Uzungu and those of Ujamaa. This last point becomes clear in the final parts of the book. Ultimately, Devota returns to the countryside to stay with her parents. Sekulu, a poor farmer but a good and hard-working man, marries her and brings her back to his home in the Dar es Salaam suburbs. They both work the field and sell its products. But (in one telling sentence) '*Sekulu hakutaka kumpotezea kisomo mke wake* ('Sekulu didn't want to make his wife lose her education'), and Devota eventually gets the chance to work in a government office. This appears to be a circular process: Devota starts out as a secretary in a government office, and she ends up working in an office again. The difference is, however, that she moves to a 'higher', literate job from within a rural, Ujamaa-inspired environment, and not on the basis of idealisations of the West ('Uzungu') as she used to do before. Sekulu proves to be a good man who realises the potential benefit of his wife's literacy for society, and gives her the opportunity to work in the administration. This again is in line with Ujamaa values, in which learning and education had to be used for the benefit of the people, not for one's own ambitions.

The same paradox as the one described in relation to Akwilombe's attitude towards English arises here. This type of booklet seems extremely unfit for a slightly dated eulogy of Ujamaa, since the book as an economic free-market product – as well as its author as a free-market entrepreneur – are both very un-Ujamaa phenomena.

How can we solve this paradox? The answer may lie in the role of Ujamaa as an all-pervasive rhetorical framework for speaking about one's society. Until the 1990s there was certainly a remarkable continuity of discursive styles in this domain in Tanzania, which can be attributed largely to the preponderance of Nyerere's rhetoric about politics, values, ideology and social life (Lwaitama 1988). Alternative forms of discourse about society were marginal and restricted to specific groups in society (for example, intellectuals, businessmen), even after the end of the Nyerere era. Their comprehensibility was low, because they did not fit into the semantic tradition established by Ujamaa discourse over the previous 20 to 25 years. Nineteen ninety-eight fell in a period of political-ideological transition, in which Tanzania gradually abandoned Ujamaa as its basic political frame of reference, but had not yet adopted full-blown economic and political liberalism. Society still showed many traces of the hegemonic profile it had known since independence, in the fields of politics (one-party state), ideology and political discourse (Ujamaa) and mass media (almost exclusively state controlled, with a virtual absence of television – commercial television stations emerged only in the 1990s). The interregnum between Ujamaa and liberalism allowed Akwilombe to publish his novel outside state-controlled channels; but, simultaneously, it compelled him to draw on Ujamaa discourse to construct his plot. So, despite the emergence of new forms of discourse, in 1988 – and in a highly unexpected context – Ujamaa discourse remained the dominant stylistic-thematic mode for talking about life in Tanzania. Akwilombe adopts this discourse, and he tells a typical Ujamaa story, full of typical Ujamaa topoi. The storyline is clear, intelligible and persuasive, because it is in line with what Tanzanians have been taught about their society through Ujamaa discourse.

5.5 CONCLUDING REMARKS

Ujamaa has undoubtedly had a very important influence on the development of Swahili literature in Tanzania. It spurred the development of a very lively and productive 'high' literary scene, in which writing was both an artistic-creative practice and a form of political and educational activity and in which stimulating literary debates took place. Writers and literature scholars (most of them intellectuals) were spurred on by the Ujamaa project to contribute creatively to the construction of a new society. Their sense of self-importance, derived from their involvement in this political project, must have galvanised their morale and self-esteem. This, however, did not mean that Tanzanian writers all became adepts of Ujamaa. Their acts of writing were made part of the general cultural Ujamaa programme, sometimes by themselves but mostly by critics and by government officials. Still, what and how they wrote was often controversial and full of contradictions, illustrating the nature of Ujamaa not as a closed system of (dogmatic) ideas but as a dynamic of interpretation in which Tanzanian writers could move and explore a variety of directions. The question as to the precise relationship between Ujamaa and creative literature can not be answered therefore by one simple proposition. Literature served a variety of functions, at various levels, in the development of Ujamaa. The output of new literature was used as an argument to illustrate the effectiveness of Ujamaa in mobilising intellectuals and in developing the cultural and artistic skills (including Swahili) of the Tanzanians. At the same time, it functioned as a rallying point for radical authors and as a medium for critique against the practice of Ujamaa, as well as an instrument for symbolic class formation among the literate, urban elites.

More surprising is the impact Ujamaa appears to have had as a compelling mode of talking about the Tanzanian society in popular or 'pulp' literature, a genre about which (Western) common sense tells us that it is not quite the preferred medium for selling high-brow political ideas. As is the case with all pulp literature, authors select simple and easily understandable storylines and avoid philosophical sophistication in the development of their plots. The point, however, is that in this process a Tanzanian writer such as Akwilombe draws on the classical Ujamaa motives. The simplest and most understandable way of telling a story such as *Dar Imenihadaa*, so it appears, is by framing it into Ujamaa discourse. A similar phenomenon was witnessed by Graebner (1989), Mekacha (1992) and Askew (2002) in Tanzanian post-independence dance music. Apart from entertaining people, the popular songs have two purposes: to educate the people about the social norms, and to propagate Ujamaa (Mekacha 1992: 99). Mekacha's analysis of the way in which women are depicted in these songs leads him to suggest that, due to their didactic and political aims, the songs present a *status quo*-oriented message: women should not be overambitious or pursue luxury, but should respect marriage (their own and that of others) and 'accept their subordinate position to men' (ibid.: 113; see also Graebner 1989: 254). This message, which is morally and politically very close to that presented by Akwilombe, can be reduced to a rejection of foreign culture and ethics, and an emphasis on simple family life. The preferred locus for these African values is the rural countryside, which is also the locus of Ujamaa; the big city indexes Uzungu, danger and antisocial behaviour. Unlike elite literature, therefore, these popular forms of cultural expression mostly present a conservative message. And to the extent that popular culture indeed serves as an index of what lives among broader masses of the people, it certainly shows the pervasiveness of a more or less dogmatised version of Ujamaa.

The overall picture is therefore fragmented and ambiguous. The attempt to gain political control over literature succeeded, but only partially, and probably in an unexpected way. The attempt to draw writers into the process of Ujamaa nation building was also an attempt to mobilise the intelligentsia. But this attempt backfired because of factors explained in Chapter 3: intellectuals found themselves in what was at best a contradictory relationship with the authorities. On the one hand, they were strongly involved in nation building endeavours, and at least an important faction of them favoured a radical left-wing political course for their country. On the other hand, the same intellectuals spearheaded the political and ideological critique and dissidence against the authorities and became a constant source of annoyance for (some) party and state officials. At the same time, however, Ujamaa seems to have penetrated deeply into non-elite, popular culture, less explicitly but all the more effectively. The state ideology provided, for authors such as Akwilombe (and doubtlessly for many other writers and artists), a normal and habituated frame of reference for discussing social issues. It was a case of successful hegemony in one layer of society combined with a partial failure to achieve hegemony in another.

At this point, a series of tentative extrapolations could be made with regard to the nature and structure of the political process in Tanzania. There seems to be a deep – but unsurprising – rift between the urban areas and the countryside, as well as – perhaps more surprisingly – between various social classes, the latter being strongly determined by access to different types of literacy. The rift is most clearly expressed in degrees of ideological penetration: the (largely rural, but also urban) subaltern classes being marked by a strong and deep penetration of Ujamaa, both as a form of state structuration and as a social-psychological frame of reference for understanding their society; and the elite classes being marked by a high degree of dissidence and anti-hegemonic critique. Much of this process has to do with the written word. As consumers of various genres of literacy, the elite classes can explore the existing doctrine and contrast it with other existing or self-created bodies of literature. They can, in other words, penetrate into the fabric of the modern literate forms of hegemonisation. The subaltern classes, on the other hand, have no access to the doctrinaire textual body, they cannot produce elements of a political-textual tradition, and therefore they cannot raise their dissent above the level of individual casuistic. 'Politics', as a textual practice, probably looks quite different at either end of the socio-economic scale, both in terms of reception (how do people perceive politics?) and in terms of production (how do people participate in the – textual – political process?). Consequently, the way in which politics is practised and performed may differ significantly, depending on the nature of rather sharply differentiated sub-audiences in the country.

This may partially account for the surprising election results of October 1995. One opposition party had manifested itself as a serious contender for power, and the Dar es Salaam intellectuals expected a victory for that opposition party. The end result, however, showed a rather comfortable victory for CCM, largely based on massive majorities in the rural areas. The cities, where modern, literate, mass mobilisation practices may work, had been carried by the opposition, while the illiterate countryside remained faithful to the only kind of politics it knew: that of CCM and Ujamaa. CCM had spent the best part of thirty years building hegemony in the villages on the basis of political-communicative practices strongly different from those applicable in densely populated urban areas susceptible to mass media campaigns. The peculiar communicative sociology in which the written word is encapsulated proved to be a political factor of major importance.

5.6 NOTES

1. Useful survey publications on written Swahili literature include Mulokozi (1985), Ohly (1985), Bertoncini (1989) and Berwouts (1991). An excellent discussion of the developments described in this section (unfortunately only accessible in Dutch) is Bulcaen (1994).
2. Sometimes this led to extreme particularism, especially with Okot p'Bitek: 'It is only the participants in a culture who can pass judgement on it' (1986: 37).
3. It should be noted that some authors dispute the novelty of the Ngonjera genre. Mwangomango (1971) traces its history back to the legendary Mombasa poet, Muyaka. Bulcaen (1994: 83) also mentions the revival of *Vichekesho* – short and humorous drama plays – in the wake of the Arusha Declaration.
4. Observe that the appeal was made to Nyerere the writer. Nyerere had translated two of Shakespeare's classics into Swahili: *The Merchant of Venice* (*Bepari wa Venisi*, literally 'the capitalist* of Venice') and *Julius Caesar* (*Juliasi Kaisari*).
5. Apart from full sentences and even conversational exchanges in English, some other English expressions appear here and there. They belong to colloquial urban Swahili, and are near-lexicalised elements. I noted *Aisee* or *Aise* ('I say') as a typical example (see, for

example, p. 47). Near-lexicalised English loans such as *Teksi* ('taxi') and *Dereva* ('driver') also seem to pose orthographical problems to Akwilombe. *Teksi* also appears as *Taksi* (with unwarranted capitals), and *Dereva* alternates with *Dreva*.

6. 'English' is of course an idealisation here. Akwilombe may be fluent in East-African English, and many of his readers may also be proficient in this English variant. On the other hand, one can expect a tendency towards purism and an attempt to use a variant of English as standardised as possible when using the language as a literary medium. There are no indications in the text that Akwilombe uses East-African English as a literary-stylistic resource. On the contrary, the English used by characters is explicitly associated with a British background. See section 6.4 below.

7. The *matapeli* phenomenon is widely known in urban Tanzania, and it is no surprise that Akwilombe can draw on it as a literary persona. There is even a neologistic verb in common Dar es Salaam speech: *kutapeliwa*, 'to be the victim of *matapeli*, to be deceived'.

Part 2 Swahili and society: the micropolitics of register and repertoire

Chapter 6

Early fragmentation: Campus Swahili

6.1 INTRODUCTION

In this chapter, and in the following chapter, we have to change the theoretical and empirical frame and look at phenomena and processes that occurred only peripherally in the previous chapters. Rather than looking at the Tanzanian state's attempt towards Ujamaa hegemony, we now turn to Tanzanian society, and we shall be able to look more carefully at things such as the occurrence of English in the novel by Akwilombe that was discussed in the previous chapter.

Language users, as we know well, are far from ideal citizens when it comes to following language policies. That is, while they can explicitly support the views promoted in legislation and authoritative discourses their language practices can and do implicitly contradict their explicit beliefs, since actual language use is governed by far more complex and diverse sets of norms and expectations, related to the actual structure of social life rather than to the desired structure sketched in formal policies. Checking the effects of language policies by looking at language practices 'on the ground' is always to be recommended because we know that analyses of formal policy texts reveal a lot about the ideological imagination of the state, but very little about the actual sociolinguistics of society (cf. McCarthy 2011; Johnson 2013). While the former usually suggests a rather stable and unified sociolinguistic system, the latter inevitably reveals a far more fragmented and dynamic system. I consider the interplay between both – the homogenising imagination from above and the fragmented and dynamic realities on the ground – to be a sociolinguistic topic of critical importance, for it grants profile and understandability to authoritative discourses otherwise seen simply as irrelevant or surreal. The interplay of power from above and reactions from below is what shapes the dynamics of social change, and sociolinguistic processes on the ground are often an extremely sensitive index of broader social change (cf. Agha 2007; Blommaert and Rampton 2011). This chapter and the following chapter will document the ways in which the hegemonisation of the Ujamaa state was accompanied by a far less homogeneous and more fragmented sociolinguistic reality (this chapter), and a far more dynamic system which continues to change rapidly (Chapter 7).

The shift from a top-down to a bottom-up view involves some significant conceptual and theoretical changes as well. We need other instruments with which to investigate the sociolinguistic processes on the ground than those we could deploy for analyses of formal language policy. So let me first introduce these instruments.

6.2 FROM LANGUAGES TO REPERTOIRES

Addressing actual situated language practices requires precision about what it is that we are observing. People do not actually use 'languages' in their traditional sense, as the named and self-contained items such as 'English' or 'Swahili'; they use specific *resources* drawn from such conventionally understood 'languages' – sounds, words, grammatical patterns and larger 'ordered' resource clusters such as styles or genres (Creese and Blackledge 2010; Jørgensen et al. 2011). The crucial notion here is 'register': a specific part of 'a repertoire that is associated, culture internally, with particular social practices and with persons who engage in such practices' (Agha 2000: 216; also Agha 2007). People 'enregister' specific bits of language and other semiotic material, configured, indexically ordered, so as to produce *specific* meanings. Thus, a formal letter will require different enregistered resources than an informal one, and a chat with our mothers will demand very different registers from those we use in talks with our colleagues or bosses – styles and genres are all driven by specific registers. It is the capacity to deploy such registers adequately, to switch from one register into another, and to rapidly and adequately enregister new resources whenever required that defines what used to be known as 'communicative competence' (cf. Silverstein 2003; Agha 2007; Blommaert and Rampton 2011).

Thus, issues of repertoire – the combination of such enregistered resources within the scope of individual agency – become crucial in understanding the social dynamics of language. The specific resources people have access to, and the resources people do *not* have access to, all reveal historically and biographically emerged social positions – elite, sub-elite, young, old, apprentice, expert and so forth – that inevitably shine through in everyday interaction (Blommaert and Backus 2013). Repertoires, therefore, are not random or accidental in structure, but reveal patterns of distribution, social stratification and power affecting individuals and their social trajectories through life.

It is useful to stress the analytic distinction between the *availability* of resources and their *accessibility*. The former concept refers to the historical distribution of linguistic resources in a particular community; the latter refers to the synchronic pattern of power-related distribution of elements of the repertoires among members of that community. Even if English is available, in theory, to every Tanzanian citizen, it may not be accessible to all of them, but only to a particular group or class. And here, of course, we should look far beyond 'English' into the *specific resources* associated with English that people can have access to.

The power that makes resources accessible to certain people also allows them to imbue these resources with power and exert power by means of them. In a more sophisticated wording: the social history of resources is the source from which these resources are indexically 'loaded'. Concretely, someone who speaks a 'rare' or exclusive code (for example 'high' English in Tanzania) can use knowledge of this code to include or exclude people from certain material or symbolic benefits. He or she can demand that his or her employees speak English; if they don't speak English, they don't get hired or they lose their jobs. It is clear that language is far more than just grammar and vocabulary here; it is a symbolic field and an instrument with which and through which social struggles are being developed. It is, in Bourdieu's words, not only a matter of 'technical capacity', but, even more importantly, a matter of 'statutory capacity' which invariably involves questions of authority, sanctioning and legitimation in usage (Bourdieu 1982: 64; cf. also Heller 1992: 124–6). In interpreting what happens when people 'do' language, the question is through what processes these resources have become accessible or remained inaccessible to certain people.

The point is that an analytical lens that stops at distinctions between conventionally understood languages doesn't help us much in our efforts to analyse actually occurring communicative practices; we need far more precision and accuracy. It is by looking at more specific phenomena and processes that we will begin to see how the monoglot ideology of Ujamaa Tanzania was accompanied by a far more fragmented sociolinguistic reality, in which phenomena occurred that flatly contradicted some of the basic assumptions of the state ideology. Campus Swahili is one such phenomenon, and in the following pages I shall return to some of my very early observations of language usage in Dar es Salaam in the 1980s and 1990s.

6.3 CAMPUS SWAHILI

Campus Swahili is the term I used for English-interfered Swahili spoken by staff members of the University of Dar es Salaam (Blommaert and Gysels 1987, 1990). When I first recorded samples of Campus Swahili in 1985 the phenomenon was neither new nor exclusive. Harries (1968) had already examined Swahili-English code-switching, and Khamisi (1974: 298) had observed a 'complex pattern of language use for social occasions . . . especially among the educated. People in their free association often found themselves having to switch from one language to another in their effort to keep company.' He also noted that '[c]uriously enough codeswitching tends to occur between English and Swahili much more than between English and tribal languages' (ibid.: 299).[1] So the phenomena I recorded in 1985 were not recent innovations, they must have been there since at least the late 1960s, and probably even earlier. Neither were they restricted to university faculty. In 1989 and 1992 I noted similar kinds of code-switching among school teachers, journalists, doctors, executives, in short, all sorts of *wasomi* ('intellectuals') with a post-primary education. Even Radio Tanzania Dar es Salaam, previously a stronghold of Swahili purism, had broadcast a report on a conference of journalists at which delegates were switching enthusiastically and profusely between Swahili and English.

The Campus Swahili register

Seen from a structural perspective, Campus Swahili involves mixing *standard varieties* of both Swahili and English into a pattern that is syntactically and pragmatically coherent and that conveys the propositional message in what appears to be an adequate way (Blommaert and Gysels 1990). By 'standard' varieties, I mean that (1) the Swahili they use is quite sophisticated lexically and syntactically, and reflects the standard variety developed at the university, and (2) the English they use is also of considerable lexical and syntactic complexity, and retains much of its semantic and syntactic integrity when it appears in mixed utterances or terms, as in:

1. waka*discourage* ('they discouraged')
2. zilizo*run* ('that were running')
3. haija*pickup* ('it hasn't picked up yet')

The degree of lexicosemantic shift (not uncommon in borrowings) is low. English lexemes keep their original, standard English lexical meanings, more or less. This does not mean that Campus Swahili speakers sound like English people. Phonetically, the English phrases may sound very African, and, overall, the phonetic pattern of English elements in Campus Swahili is that of Swahili. Shifts in language do not entail shifts in pronunciation. The accent used in speaking may on the one hand be typical of East-African English in general. On the other hand, it may be due to the overarching phonetic influence of Swahili on the embedded English elements. So even though Campus Swahili may sound eminently African, academics display their proficiency in both a 'high' variant of Swahili as well as in a 'high' variety of English, albeit that the English elements have been phonetically 'contaminated' by Swahili.

When I observed Campus Swahili in the 1980s and 1990s among university staff members, Campus Swahili was used in informal and off-the-record conversations. During formal meetings, standard Swahili was used throughout, although some functional borrowing of English lexemes that were felt to be untranslatable would occur. Thus, staff members would use Campus Swahili at home among fellow academics, in conversations on and off campus, and during leisure hours in the afternoon or evening. People of whom their identity was not immediately known would be addressed in standard Swahili; as soon as it was established that the interlocutor was either a colleague or someone who would qualify as a *msomi* ('an intellectual'), shifts into Campus Swahili followed. It was therefore clearly an in-group variant, requiring and indexing membership of the educated elites. As a consequence, it was rarely used at home in conversations with family members. There, either standard Swahili would be used (for the children would grow up in a standard-Swahili environment), or the ethnic mother-tongue would be used, mostly between husband and wife and other family members or kinsmen. In the latter type of conversations a limited number of English borrowings could occur (as noted by Khamisi 1974).

Let us now take a closer look at how Campus Swahili is configured as a register. English elements in Campus Swahili speech serve a number of pragmatic functions. They may signal topic and focus, or various forms of emphasis. Consider this sample, where the English lexemes 'private schools' and 'nationalised' mark the topical string in the conversation:[2]

A1   Kana kwamba *private schools* zote baada ya kupata uhuru au baada ya Azimio la Arusha zilikuwa nationalised
      [as if all private schools after independence or after the Arusha Declaration were nationalised]

B1   Shule zilikuwa *nationalised* . . .
      [The schools were nationalised. . .]

A2   . . . zote? Hapakuwa na *private schools* zozote?
      [. . . all of them? Were there no private schools at all?]

B2   I say, shule zilikuwa *nationalised* karibu zote. Nasema karibu zote, huenda kuna nyingine zilizobaki, lakini *private schools* zilikuwa za akina nani, si hizi za misheni . . .
      [I say, almost all schools were nationalised. I say almost all, there are always some that remained, but the private schools were of what affiliation, not those of the missions . . .]

A3   . . . na za Wahindi chache . . .
      [. . . and some of the Indians . . .]

B3   . . . na za Wahindi ndiyo, akina Azania hizi na nini, na nini . . . na Azania zilikuwa *nationalised*
      [. . . and of the Indians, yes, those Azania schools and what, and what . . . the Azania (schools) were nationalised]

A4   Zote?
      [All of them?]

B4   Zilikuwa {hi} *nationalised* . . . za Wahindi chache ambazo zili . . . *private schools* kamaaa . . .
      [They were nationalised! Some of the Indians that were . . . private schools liiiike . . .]

The use of the lexemes 'private schools' and 'nationalised' signals topic continuity in this fragment. They are not near-lexicalised borrowings, as can be seen from the fact that as soon as the topic of conversation shifts from 'the nationalisation of schools' to the next topic ('building schools'), the English lexeme 'private schools' alternates with the mixed phrase '*shule za private*', and 'nationalised' alternates with the (almost puristic) Swahili verb '*kutaifisha*', as in:

B7   Moshi kulikuwa zimeshajenga tayari, lakini *zilizotaifishwa* ni nyingi
      [In Moshi they were already built, but there were many that were nationalised]

The information-structuring functions of English elements, especially emphasis-related functions which derive from the contrastive focus-effect of embedded English elements, can be judged from this fragment, taken from a later stage of the same conversation:

A1   Manake . . . shule hata *chakula hawapati siku hizi . . . cha-chakula stand-ard hawapati kule . . . basi imebidi wa*withdraw* . . . wanasema {hi} ooooh nijilimie mewnyewe .. na kila mwanafunzi wanacholima hakitoshi {hi} *even for *two months* . . . basi mambo yame*deteriorate* . . . basi unakuta . . ndiyo.
[Because the schools don't even get food nowadays, standard fo-food, they can't obtain it there. So it was necessary for them to withdraw. They say oooh! I'll work the field myself. But everything the students were farming, even that isn't enough even for two months. So things have deteriorated. And so you bump into . . . yes.]

B1   Sasa hivi wana-wanaanza kuamini . . . lakini sasa haija*pickup* . . . haija*pick* . . . ni hali ambayo kwa kweli it is *still deteriorating* . . . lakini kwenye *situation* kama hiyo hata kama umepata nafasi ya kusoma nafikiri *it's just low* . . . *they {lo} can't go on* . . .
[Right now they-they start to believe . . . but now it hasn't picked up yet, it hasn't picked . . . it's a situation which really is still deteriorating. But in a situation like this, even if you got the opportunity to study, I think it's just low, they can't go on . . .]

A2   Nchi ambayo ina *population* inayoongezeka *by *three percent* . . . lakini *intake* yake ya *university* inapungua *by {hi} *seventy percent* . . . na kuna wakati imefika hapa watu walikuwa wamechukuliwa mia tano . . . {hi} *intake ya university* . . . {hi} *five hundred* . . . *that wasn't what it was before.*
[A country that has a population which increases by three percent, but the intake of its university goes up by seventy percent! And there was a time when there came five hundred selected people here. The intake of the university, five hundred! That wasn't what it was before.]

Campus Swahili was a 'normal' code among academics. Whenever they found themselves in informal conditions with fellow academics, Campus Swahili would be the preferred or 'unmarked' code for conducting the conversation.[3] When I visited Dar es Salaam after the publication of the first reports on Campus Swahili, academics had become very much aware of their code-switching behaviour, which gave rise to amusing incidents. However great their efforts to speak standard Swahili were, they still lapsed into Campus Swahili every now and then, provoking laughter from me and from their colleagues. The near-automatism with which Campus Swahili was used sometimes produced quite funny or ironic utterances, such as:

Sisi tunasema *practically* Kiswahili sanifu.
[We speak practically pure/standard Swahili.]

Note that this line was spoken in response to a challenging question from me, as to why they switched so frequently from Swahili into English. In the very act of explicitly denying this, they implicitly confirmed it.

The emergence of a class variety

What does this kind of code-switching tell us? There is a macro level to this, at which code-switching takes on an ideological and political load. Switching codes involves playing with elements of the speech repertoire, in which unequal access to linguistic resources by speakers is crucial. When a code is used, the access to which is restricted to only some of the group of participants, others are excluded from the interaction. At a wider societal level, the use of codes – access to which is restricted to specific status groups in society – excludes the rest of society as potential participants in that type of interaction. So before people use code-switching as a cooperative enterprise in conversation, a lot of socially negative work has been done: they have selected linguistic resources which mark them as a separate group in society, and the use of these resources creates an insurmountable barrier to all those who have no access to them. Translated into social identity construction processes, this means that, first, an antisocial phase must be passed in which identities are created by exclusion, before the second cooperative and socially constructive phase can be entered; the *con*textual phase of communication is preceded by a *pre*textual stage in which people must draw on whatever is contained in their repertoires (cf. Blommaert and Maryns 2002). The process mobilises certain symbolic meanings, at the same as time demobilising others.

How does this pattern develop in Campus Swahili? Here, the Tanzanian language planning history, and specifically the role of English in education, will be a critical contextual feature. Academics use sophisticated varieties of English in their Swahili, and such English was a very rare commodity, certainly until the mid-1970s but also much later. Access to it was (and largely remains) strongly conditioned by education: the higher one's education, the greater the exposure to English. In the education system in operation in Tanzania at that time, this meant that extraordinarily *few* people could get access to status varieties of English. Figures from 1995 showed that about 5 per cent of students who finished the Swahili-medium primary school would pass into the first year of the English-medium secondary school; of this small group, about 15 per cent would actually finish secondary school – which means that a minute fraction of Tanzanian youth would have access to higher levels of English proficiency. Needless to say, an even smaller group of those who completed secondary education progressed to the university, where advanced professional registers in English could be learned (Neke 2002: Chapter 3). Therefore, the fact that Campus Swahili is a type of language behaviour restricted to the *wasomi* is not trivial: they are the only ones who, for sociological and political reasons, *could* acquire the resource that became a prerequisite for using Campus Swahili: English. Furthermore, they do not use just any kind of English. The English they use is locally experienced as standard English, a status variety – English which is perceived as grammatically correct and sophisticated, the mark of an educated person.

We will shortly turn to look at the English resources that were available to sub-elite groups in the population. At this point, it is enough to see the specific pattern of distribution that enables Campus Swahili to emerge as an elite variety of vernacular Dar es Salaam speech. English in itself seems not to be the crucial resource used for the construction of an in-group code among academics, but a variant of English which is highly valued because it is inextricably linked to that key element in upward social mobility in Tanzania: higher education. It is that particular variety of English, mixed with a variety of Swahili which also stands out because of its degree of elaboration and sophistication, which signals membership of the elite class of highly educated professionals.[4] The variety of Swahili should not be overlooked either, as standard Swahili is also connected to education, although to a lesser degree than English. We have seen that the higher one climbs on the ladder of education, the greater one's proficiency in Swahili is likely to become. The combination of both elements, 'good' Swahili and 'good' English, excludes the overwhelming majority of Tanzanians (the 'masses') from the possible range of in-group members. It creates within Campus Swahili a very exclusive, antisocial medium of communication, completely restricted to (and therefore indexical of) intellectual elites. A specific professional class – the intellectual elites – became marked by a specific variety of speech, and the use of that speech would be a maximally transparent signal of class belonging.

Campus Swahili, seen in this light, testifies to the emergence of a strong sociolinguistic diacritic of class in a society otherwise saturated with an overtly classless self-imagination. The power and pervasiveness of this diacritic can best be understood by looking at the kinds of English resources accessible to Tanzanians who did not belong to the narrow intellectual elites on University Hill. So let us now turn to someone we have already encountered above – Rashidi Akwilombe, and his novel *Dar Imenihadaa*.

6.4 ENGLISH IN *DAR IMENIHADAA*

In the previous chapter, I discussed the ways in which a rather unlikely cultural product – a post-Ujamaa popular novel – proved to be deeply influenced by Ujamaa frames and discourses upon closer inspection. Ujamaa, I argued, was the most transparent and effective pattern for discussing Tanzanian society available to a writer such as Akwilombe. Part of the evidence for this was the specific ways in which the use of English was depicted in the novel: it indexed – in line with the most rigorous versions of Ujamaa language ideology – the anti-socialist, anti-egalitarian and 'Westernised' dimensions of character and behaviour. English was *bad* in Akwilombe's novel.

In creating and shaping this specific motive, Akwilombe uses actual English phrases and expressions, as spoken by the leading characters in the novel. The English phrases are invariably followed by a Swahili translation; Akwilombe, with sound sociolinguistic intuition, does not expect his readership to be fully fluent in English. A total of twenty-nine such English fragments occur in the novel. Here they are (page numbers added).

1. 'Hello Darling D. Where are you going Honey? Can I call myself the luckiest person in the world to be with beautiful girl again?' (p. 8)

2. 'Thank you, Darling. As I told you earlier, I am going to start work in Dar es Salaam as a Secretary.' (p. 8)

3. 'Darling, there is transport waiting for us outside. I will escort you to Ilala before I proceed to my home at Oysterbay. Let us go Dear.' (p. 11)

4. 'Darling D., I have very good news for you. As I had promised, I have managed to secure accomodation for you at Ilala Flats. I have furnished the place and you will get everything that you need. Do you now believe that I love you.' (p. 12)

5. 'This is your new home Darling. I hope you will find everything that you need in here. In case there is something missing, just inform me and you will get it promptly. Do you like this place? Do not mind about the House Rent because I will always be paying it for you.' (p. 13)

6. 'Darling, I like this place very much. I am even prepared to come and live here with effect from today.' (p. 13)

7. 'What are you? What do you want in my house, you idiot.' (p. 15)

8. 'What do you want here, poor old stupid man? I do not know you and I do not give arms to the poor except on Friday. Go away at once.' (p. 16)

9. 'Do you have the shape or Education to cope with me? Do you expect me to love a poor stupid hooligan like you? To hell with your silly words. Do not come near me you fool?' (pp. 16–17)

10. 'My name is Dezo. I am a Librarian by profession and I am now taking a Master's Degree in Librarianship at the Polytechnic of North London in the United Kingdom. I am about to finish that Degree but I am required to write a thesis as part of the fulfilment of the Course. I have come to understand that you have a very good Library in your Organization. Would you therefore allow me to see your Manager so that I talk to him on the matter. Might be he may allow me to do my studies here for some time.' (pp. 20–2)

11. 'Wait a moment Sir. I am going to tell the Manager about you and I will be back soon.' (p. 22)

12. 'Thank you Sister.' (p. 22)

13. 'I thank you very much for your hospitality sister. I am pleased to inform you that I have been allowed to come and prepare my thesis in your Library as long as I like.' (p. 22)

14. 'I am very pleased to hear that you are coming to work with us here for some time. I wonder whether you would allow to come and prepare my thesis in your Library as long as like.' [error] (p. 23)

15. 'I am lonely as I have told you Would you be kind enough to join me and break my loneliness and at the same time show me various places of you noble city of Dar es Salaam? I am very sorry and please accept my apologies Madam if I am offending you by asking such favour from you.' (p. 23)

16. 'You are not offending me Sir. I am prepared to join you and walk around Dar es Salaam but how will get you?' (p. 24)

17. 'Just ring the Kilimanjaro Hotel and ask for me. I will be available at any time.' (p. 24)

18. 'Mr. Dezo, I think I am free today. Would you kindly come and collect me outside my office after office hours?' (p. 24)
19. 'Excuse me Madam if I have kept you waiting. I have come to collect you as per our telephone conversation.' (p. 25)
20. 'Do not mind about my waiting Sir. I have not been here long enough to be irritated. How can you say you have kept me waiting if I have just arrived here? Never mind Sir.' (p. 26)
21. 'You see, Miss Devota, I have got a very big problem but before I tell you what it is, may I kindly ask if you are married.' (p. 27)
22. 'Miss Devota, may I confess that I love you immediately I saw you in your Office. In addition to my coming to prepare for my Degree in Librarianship, my parents have allowed me to come and marry in my country. Would you kind enough to accept to marry me and go back with me to the United Kingdom? Once again, I apologize if I have offended or insulted you Madam.' (p. 27)
23. 'I also loved you when I first saw you. In short, I am prepared to marry you and I am ready to go anywhere with you, Darling. Are you happy now?' (p. 28)
24. 'You poor old man, what do you want with me? Do you expect a young and beutiful girl like me to have love affairs with you. You are like my father and I can no longer continue loving you. Go away, you Rat.' (p. 31)
25. 'Darling, I think I have a very big mistake. I had booked myself at the Kilimanjaro Hotel for the weeks, that is from the day I landed at the Dar es Salaam International Airport, While coming from UK. up to and including the day we traveled to Iringa. I did not renew my booking and I think my room will have been occupied by somebody else. However, I will make arrangements at another lodging until I renew my booking at the Kilimanjaro. Is that alright with you Darling?' (p. 37)
26. 'What will you do if your fiance does not come back? I have got a feeling that this Mr. Dezo of you is not coming back.' (p. 45)
27. 'I am reporting to my place of work tomorrow because my leave is finished. By then, I will be in a position to decide what to do.' (p. 45)
28. 'The Taxi which we used yesterday is waiting outside. I will escort you to your office and then I will continue with my daily Routine. Let us go if you are ready Madam.' (p. 46)
29. [part of sentence omitted] 'know, you are supposed to be a Librarian to go back to England Why didn't you return to the Hotel and settle the Bill? Why leave me alone?' (p. 49)

A sociolinguistic look at 'errors'

Undoubtedly, the twenty-nine fragments presented above offer a somewhat strange picture. No one will dispute the fact that this *is* English. And leaving aside simple qualifications of 'good' or 'bad' English, it certainly is *peculiar* English. For one thing, the fragments contain numerous 'errors' when approached from the punitive perspective of the (standard) English language teacher. At the same time, we can assume on the basis of the generic characteristics of the text that Akwilombe has attempted to write *good* English, the *best* English he could mobilise for the stylistic and communicative purposes served by the passages in the novel. This is the point where perceptions and resources interact: Akwilombe has realised a stereotype of English language usage by means of the various kinds of English to which he has access. This is also the point at which errors become interesting ethnographic objects, highly informative about the way in which English or Englishes (and other linguistic resources) are distributed across different layers in society, as well as about the ways in which these unevenly distributed resources become instruments of cultural expression among those who have access to them.

Let us take a brief look at some of these errors. I will not comment on the typographic and punctuation problems, although some of them certainly merit deeper investigation (for instance, the unwarranted use of capitals in terms of address such as 'Darling' and 'Honey' (1) or 'Rat' (24), terms such as 'Degree', 'Course', 'Library' and 'Organization' (10) or 'House Rent' (5) and 'Taxi' (28)) and can be indicative of inter-language influence (for example, the l/r confusion in 'I do not give *arms* to the poor' (8)).

First, there are quite a few syntactic errors. The deletion of definite and indefinite articles is quite common (see for example (1) 'with beautiful girl again', and (25) 'from UK') and can even be found in scientific papers published in English by Tanzanian scholars. This, like the l/r confusion noted above, may be an instance of inter-language influence (Bantu languages have no definite/indefinite articles). Further syntactic errors include:

1. errors in verbal inflection: 'start work' instead of 'start working' in (2);
2. other inflectional or concordance errors such as with the possessive pronouns in 'you [= your] noble city of Dar es Salaam' (15) and 'this Mr. Dezo of you [= yours]' (26);
3. the deletion of personal pronouns in, for example, 'as long as [I] like' (14) and 'but how will [I] get you' (16);
4. the deletion of prepositions in, for example, 'I love you immediately [when] I saw you' (22) (the whole sentence would sound more familiar if it were written as 'I loved you from the moment I saw you');
5. errors in the selection of the predicate, as in 'I have a very big mistake' (25) which should be 'I made/have made a very big mistake'.

More frequent, however, are problems with lexical selection and, ultimately, with *register*. 'I have come to understand' (10) could be replaced by 'I have come to know' or 'I have learned'. 'I am going to tell the Manager about you' (11) sounds as if Devota is going to say bad things about Dezo to the manager, and would benefit from a cosmetic operation using 'to inform' rather than 'to tell'. 'How will [I] get you?' (16) could be 'how will I find you?' 'I had booked myself at the Kilimanjaro Hotel' (25) might sound to some people as if Dezo has arrested himself at the

Kilimanjaro Hotel – mentioning the true object of the booking, 'a room', would work wonders. The phrase 'to cope with me' (9) probably means 'to go out with me' or something related to that. And finally Shuga Dedi's immortal question, 'Can I call myself the luckiest person in the world to be with [a] beautiful girl again?' (1) is a fine indirect speech act, but a rather unconventional one.

Other lexical problems, but of a different sort, are those that are the result of 'calques' from Swahili into English. In a number of cases, Akwilombe provides literal English translations of common Swahili utterances. The word 'shape' in 'Do you have the shape or Education to cope with me?' (9) is a translation of '*sura*', a term meaning 'appearance' and referring to a broader concept of physical characteristics including body posture and elegance. The term of address 'Sister' (12) is a calque of '*dada*', a common Swahili term of address for young women. These calques all feed the suspicion that Akwilombe started with Swahili conversations which he later translated with the help of a dictionary or sets of stock phrases.

The most striking phenomena in the fragments are *cross-register transfers*. While depicting a courteous but intimate spoken interaction, Akwilome puts elements from a highly formal, literate style into the mouths of his characters. Some phrases could be picked directly from official letters:

'. . . with effect from today' (6)

'I am pleased to inform you that I have been allowed to come . . .' (13)

'. . . as per our telephone conversation' (19)

Others phrases present such extreme cases of deferential or distancing language use that they are quite unrealistic when set in the situations in which they are supposed to occur:

'Might be he may allow me . . .' (10)

'. . . you[r] noble city of Dar es Salaam' (15)

'I am very sorry and please accept my apologies Madam if I am offending you . . .' (15)

'Excuse me Madam if I have kept you waiting.' (19)

'may I kindly ask you if you are married.' (21)

What happens here is that conventional, enregistered features from one zone of linguistic activity – invariably that of highly formal and semi-routinised (written) interactions – are projected onto a situation that would require a very different register. The conversational dimension is lost; what is left is a caricature of spoken deferential English – indicative of Akwilombe's limited knowledge of English register variation.

Let me now summarise some of the observations made so far. The English used by Akwilombe to sketch and moralise about characters and forms of behaviour in his novel is littered with various types of errors or unconventional wordings, seen from a normative standard-English viewpoint. To some extent, the errors can be related to material conditions of production such as deficient editing and typesetting. However, other errors point towards gaps in the repertoire of the language user: grammatical errors, problems in lexical selection, pragmatic problems such as the cross-register transfers. Having said all this, we need to bear in mind that Akwilombe displays considerable proficiency in English. Most of what he writes is 'technically' correct. When compared to the Swahili translations accompanying each fragment, the English phrases are always to different degrees 'correct' – at least, when 'correctness' is taken to be a continuum of acceptable and communicatively appropriate choices rather than as a fixed and narrow category. This is by all standards 'English'. But it is English that has been re-ordered and restructured in a particular (local) communicative economy not governed by the codes and norms of standard English. Its conventions and norms have been relocated in relation to other elements of Akwilombe's speech repertoire, and therefore the English he uses can pass, locally, in a society in which English is a rare commodity, as an adequate picture of what people would really say in English.

So whereas we saw that academics draw on status varieties and sophisticated English registers, we see that the English resources on which Akwilombe can draw have different sources and reflect different patterns of distribution of 'English' in Tanzanian society. Akwilombe's English phrases have their stylistic and generic roots in formal written correspondence in English – a very specific register that is 'generalised', so to speak, to cover scenes of informal spoken interaction in his novel, in a process I called cross-register transfer. These two complexes of English resources occupied different positions in the economy of English in Tanzania. Whereas Akwilombe's formal written register builds on the competences acquired in secondary school and could, with some effort, be further developed informally and on one's own – by reading business correspondence books, for instance, or by becoming familiar with institutional correspondence in administrative or work contexts – the English resources deployed by the academics reflect patterns of disciplined learning patterns in a strong and cohesive professional peer group. The first set of resources, thus, can be qualified as 'democratic' while the latter is a 'members only' resource. The sociolinguistic differences between the two varieties of English bespeak larger patterns of social and political fragmentation; they reflect a non-unified and class-stratified society, and they do this in spite of the strong and overt acceptance of Ujamaa principles by their users.

6.5 A FRAGMENTED SOCIOLINGUISTIC SYSTEM

Let us now return to Campus Swahili and consider its analytic value. The class dimension I identified in relation to it is, of course, merely a description of the effects of Campus Swahili in terms of the overall make-up of Tanzanian society in the 1980s and 1990s; it is not an imputation of intentions. It certainly tells us something about Tanzanian society and its class dynamics, but I am not ready to go as far as to connect Campus Swahili to class consciousness or class-conscious behaviour.

Campus Swahili is a 'normal' way of speaking among academics, intrinsic to their class position or, to use Bourdieuan terminology, to their habitus as academics or intellectual elite members. In their in-group, using it does not constitute a 'hard' identity signal since available identities in that period in Tanzania tended to be pre-established: those who spoke Campus Swahili were all *wasomi*, and class membership was a prerequisite to being able to use Campus Swahili. It only indexed their class affiliation to outsiders, and at the macro-dimension of code choice and the accessibility of parts of the speech repertoire. In that sense, Campus Swahili was a *structural* symptom of class formation and exclusivism in a society professing classlessness and egalitarianism.

However, the world should not be turned upside down. It is not language which creates class in this case. The major factor in the rise of an intellectual elite, which symbolises itself, among other things, by means of specific language usage, is the hierarchical, pyramidal stratification of the educational system – of which, the base is very large, and the top is very small. In the 1980s and 1990s, the top of the pyramid, the academic *wasomi*, was a very small community of urban professionals drawn from all parts of the country, and who, in the case of the university staff, lived on or around a geographically separate area: the main campus on University Hill. The fact that a specific form of language behaviour became one of their class-marking paraphernalia is largely due to factors over which they had hardly any control, but that were part of the larger social history and structure of Tanzania. In the course of becoming members of the intellectual elite, the academics acquired not only technical or scientific skills, a middle-class way of life and facilities to travel abroad, but also a deepened competence in standard Swahili, their political medium, and status varieties of English, their professional medium. The latter skills turned out to be so exclusive that they can hardly be mimicked by non-members of their class; more than their wealth – expressed in cars, clothes, watches and other material goods – the specific, exclusive language resources they used marked their elite status.

I am therefore also very hesitant to follow a popular line of scholarship and qualify Campus Swahili as a form of *contest* or *resistance* against the dominant egalitarian state ideology. The issue, again, can be addressed from different perspectives. For as far as contest and resistance presuppose conscious and deliberate action, the intellectuals who used Campus Swahili in the past gave ample evidence of a willingness to incorporate Ujamaa assumptions into their professional practice, and they actively seemed to adopt a posture of an intellectual vanguard in the process of nation building. We have encountered them doing precisely that in earlier chapters. Furthermore, using Campus Swahili was very much a speech routine in certain situations, developed with a low level of metapragmatic awareness (remember the '*practically* Kiswahili Sanifu' of my interlocutors) and *not* using it required conscious and deliberate effort from the speakers.

But looked at from a more detached perspective (the perspective of, for instance, language planning scholars), Campus Swahili and its elite dimensions may serve as an index of some basic weaknesses in the ideological complex. It may indicate that the linguistic and cultural philosophy contained in Ujamaa did not work, because some of the linguistic and cultural symbols (foremost, Swahili) could, in practice, be used in ways that fundamentally contradicted several key principles of Ujamaa. Swahili was not *in itself* an egalitarian vehicle that incorporated and diffused Ujamaa values by its sheer usage. It was distributed and acquired in different varieties (the registers we mentioned above), all of which could be related to, and made indexically expressive of, forms of social stratification: the higher one's education, the better one's Swahili becomes, and the better one's Swahili-English code-switching becomes. Thus the diffusion of Swahili varieties correlates (and documents) processes of class formation in Tanzania in the period described here.

Further, the decision not to implement full Swahilisation in post-primary education (also discussed earlier) magnified the class effects of Swahili. Academics who were questioned about their use of Campus Swahili frequently referred to the fact that they had to teach and carry out research in English, and therefore that certain topics could only be discussed adequately by means of frequent switches to English. This is not the whole story, as I hope to have shown, but it is certainly an important factor. The fact is that the academic environment was strongly permeated by Anglophone ways of speaking, or, that Dar es Salaam University was essentially and effectively (even if not officially) an *English*-speaking university.

This then created conditions in which the privileges of Swahili came under pressure and a more ambivalent pattern could emerge. On the one hand Swahili was the national language, the usage of which was the rule in all social and formal occasions (the graduation ceremony, for instance, was performed in Swahili), and the usage of which was normative for those people who since independence had been granted such a prominent role in the rhetoric about society. On the other hand it was not the language of professional business at the university. If Swahili was supposed to stand for the new Tanzanian culture, then science was apparently not part of it. Therefore, rather than a symptom of elite resistance and class consciousness, Campus Swahili was a symptom of the *failure* of Ujamaa ideology in the domain of language hegemony. While the ideology of the state prescribed (and predicted) a monoglot Swahili-speaking society unified by Ujamaa principles and ways of life, a far more fragmented society developed 'from below', marked by social class distinctions articulated strongly around indexically-ordered ways of using language, converging in strongly different repertoires.

6.6 CONCLUSION: THE FAILURE OF A LANGUAGE IDEOLOGY

At this point, we stumble over an argument we have encountered previously: the ideological conceptualisation and imagination of language. The paradoxical fieldwork observation which I came across in the academic circles of the University of Dar es Salaam was that the very same people who devoted the best of their efforts to standardising and promoting Swahili and advocating a monolingual Swahili-speaking Tanzanian society, simultaneously defeated this monolingual ideal in their own speech behaviour. They themselves did not perceive this situation as a paradox.

Their everyday speech was just that: everyday speech, with all its vernacular, dialect- or sociolect-like qualities. It had nothing to do with the national language they were working with, because this national language was the 'real' language. They mastered that 'real' language brilliantly, and even exhausted its indexical potential by deliberately choosing an Arabised pronunciation (a mark of purism) when speaking in formal or out-group situations.

So, at an implicit level observable only when scrutinising various forms of language behaviour, these people allocated symbolic statuses to standard Swahili in a flexible, situational and functional way, always as part of a broader repertoire. At an explicit level, however, these various elements of the repertoire were given a normative connotation: one was a 'language', others were just 'speech', or 'ordinary talk'. The tension between a normative and monoglot conception of Swahili and other elements of the repertoire, and a situational and functional conception of these various elements, was neutralised in their work and did not become a topic of theoretical reflection until later, when scholars started calling into question the monofocal orientation of Tanzanian language policies in the light of new research on the relationship between Swahili and local languages. For their own speech behaviour, various kinds of rationalisations were offered, ranging from the power of habituated behaviour to the professional strain of having to work and teach in English. However, none of the rationalisations was powerful enough to challenge the normative, monofocal conceptualisation of language and its ideological underpinning of a Swahili-speaking Tanzanian nation.

This preference for a normative (deductive) conception of language over more 'realistic' (inductive) conceptions is, on the one hand, part of the linguistic ideology handed down to Tanzanians by previous generations of scholars. As argued earlier, it is part of their colonial legacy. But this colonial legacy is not restricted to linguistic conceptualisations only. It also encompasses broader notions of society and its features, of a people and its identity. The normative conception of a language is, I believe, a typical ingredient of European nationalist thought, and it was integrated into the Tanzanian idea of nation building. The Tanzanian intellectuals were trapped into adopting this frame of reference for discussing the sociolinguistic realities of their country, and the result was that they failed to look at some extremely relevant parameters of language spread, the social stratification of language, the efficiency of Swahili as a medium of everyday communication, and, most of all, the conditions for distributing various forms of Swahili (and English) into the language repertoires of Tanzanian citizens.

This observation teaches us that the ideological hegemonisation of the country used deficient theoretical tools as far as Swahili was concerned. To the extent that language spread – Swahilisation – was seen as an ingredient of the process of nation building-as-ideological-hegemonisation, an irrelevant ideology of language was used, one which drew attention away from the actual speech behaviour of people and focused, prescriptively, on what they *should* speak. Note that code-switching is in itself not hard counter-evidence for hegemony. On the contrary, the speech of the intellectuals demonstrates the extent to which Swahili had been accepted as a cross-ethnic medium, used by people who otherwise had to perform in English. But it challenges the parameters along which hegemony was measured in Tanzania: it challenged the association between ideological hegemony and monolingualism. In that sense, it is evidence of the failure of the theoretical instruments of the cultural philosophy.

6.7 NOTES

1. Abdulaziz's seminal paper (1972) also gives examples of Swahili-English code-switching (pp. 207–8). But although the examples given are clearly sampled in an academic context, he relates them to more general features of life in a multi-ethnic urban environment.
2. Transcription conventions are kept to a minimum in the transcripts of this tape-recorded conversation. The symbol {hi} indicates a rising pitch, {lo} a lower pitch, * marks sentence stress, and two or three dots indicate hesitations or pauses, depending on the duration of the hesitation or pause. The conversation took place in August 1985 in an office in the university, and four interlocutors were present. However, in the fragments presented here only two interlocutors (A and B) talk.
3. I noted very few exceptions to this rule. One of these was a multilateral conversation which was conducted in Campus Swahili, until the group was joined by a known Swahili purist who enjoyed great status among the group. From then on, efforts were made to speak standard Swahili.
4. The importance of distinguishing *varieties* of languages used in code-switching is also emphasised by, for example, Heller (1992: 139). Canadian Francophones use Canadian French as an ethnic mobilisation strategy, because Canadian French sets them apart from both the Anglophone Canadians and the European speakers of French.

Chapter 7

Enregistering the globalised nation

Ujamaa was a political ideology aimed at unity, or, better, at political, social, cultural and linguistic homogeneity. The previous chapter has shown that this homogenising tendency could not control sociolinguistic differentiation; we have seen the emergence of specific registers among social groups, differentiated both by objective aspects – highly educated Tanzanians versus less educated Tanzanians – as well as by subjective aspects – desires and images of identities brought out through practices of 'distinction'. Of course, we can expect such forms of register differentiation to expand when the homogenising drive of a singular political ideology and a monofocal nation vanishes, and in this chapter I will turn to these escalating patterns of sociolinguistic differentiation.

7.1 A CHANGED ENVIRONMENT

When I returned to Dar es Salaam in 2012 after an interval of several years, I found the city to be superficially different. For one thing, Dar es Salaam had grown explosively and is now supposed to harbour approximately 4–5 million people. Thousands of cars create a permanent traffic catastrophe, because the roads – now much improved – were not designed for the capacity currently required. Reconditioned cars, mostly Japanese and with a remarkable frequency of rather expensive SUVs, mix with school buses and Indian motorcycle-taxis called *Bajaj* – two things I never encountered before. New tall, fancy buildings dominate the city, and much impressive construction work is going on. An immense quantity of natural gas was discovered off the coast of Tanzania, and investors and speculators (notably from the Emirates and from China) obviously consider Dar es Salaam to be the East-African boomtown of the future.

There is adequate Internet provision in the city now and roads are lined by posters advertising cheap mobile Internet rates offered by the multitude of mobile phone providers now active there (of which, more below). People in downtown Dar es Salaam are using their mobile phones liberally, and, as in most other metropolitan cities in the world, one can easily overhear loudly articulated phone conversations in bars and restaurants. There is a new middle class, including a considerable number of what we could call Tanzanian yuppies, and this middle class dominates the cityscape. The media companies offer a large range of television networks and channels, many of them international and with several domestic channels operating in Swahili and English. In addition, private schools and universities are booming, as the elites prefer to pay for an education they themselves can control. Money is now counted in *laki* (100,000) and *milioni*, because the Tanzanian Shilling dropped from 15:1 against the US Dollar in 1985 (150:1 on the black market) to a staggering but stable 1500:1 in 2012. A beer in an ordinary bar now costs 2,000TSh, rising to 7,000TSh in more exclusive places.

Contrary to the sometimes extreme paucity of supplies in shops in earlier days, the city now has several shopping malls in which one can see the effects of economic globalisation: Heinz Ketchup manufactured in Hong Kong and Heinz Corned Beef made in Brazil; vegetable oil from Kenya; peeled tomatoes and Buitoni pastas from Italy; American Garden mayonnaise imported from the US; Kellogg's cereals packaged in Manchester, UK; MAGGI ketchup from Malaysia; sushi rice from Thailand; basmati rice from Dubai; garlic from China; pears from Somerset West in South Africa; and, to top it all, the iconic South African sausage called *boerewors*, manufactured in Kenya. Tanzania's trade doors are obviously wide open, while locally-produced goods, suffering from poorly designed and uninspiring packaging, look uncompetitive next to the global trade commodities on the shelves of the new supermarkets. These supermarkets, needless to say, sell their goods at prices that exclude almost everyone except the truly affluent. The Kenya-made sausage costs 15,000TSh (about 7.5 euro) per kilo; imported lemons are sold at 2,000TSh (about 1 euro) per kilo; and even humble stock vegetables such as onion and garlic are offered at prices of around 1,800TSh per kilo. Local average salaries don't take you far in such shops.

The change is superficial though. As soon as one leaves the central district of the city and wanders towards traditionally poorer areas – the Kariakoo market area, for instance, or districts somewhat farther from the centre such as Mwenge and Sinza – one enters a city quite similar to that of two decades ago. The shops and kiosks are now better supplied, that is true; but the people running them are still poor, and they complain about the rising prices of commodities now distributed not by the state but by private companies. Thus, the Makonde woodcarvers in Mwenge now have to procure their ebony wood from a private foresting and lumber company and ebony prices have soared enormously, endangering their tourist-oriented trade. There are new forms of employment – the affluent middle class demands protection and the private security business is exploding in size and profitability; the same is true for car maintenance and Internet/mobile phone provision, new forms of journalism and, for the hopeful, a new tourist business attracting a wealthy population interested in luxury beach hotels and well-equipped golf courses, rather than the Lonely Planet backpackers of some decades ago. The majority of the people, however, still live outside the formal economy, and the Tanzanian Ministry of Education reports on its website that the illiteracy rate in the country has grown from 9.6 per cent in 1986 to a dramatic 31 per cent in 2007. An economic growth rate of 6 per cent has obviously not done much to alleviate the poverty of the Tanzanian masses.[1]

The government has changed face as well. Nyerere's *Chama Cha Mapinduzi* (CCM) still rules the country – the introduction of a multiparty system has not changed the structures of power – but its executives now dress in smart Western suits and occupy large mansions in exclusive areas alongside diplomats and business tycoons. Political power has very much been 'normalised', so to speak: its formats and appearances do not articulate much difference anymore to that in advanced capitalist countries. Nyerere is still worshipped as the *Baba ya Taifa* ('Father of the Nation') and claims to moral leadership still orient to him, but the socialist idealism and voluntarism of his generation have been replaced by a pragmatic managerialism of the Executive, as we shall see later in this chapter.

I will document and discuss some of the sociolinguistic changes accompanying the transformation of the country. And the argument I shall build is that Tanzania has now become a globalised nation whose political, social and cultural profiles must be understood in relation to the different scales that characterise globalised socio-political and cultural configurations. We will have to consider the impact of globalised scenarios and frames for identification – an important and qualitatively new scale level – as well as those of a repositioned nation-state and of repositioned subnational dynamics. The local and the national have both shifted their relative positions due to global forces: this argument was central to *The Sociolinguistics of Globalization* (Blommaert 2010) and can be elaborated, albeit sketchily, with respect to Tanzania. I also recapitulate the central claim made in *The Sociolinguistics of Globalization*: that attention to sociolinguistic detail offers us a privileged and uniquely sensitive diagnostic of wider patterns of change and development (cf. also Blommaert and Rampton 2011). By looking at what many others would consider irrelevant details, we are sometimes able to get to the very heart of such processes.

In particular, and here I recapitulate points made in the previous chapter, we see that social processes have patterns of enregisterment as their sociolinguistic correlate (Agha 2007). Particular 'chunks' of language and other communicative and semiotic resources are 'ordered' in such a way that they indexically point towards the specific social practices and actors' identities with which they occur. The relationship is not just reflective: processes of enregisterment construct such social practices and identities. Talking in a political register, for instance, constructs meanings as 'political' and speakers as 'politicians'; the same goes for lawyers, doctors and other neatly identifiable social categories, but also for hip youngsters, yuppies, hip hop fans, and so forth. Enregisterment is the social order we find in communicative practice; the requirement (or desire) to be recognisable-as-someone ensures a relative stability and recurrence for the orders of indexicality that construct the practices and identities within which one wants to inscribe oneself (see Blommaert 2005: Chapter 3). Thus, following up on the previous chapter, we shift the debate and the analysis from differences between 'languages' (for example, Swahili and English) towards differences *within* languages – 'ways of speaking', genres, styles; in sum – the patterns of order we can observe in processes of enregisterment.

In what follows, I shall offer a series of three vignettes illustrating the multiple processes of enregisterment we observe in contemporary Tanzania. I will first document the new culture of managerialism of the Tanzanian state (in section 7.2). It is a feature of global ideoscapes in the sense of Appadurai (1996), and its usage indexes the incorporation of the Tanzanian state in a worldwide model of business-oriented public governance. Next, I will engage with new forms of advertisements for Internet and mobile phone provision (in section 7.3). These articulate a range of new images of middle-class identities, and they – remarkably – do so in Swahili. The first two sections, thus, will discuss the emergence of new registers targetted at new complexes of social and political practice. Thirdly, I will turn my attention to the emergence of heterograhic practices among Tanzanians on Facebook (in section 7.4) – their 'languaging', so to speak (cf. Jørgensen 2008; Creese and Blackledge 2010; Juffermans 2010; Blommaert and Rampton 2011). This, too, will show global affordances turn into locally enregistered codes (Pennycook 2010; Blommaert 2012).

After these three descriptive sections, I will pull the different pieces of the argument together in a discussion of the complex forms of enregisterment that characterise the globalised society that Tanzania has become (in section 7.5; cf. Agha 2007; Møller and Jørgensen 2011). Throughout the different examples we shall see the gradual emergence of register, rather than language, as the key notion for understanding contemporary sociolinguistic processes in Tanzania. This argument will be more fully developed in that final section, and we will see how more complex repertoires answer the demands of more complex forms of identity work now performed.

7.2 VISIONS AND MISSIONS

The present rulers of Tanzania, both in the public and private sectors, are people who were educated under *Elimu ya Kujitegemea*, the educational policy of Ujamaa discussed earlier in this book, in which primary education was generalised and improved so as to create (certainly until the oil crisis of the mid-1970s) an education system unique in scope and quality (Mushi 2009). These leaders, consequently, are all fully literate, multilingual and highly educated, and these features set them apart from the previous generation of leaders, many of whom had just modest educational backgrounds often acquired under colonial rule. Abeid Karume, the first President (and dictator) of Zanzibar and Vice President of Tanzania, was at best semi-literate, and he took pride in the fact that most members of his Zanzibar Revolutionary Council likewise had enjoyed very little formal education (Shivji 2008: 109). The present leaders were also among the second wave of promising youngsters handpicked and sent off to the University of Dar es Salaam and other higher institutions in Tanzania and abroad for advanced education. They returned in the 1980s with Business Administration or Law degrees and set out to construct post-Ujamaa Tanzania.

The slowness and inadequacy of Tanzanian public administration used to be the stuff of legends. A good friend of mine started working at the University of Dar es Salaam in 1979 and retired some years ago after a career of over three decades;

recently, to his infinite joy, he received the letter appointing him to tenure at the university, backdated to 1981. Changing foreign notes into Tanzanian Shillings in the 1980s required about half a day in the bank, because the form used for this rather simple transaction required no less than three stamps and signatures. I kept some such densely belaboured slips of official paper as souvenirs of the many, many desperate hours in banks, waiting for the Deputy Chief Teller Clerk to arrive and put his signature and stamp on the exchange form. Mountains of paper would cover the offices of ministries and very little could be achieved without elaborate explanation and, occasionally, some 100TSh notes offered in hierarchical sequence to officials. And I also have vivid memories of that perplexing event in 1985, when the government decided to change *all* bank notes in the country to a newly printed series over a period of just a few days, forcing all citizens to stand in phenomenal queues by the banks with their cash possessions in hand – a genuine Eldorado for pickpockets and corrupt bank managers, and possibly the most chaotic instance of public management I have ever witnessed.

Today, ministries are housed in new tall glass-and-steel buildings in downtown Dar es Salaam as well as (the smarter ones) in some suburbs. The ministries now have websites and offer e-facilities to citizens, and the facades of their buildings are, like those of some large businesses, adorned with boards announcing the ministry's vision and mission solemnly written in Swahili and English (see Figure 1).

Figure 1   The vision and mission of the Ministry of Energy and Minerals, Samora Street. (Source: © Jan Blommaert)

These vision and mission statements indicate a change of seismic proportions in public management. From a hegemonic and monopolistic state in the days of *Ujamaa na Kujitegemea*, Tanzania's public policy texts now overflow with references to cooperation – first across national boundaries and second between public and private actors – and it inscribes itself into a familiar globally aligned discourse. Consider the following fragment from a policy document, *Public Financial Management Reform Programme – Strategic Plan*, issued by the Tanzanian Ministry of Finance and Economic Affairs (2008: 31):

> The PSRP (Public Service Reform Programme) has a wide mandate. It covers restructuring, private sector participation, executive agencies (of government), Performance Management, Programme coordination and M&E (Monitoring & Evaluation), MIS (Management Information System) and Leadership Management and Development and Coordination. Each of these touches upon aspects of PFMRP (Public Financial Management Reform Programme). Investment Management component of PFMRP deals with Parastatals, so there is common interest on executive agencies. Information Technology (Computer Services) deals with management information and so needs to relate to overall MIS within government.

This Reform Programme has a vision and a mission itself (ibid.: 38). The vision is formulated as follows: 'To excel in and sustain financial management and accountability, fiscal control and provision of quality Treasury Services.' And the mission statement reads: 'To achieve and maintain sound financial management, fiscal discipline, accountability resource mobilization and allocation, public debt management, Government asset management through developing robust fiscal and monetary policies, efficient and effective provision of Treasury Services and enhancing professionalism' (ibid.)

Clearly the Tanzanian officials have taken advanced lessons in the jargon of new public management. Their discourse has been streamlined and polished into what can best be seen as a global discourse model of managerialism, a typical 'ideoscape' in Appadurai's well-known vision of cultural globalisation (Appadurai 1996). This model of managerialism, certainly in its Anglo-Saxon variety, has blurred the boundaries between public and private management, as Du Gay (2008: 235) observes, since public administration is now supposed to operate in identical fashion to the private sector. Public sector institutions are to be run on an entrepreneurial basis, and 'culture change' – a transition from a supposed archaic management culture to a new entrepreneurial one – is seen as a key feature of the model (O'Reilly and Reed 2010: 962). Discourses, images and metaphors such as those we encounter in the fragments above are central features of such culture change. In the ideology of managerialism, they emblematise the transition from an atrophied statist public service to one in which the 'client' (the citizen) is focal, in which rational planning, process management, efficiency monitoring and permanent quality control are the instruments of public governance, and in which public services are seen as commodities offered in a competitive market.

Let us return briefly to the document quoted above, and consider the densely packed jargon in the following fragment (Tanzanian Ministry of Finance and Economic Affairs 2008: 36; naturally the fragment is followed by a flow chart):

There is therefore a logical sequence to the implementation of improvements in PFM, which entails getting the basics right first. If initial effort is directed at implementing a sound set of control systems, this will then enable policy to be put into practice and, subsequently, the delivery of services in an effective and efficient manner.

Or – there really is no dearth of examples in this document – consider this fragment (ibid.: 39):

PFMRP III therefore will all be about operationalising best practices, i.e. making the tools, techniques, methodologies and systems, developed under PFMRP II, work in Tanzania. The majority of the tools are now in place for a robust PFM structure, however in many cases there is little or no integration between these various supporting systems and procedures, causing inefficient and incomplete operational processes that are hindering further PFM reform. In addition, it is necessary for PFM capacity in Government to catch up with the latest techniques and methodologies to be able to take advantage of the facilities they offer. This Platform will therefore be reinforcing the second PFM reform objective, namely allocative efficiency.

Here is the culture change in public management in Tanzania: it is a shift into discourse and practice formats that are entirely in line with globally circulating normative templates, and it is via such templates that Tanzania now presents itself to the outside world as an efficient, late-modern globalised state, driven by 'core values' which, inevitably, include things such as the following, taken from the website of the Ministry of Finance and Economic Affairs (available from: www.mof.go.tz/ index.php?option=com_content&view=article&id=141&Itemid=173):

• Innovativeness
• Professionalism
• Customer focused
• Commitment to work
• Efficiency
• Participatory management
• Teamwork
• Timely service delivery
• Integrity

Note, of course, that a change in discourse and public semiotics is not immediately equivalent to a change in the actual practices and culture of work; quite often, old features of organisational culture persist under a veneer of new managerialism (Kirkpatrick and Ackroyd 2003). People in Tanzania still complain about the erratic service delivery they receive from their public institutions, and diplomats and expatriate business people will still volunteer an avalanche of hair-raising anecdotes whenever requested to share their experiences of public administrations in the country. The point, however, is that we see a discursive change in the discourse of public administration, which represents a complete break with the past and now orients fully to the rest of the world. Whereas the previous regime wanted to be understandable primarily to all Tanzanians, the new regime wants to be understood by the global business and political community.

Such global orientations naturally proceed overwhelmingly in English. The document quoted here is in English, and several of the ministries' websites contain massive amounts of English and have their design entirely in English. Swahili, though, continues to be used whenever the ministries produce documents for local and national circulation – speeches by a minister or senior aides, parliamentary interventions and committee reports, press releases drafted for national consumption, local interviews, and so on.

Much of this discourse in Swahili is reminiscent of earlier Tanzanian political styles – the core vocabulary of the state and society has remained stable – yet we see new patterns emerge. One example is the use of terms distinguishing the 'public sector' (*sekta ya umma*) and the 'private sector' (*sekta ya binafsi*), previously an unknown distinction. Similarly, *kubinafsisha* is a new and widely used official term for 'privatisation'. *Uwekezaji* is another new term, meaning 'investment', *ujasiri-amali* entered Swahili vocabulary as the term for 'entrepreneurship', *kubuni miradi* means 'project design' (or 'project development'), the key term *mteja* ('customer') is used in every imaginable context, and, of course, the mother of all business terms, the term for 'management', is *usimamizi*, not, as it used to be, *utawala* ('governance' or 'administration').

Thus, even in Swahili we see the emergence of a new managerial register used to convert the global frame into the national language. This register consists of a mixture of familiar political terminology and a new core vocabulary for denoting key concepts from the global managerial frame blended into a new managerial discourse. The new vocabulary is in pure and 'High' Swahili, and it is the product of precisely the same procedures as those described in Chapter 4: word coining and vocabulary development. And. as with Campus Swahili, this new vocabulary and the new managerial discursive templates it supports are a register – a specific and specialised set of functionally- and indexically-ordered communicative resources that identify specific complexes of activities and actors in relation to others. The new Tanzanian political culture, the post-Ujamaa shift into a globalised neoliberal universe, is being enregistered in a new way of talking – one that sounds distinctly less political than the previously dominant one, but one that evokes recognisable attributions of modern global business-minded state leadership.

7.3 INTANET BOMBA

As mentioned above, one of the most conspicuously different features of contemporary urban life in Dar es Salaam is the generalised use of mobile phones. As in other places in Africa, mobile phones solve a perennial problem, offering a means of long-distance communication cheaply and effectively, without requiring the massive investments required for landline networks. In the developing world, mobile phones represent a genuine revolution and are seen by influential policy-makers as crucial tools for future economic, social and political development. In the words of a World Bank-related researcher:

> Mobile telephones are revolutionizing the formative processes of economic development. These relatively cheap handheld personal communicators are empowering the most basic development agents, turning former functionaries reliant on erratic and remote external inputs into key decision makers with direct access to the facts they need. (Lambert 2009: 48)

New providers, consequently, are almost all located in the developing world (ibid.: 49), and the range of services they offer do not lack sophistication: m-banking can be found in several developing countries while still being rare in Europe; job advertisements and access to social and administrative services are also offered via mobile phones in several countries, as are cheap chat services.[2] Another World Bank-connected researcher, Elisabeth Littlefield (2009: 50), thus reports:

> The biggest success in customer adoption to date has been the M-PESA network in Kenya, which has reached more than 6.5 million customers in just over two years. It has become the preferred method for moving money for 50 percent of Kenyans. An average of 150 million Kenyan shillings ($1.96 million) is transferred through the network every day, mostly in small amounts averaging just over KSh 1,500 ($20) per transaction. CGAP [Consultative Group to Assist the Poor] analysis and a survey by the nongovernmental organization Financial Sector Deepening Kenya show that users like the fact that the network is faster, easier to access, and safer than the alternatives. But cost probably trumps other factors as it beats the cheapest formal alternative by 45 percent. To send $25, the post office charges 5 percent and Western Union charges 57.5 percent, but the fee with M-PESA would be 2.8 percent. In other words, using M-PESA puts $4 million a week into the hands of poor Kenyans.

In the next sentence, however, this optimism is instantly qualified:

> However, fewer than 1 in 10 mobile phone banking customers are actually poor, new to banking, and doing anything more than payments and transfers. Most of the new offerings, especially when led by existing banks, have served to provide more convenient bill payments for existing customers and to decongest branches. (Ibid.)

Thus, the sophisticated m-services are largely an affair of the urban middle classes, including the lower-middle class, as we shall see shortly.

The March 2012 statistics released by the Tanzania Communications Regulatory Authority reported almost 27 million subscriptions to mobile phone operators.[3] Set against a population estimated at around 46 million, this number is impressive, but let us not forget that people sometimes have to take subscriptions from several providers to compensate for inadequate network coverage. Several such operators are active, with the global player Vodacom (locally nicknamed 'Voda') being the largest, the state-run TTCL holding a middle position and the privately-owned Benson being the smallest. Competition among the providers is fierce and has led to a steady decrease of the rates for using mobile phones.

Apart from basic services – calls and SMS – the providers all offer mobile Internet services. These Internet services, however, are used by only a small minority of mobile phone subscribers. According to the business newspaper *The Citizen* in January 2012, approximately 11 per cent of the Tanzanian population have access to the Internet, 45 per cent of whom – around two million – use mobile Internet.[4] Internet subscriptions – compared to basic mobile phone services – are still very expensive: an average domestic (landline) subscription from TTCL in Dar es Salaam cost 100,000TSh (around 50 euro) per month in September 2012.[5]

We begin to understand that such figures point towards an elite, even if the term is used with some degree of elasticity here. We also understand that this elite is concentrated in the large urban areas, if for no other reason than the fact that the Internet requires electricity. And when it comes to electricity, the Energy and Water Utilities Regulatory Authority of Tanzania warns us that '[w]ith about 660,000 customers, electricity was available to only about 11% of the population by [the] first quarter of 2007, with more than 80% supplied in the urban areas'.[6] Roughly nine out of ten Tanzanians have no access to a regular electricity supply, and that figure corresponds to more than 90 per cent of the territory of the country. Access to the Internet is a rather exclusive feature of urban life in Tanzania.

It also plays strongly into that urban life world; even more: it has become an icon of the culture of urban life. And, again, we will see that a key element of this culture is a new register of 'cool' Swahili. As with the case of public service managerialism discussed in the previous section, a new lexicon of terms referring to mobile phone and Internet use has emerged very quickly, including terms such as *intanet* itself, *kuperuzi* ('to surf the internet', from the English 'peruse'), *vocha* ('voucher', that is, a prepaid card), *bomba* ('connection'), *hudumu* ('subscription'), *mtandao* ('network'), *m-pesa* (mobile 'banking'), *kufuatilia* ('to follow' on Facebook or Twitter), as well as globally circulating loan codes such as SMS, PIN and MB all now firmly entrenched in the cool register of mobile connectivity, and emerging slang terms such as *mrembo wa Facebook* ('Facebook darling', a woman attracting significant amounts of male attention on Facebook). Providers market their products under labels such as *ezy pesa* ('easy money' – a phone banking application) and *Epiq Nation* (an image slogan from the Zanzibar-based Zantel, see below).

Publicity for mobile phone and mobile Internet providers – which is extraordinarily dense, testifying to the price wars among providers – shows happy young people. References are made to happiness and joy throughout, in slogans such as *Ongea kutwa nzima na cheka* ('Talk the whole day and laugh'). We see a young man screaming with joy when opening his *Tigo Internet Mega Boksi* – a box containing applications for mobile Internet (Gmail, Facebook, Chrome, Firefox, and so on)

Figure 2   Wajanja wa kuperuzi ('expert Internet surfers'). (Source: © Jan
Blommaert)

from the Tigo provider. And we see young girls gazing enthusiastically at a smartphone who are announced to be *wajanja wa kuperuzi* – 'expert Internet surfers' (see
Figure 2). These are happy, successful young people, and they are very much in the
world.

As with what we encounter elsewhere in the world, mobile phone advertisements
suggest success derived from global mobility. Thus, Zantel's Epiq Nation campaign
features Mwisho Wampamba, a Tanzanian actor who appears in a popular South
African television series offered on commercial networks in Tanzania – an icon
of the mobile, successful, young Tanzanian (see Figure 3). Large Vodacom and
Epiq Nation campaign events feature Chidi Benz and Juma Nature AKA Kibla
– Tanzanian hip hop stars who attract audiences all over East Africa – and Epiq
Nation sponsors a *Bongo Stars Search* programme, comparable to *American Idol* or
The X Factor and aimed at recruiting new and hip popular culture celebrities.

The exploitation of Tanzania's vibrant 'Bongo Flava' hip hop scene in mobile
phone marketing campaigns has been noted already by Christina Higgins (2012)
in a remarkable paper. Higgins observed that providers deployed the urban Swahili
youth slang in their campaigns, a variety of which Bongo Flava artists are the
epigones, popular hip hop song titles likewise found their way into marketing
slogans, and a popular brand of beer has '100% TZ FLAVA' printed on its bottles.

The point Higgins made, and which can be confirmed here, is that the connec-

Figure 3 Epiq Nation Moto. (Source: © Jan Blommaert)

tion between popular culture and marketing moves Swahili into a privileged position *vis-à-vis* the young, urban middle-class consumers targetted in campaigns. But
it is not just *any* Swahili: it is the cool slang-ish Swahili characterising local youth
cultures in Tanzanian cities, driven by the media and (as we shall explore more fully
in the next section) the Internet. The medium for such campaigns is thus not a

language *per se*, but a specific register. The amount of code-mixing in mobile phone providers' publicity should already make clear that 'language' is not the best unit to describe what goes on. As we can see in Figure 3, the English term 'Epiq Nation' is followed by the Swahili term *moto* ('heat'): Epiq Nation is *hot*, and the blend of English and Swahili brings that message about.

We are thus witnessing fully-developed lifestyle branding targeting a young urban audience of consumers, and this fully-developed form of branding follows global templates. Look at how the companies behind Epiq Nation announce their campaign:[7]

> 'Etisalat Zantel' has partnered with 'Mobilera' to offer 'Epiq Nation' the new youth lifestyle product which is much more than just great rates for mobile phones and Internet services.

> 'Epiq Nation' will provide the Tanzanian youth with unprecedented services where they can have access to exclusive deals, discounts, experiences and competitions. This offer aims at improving the lives of the youth in Tanzania and meets their hunger for new technologies and products.

The lingo is that of advanced consumerist marketing, and the approach is that of sophisticated branding strategies aimed at complementing the product ('great rates for mobile phones and Internet services') with an avalanche of 'exclusive deals, discounts, experiences and competitions', so as to shape entire identities and life projects centred around particular commodities (Blommaert and Varis 2012a, 2012b). We have seen that post-Ujamaa politics has been inserted into global ideoscapes of public managerialism; here, too, we see how mobile phones and Internet products are advertised in ways fully integrated into global scenarios for branding and marketing, centred around the commodification of entire identities and life projects via the purchase of a product.[8] Choosing Zantel's Epiq Nation products is not just a choice for a particular product in a competitive market – it is a choice for a specific lifestyle, a self-imagined identity constructed through consumption. People who make this choice are not just *wateja* ('customers'), they are laughing and smiling, happy, young, affluent *wajanja wa kuperuzi* ('expert Internet surfers') and, perhaps, *warembo wa Facebook* ('Facebook darlings').

We have seen that providers target a young urban audience, and that they do so by means of complex campaigns turning products into lifestyle choices. Given the cost of Internet subscriptions, the audience for the full package is relatively restricted. And this is where we see providers 'opening up', so to speak, and attempting to bring their products to customers in less well-off areas of the cities, to the struggling urban lower-middle classes who earn a modest salary but who are nonetheless fully integrated in the networks of contemporary urban life. A taxi driver, for instance, needs a mobile phone to conduct his business, because taxis operate on an individual lease basis and without a central radio dispatching system. The same is true for small traders and shopkeepers: contact with customers and providers is maintained through mobile phone communication. Further, given the relatively

Figure 4   Advertisements in Mikocheni village. (Source: © Jan Blommaert)

high cost of cross-network calls, these lower-middle-class people can be seen to be equipped with more than one handset, each of them connected to one provider network and all of them used to make network-internal calls. More affluent customers, less worried about the prohibitive costs of cross-network communication, typically have a single smartphone.

With this in mind, consider Figure 4.

Mobile phones, subscription packages and prepaid cards are not just sold in hip downtown shops and malls; they are sold almost everywhere in the city. Small groceries, restaurants, post offices, bars, kiosks: one can read everywhere that *vocha* are available, and *vocha jumla* ('every kind of prepaid card'), followed by a list of brand names – 'Voda', Airtel, Tigo, and so on. Mobile phone provision stretches into the poorest corners of the city. Naturally, the cost of full-subscription packages with mobile Internet access far exceeds the budgets of most people in such areas; essentially, what is sold there are the cheapest prepaid cards, enough to make local calls and send some SMSs. But they can be found everywhere alongside other standard household products such as soap, maize flour, cooking oil, onions, fruit or water. Thus, while we can say that the spread, the availability, of mobile phones in Dar es Salaam is 'democratic', their distribution or accessibility – the specific ways in which they are being appropriated and used – is not democratic at all and follows clear class lines.

The democratic spread, nonetheless, necessitates an open format of marketing communication. A more detailed look at Figure 4 reveals something quite interesting, and in order to grasp its relevance some explanation needs to be given about advertising culture in Tanzania. To begin with, advertising was a relatively rare thing in Ujamaa Tanzania. The reason was quite simply that consumer commodities were rare in the days of *Kujitegemea*. One would see professional beer advertisements, some Pepsi publicity boards (also in Figure 4) and some for other international products – more about that in a moment – but, often, products were advertised by locally manufactured paintings on facades and fences, done by professional signwriters. Commercial slogans did not circulate widely, with perhaps the exception being a slogan for a local *pombe* (indigenous beer) called Chikubu. The slogan was *Tumia Chibuku, ni pombe bora* ('Use Chibuku, it's excellent beer') and it was played before and after a popular humorous radio play that aired every night on Radio Tanzania Dar es Salaam for years on end. Most people still know the slogan today, and note that the slogan was in Swahili.

Prestige products – a synonym for products manufactured abroad – were almost invariably accompanied by English publicity items. Thus, in Figure 4 we see a small and older sign promoting Nivea cream with English text; we also see the older Pepsi sign, also in English. Driving through Dar es Salaam, we still see English widely used whenever prestige products are being promoted: hotels and spas, wines, brandies or whiskies, imported beers, some banking facilities, insurance, and so on. Mobile phone adverts, by contrast, are overwhelmingly in Swahili, and the English Nivea sign in Figure 4 is juxtaposed with several Swahili mobile phone signs, as the more detailed Figure 5 will show.

Even when the advertisers target the affluent Tanzanian yuppies, as we have seen, the new Swahili register is used rather than, or at least in conjunction with, English

Figure 5   Mikocheni village, detail. (Source: © Jan Blommaert)

(as in, for example, '*Ezy Pesa*'). Monolingual English mobile phone advertising boards can be found, not by coincidence, in the vicinity of expensive shopping centres attracting a largely expatriate community of customers. Thus, the English Epiq Nation poster featuring Mwisho Wampamba (Figure 3) could be found near Shopper's Plaza, Masaki, a supermarket tailored to the demands of the international business and diplomatic community in Masaki, and incorporating a Subway sandwich shop on its premises.

The Mikocheni kiosk in Figures 4 and 5 displays two generations of prestige products: an older one (Nivea cream) in English, dating back to the time where 'international' was still a synonym for 'outside of Tanzania' and therefore 'in English'; and a newer one (mobile phone services) in which global commodities have been turned into *local* status-hierarchical emblems – they have been 'reterritorialised' to adopt Higgins' (2012) terminology. Such forms of localisation, as we now know, are defining features of cultural globalisation. They enact the 'vernacular globalization' that Appadurai (1996) had already announced, and that accounts for the tremendous frequency with which we see local 'accents' added to global cultural templates (see Pennycook 2007, 2010; Higgins 2009; Blommaert 2010: Chapter 3; Blommaert and Varis 2012a). The use of mobile phones is a global status emblem cleverly and skilfully 'translated', so to speak, into a local stratification of symbols and values. The cool Swahili register that accompanies it and enacts it is the key to this localisation practice, and is no doubt also the key to the success of mobile phones in Dar es Salaam.

7.4 TANZANIANS @ FACEBOOK

We can notice such 'accents' in other globally circulating status registers as well, and one such register is the playful heterographic languaging we find in various new media niches: Internet chats, SMS codes, Facebook and Twitter messages. I have previously described such forms as 'supervernaculars' (Blommaert 2012). Before engaging with some Tanzanian examples, let me briefly clarify some conceptual issues, because the first sentences of this section contain some relatively recent jargon.

'Supervernacular' is a term we coined in order to describe rapidly emerging and developing codes widely used among 'supergroups' – huge network and/or online communities in which new and locally constructed ('grass-roots') vernaculars circulate thanks to new communication technologies such as the Internet and mobile phones. These supervernaculars are:

> patterned sociolinguistic resources . . . adopted by communities of users that share none of the traditional attributes of speech communities – territorial fixedness, physical proximity, socio-cultural sharedness and common backgrounds. People now use similar sociolinguistic resources without sharing any of these traditional features of community. And such loose, elastic, dynamic and deterritorialized communities are among the key features of superdiversity. (ibid.: 3)

Supervernaculars are a typical instance of register: the symbolic resources of languages and scripts are explored, exploited and ordered in such a way that they create a distinct but shareable code, considered to be 'normal' (hence normative) among members of the supergroup in which it circulates. It is a script which transmits both denotational meanings – one can 'say things' in the code – as well as a dense package of indexical meanings: joint identity frames are being activated, speaking positions and stance can be flagged (for example by means of emoticons), degrees of expertise and seniority of group membership can be displayed. Using the script, therefore, is much more than just another form of 'writing'; it is inevitably an act of identity in relation to specific social settings. The script becomes a register, and that register is 'cool', creative and subversive.

As to the creative and subversive aspects: supervernaculars such as chat codes and mobile phone texting codes are often 'heterographic': they stretch the affordances of conventional scripts in such a way that a new, deviant system of normative writing emerges, different from the 'orthographic' one and therefore 'heterographic' (Blommaert 2008b). Thus, orthographic 'See you at four o'clock' can become, in mobile texting code for instance, 'CU@4'. And note the normativity of this heterographic system: writing 'SU@4' is meaningless because it contains an error ('S' instead of 'C') which is as catastrophic as major errors in 'orthographic' writing. The codes of conduct of subcultures, we can notice, are as normative as those of any 'mainstream' community.

This creative deployment of semiotic resources, in defiance of established norms and expectations (but simultaneously constructing alternative ones) has been called 'languaging' in recent literature (cf. Jørgensen 2008; Creese and Blackledge 2010; Jørgensen et al. 2011). People do not 'have' or 'use' language, they *do* language, they *perform* and *enact* language, sampling and assembling any available resource that has the potential of conveying the intended meanings and indexical effects. Such meanings and effects draw intertextually on existing traditions – of heterographic practices for instance – and creatively re-perform and reorder such traditions.

There are such traditions of heterography in Tanzania; in fact, I discuss several instances of it in earlier work (e.g. Blommaert 2010: 190–3), observing several different phenomena. One was the playful and witty exploitation of English expressions so as to create ambiguities and pun: the owner of a (rather battered) minibus, for instance, writing 'Con Ford' on his windscreen and thus flagging (1) the brand of his vehicle, (2) the comfort it offers to passengers, who should be mindful, however, because (3) this is a *con* Ford – a possible 'tapeli' trick. While producing these multiple and layered meanings, the author of 'Con Ford' displays his linguistic skills, his ability to twist common English expressions in such a way that they generate irony, humour and so on. We encounter here a typical instance of what Higgins (2009) understands by 'English as a local language' in Tanzania: English language resources are 'brought down', so to speak, to a local universe of indexical meanings and attributes, and they make sense *hic et nunc* on the windscreen of a Dar es Salaam minibus.

A second phenomenon was global. The Bongo Flava hip hop movement of the 1990s imported the heterographic codes widely circulating in the global hip hop scene – in artists' names, song titles, graffiti and slogans. A famous early hip hop band, thus, was called 'II Proud' ('too proud', cf. '2Pac' – 'Tupac'), another was called 'Da Dee-polw-matz' ('the diplomats'). Note the 'eye dialect' in the former ('da' for 'the'; see also the 'Flava' in Bongo Flava itself) and the plural ending '-z' in the latter. These global features of hip hop and (later) broader pop-cultural writing ('colorz', 'niggaz', 'gangstaz', 'Gorillaz', 'rapz') penetrated all the way down to small and local Dar es Salaam youth gangs, who called themselves *wahuni* (the Swahili equivalent of 'gangstaz') and proudly displayed their slang vocabulary to me (Blommaert 2010: 191–2). While dictating their words and expressions to me, they took care that I wrote these words down *correctly*, even if that correctness was heterographic. Thus the plural of the slang term *toto* ('girl') had to be written as *totoz*, with the '-z' plural ending. The '-z' was cool.

So cool that in Dar es Salaam even now a good number of quite respectable businesses can be found using this heterographic feature in their names: 'Mamboz Corner BBQ' and 'Choma'z Grill', for instance, or the cleaning firm 'Spiknspanz'. The '-z' was also there, as we saw earlier, in the mobile phone brand slogan 'Ezy pesa' – in which 'ezy' is an entirely heterographic reconstruction of 'easy'. The 'Epiq' in Epiq Nation is of course another instance; and I have also already noted the '100% TZ FLAVA' slogan on bottles of Kilimanjaro beer. The cool heterographic codes of Bongo Flava and its global sources of inspiration have become fully integrated into corporate marketing discourses.

With this under our belts, let us now turn to the languaging of Tanzanians on Facebook. Of course, the earlier observations on the spread and distribution of the Internet in Tanzania apply here as well: Facebook users are a small minority of predominantly young people from the more affluent middle classes, clustered in the urban centres of the country where they have access to the rather expensive Internet provision. Let me now present some observations.

To start with, Facebook is obviously a tool by means of which some young Tanzanians enter a fully globalised world of objects, commodities, meanings and values. Young Tanzanian males express very strong opinions for or against international soccer teams, often from the English Premier League – Manchester United, Everton and Liverpool top the rankings. Young women post top designer clothes and shoes on their Facebook walls, and several Tanzanians appear to be entirely *au fait* with the curious world of Internet 'memes'. I noted a status update in which we encounter the so-called 'Lolcatz' – pictures of cats accompanied by (often heterographic) English statements that have rapidly become one of the most popular Internet memes ('Can I has cheezburger?'). Figure 6 shows how 'funny animal' pictures are used in Tanzania as elsewhere to good effect:

Figure 6 already shows some of the intriguing linguistic features of Facebook in Tanzania, to which I can now turn. In general terms, of course, Facebook usage is a distinctly multilingual enterprise in Tanzania, and we can see various different varieties side by side on a kind of continuum with 'standard English' at one end and 'standard Swahili' at the other. In between, we notice a wide variety of heterographic forms of languaging.

kwetu mbezi ipo hii saloon

HAPO KWA MASHOST MMEFUNIKWA NA NYANI KWA MITINDO

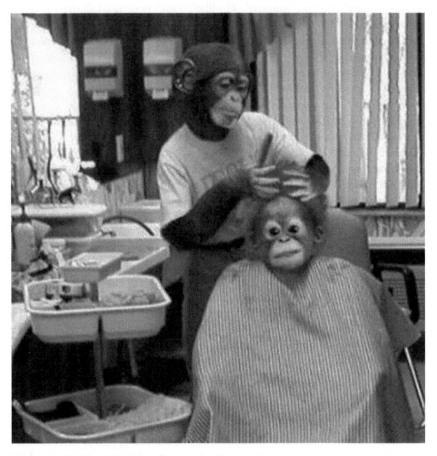

Figure 6   Funny animals on Tanzanian Facebook

Let us first have a closer look at 'standard English'. It is not Her Majesty's variety which we encounter here, since 'standard' stands for what counts locally as standard. A particular degree of fluency appears acceptable as 'standard', even if it contains odd syntactic or other forms. Thus we encounter examples such as:

very girl has three guys in her life.the one she love.the one she hate and the one she can't live without . . .

They say in every successful man, there is a woman behind it.
Question: What is behind unseccessful men??

Never to die unnoticed, nothng drops from air . . . hardwork!!!!!!!!!!

'Standard' here is an aspirational description: people consciously try to write 'stand-ard', as opposed to other forms. These other English forms are, by and large, globally circulating heterographic signs, as we can see from the following examples:

choose 2 be single is selfish its just smarter to be alone than with wrong person

. . . mornin guyz . . . on ma way 2 college!

am proud 2 b man u fan!

Gud mornin 2 al friend of myn

. . . ooh ma God help me!

Thanx You

in da office

We see a supervernacular here: the young Tanzanian Facebook users have absorbed the heterographic rules of a range of varieties of English that one now encounters all over the world and in a variety of channels. They have very clear ideas of the affordances offered by these heterographic scripts – they know, for instance, that '2' can stand for 'to' and 'too', they know that eye dialect is best done when it sounds 'black' ('ma God', 'da office') and they know how to shorten orthographic forms by slotting in homophonic heterographic symbols, as in 'Gud morning' ('Good morning') and 'myn' ('mine').

This supervernacularised English can of course be mixed with Swahili, yielding a variety in which almost every aspect of language usage is dislodged and blended:

how?? watever botherin yu weka kando thats lyf ups nd down ni kawaida. [Whatever is bothering you, set it aside, that's life, ups and downs, it's normal.]

And Swahili itself can be turned into a heterographic code by using exactly the same affordances as the ones we noticed in English. Thus, '2' can stand for the Swahili syllable 'tu' in, for instance 'wa2' (*watu*, 'people'), or it can replace the first person plural marker 'tu' as in '2ngoje' (*tungoje*, 'let's wait'). The symbol 'w' stands for 'we' as in 'ww' (*wewe*, 'you'), and 'c' can replace 'si' in, for example, 'cc' (*sisi*, 'we') and 'cendi' (*siendi*, 'I'm not going'). Further, we notice local idiosyncrasies – a 'dialect' of the supervernacular in the sense that the general rules of supervernacularisation are complemented with some local ones. Final syllables or vowels can be dropped from words, as in the following example:

ulienda wapi ten ww any way 2ngoje but i wixh itakuw pouwa xan

Orthographically transcribed, we would get something like:

ulienda wapi tena wewe; anyway, tungoje, but I wish itakuwa poa sana

Apart from the switches into supervernacularised English, which we have already pointed out, we also see a shift into urban slang, where the term *poa* is used (written here as '*pouwa*'). *Poa* is the Dar es Salaam urban slang term for 'cool'. Thus what our Facebook user writes here can be translated as:

> where did you go again, you? Anyway, let's take it easy but I would like it to be very cool

Such expressions are not necessarily reserved for exuberant language display; the heterographic forms are routinely used in mundane utterances and interactions; thus a young woman responds to the counsel of a friend as follows:

> . . . *malez yak bora yananifany niwez kuish n wa2 w ain tofaut tofauti maishan*

In an orthographic rendering this would read:

> *maelezo yako bora yananifanya niweze kuishi na watu wa aina tofauti tofauti maishani*
> [your excellent advice enables me to live with all sorts of different people in my life]

And elsewhere we read: *Gud nyt pipo n nawatakia njoz njema!* – which can be converted to *Good night people na nawatakia ndoto njema* ('Good night people and I wish you wonderful dreams'). The heterographic code, thus, is an instrument for a wide variety of interactions.

We observe intense languaging, exploring the affordances and the limits of heterographic writing and blending standard and slang varieties of any origin – in short, assembling any and all useful resources in the construction of a register that identifies the skilful Facebook user: the *wajanja wa kuperuzi* we encountered earlier. Facebook in Tanzania, as elsewhere, is a laboratory of new identity work, drawing on a range of semiotic means that can be ordered and reordered within the limits of communicability (cf. Varis and Wang 2011). While transferring messages and their content – not necessarily devastatingly relevant content, as in *gud nyt pipo* – the Facebook users also display their semiotic skills and their fluency in the cool register that marks and distinguishes identities in this new medium. They are a community, and they have a language of their own. Not a stable one and neither a unified nor a uniform one, but a language nevertheless.

7.5 WHO IS THE TANZANIAN NOW?

In an exceptionally insightful ethnographic study, Sabrina Billings (2006; also 2009, 2011a, 2011b, 2013) explored the language hierarchies that emerged in post-Ujamaa Tanzania in that archetypal global format of feminine competitiveness: the beauty pageant. Beauty pageants have arrived in Tanzania along with the free-market economy and commercial media, and they have been (and are) spectacularly successful events. This success goes hand in hand with controversy, and there has been perpetual debate over both the feminine aesthetics expected from contenders during these events and the more specific aspects of their presentation, dress and demeanour (see also Higgins 2009: Chapter 4). The format, as suggested above, is a global template with a local accent: the contenders have to go through the routines found in similar contests elsewhere in the world, and the winner progresses to the Miss World contest. Becoming Miss Tanzania, thus, is seen as a step-up towards competing for the crown at the global scale level.

Billings shows how language creeps into this globalised pageant format and plays a decisive role in it. In addition to displaying their physical beauty candidates also have to display intelligence and wit in an interview. They are asked whether they wish this interview to be conducted in Swahili or English, and the choice appears not to be one between equals: winners rather systematically opted for English as the medium for conveying their thoughts and views. Further, in such choices English appears to be an immediate pointer towards education, and girls produce English discourse modulated by school-based templates for speaking and arguing. Whoever speaks English must be educated, and a beauty queen should be well-educated – that is the logic.

This logic is compelling and oppressive, because it opens a scale of judgement about the 'quality' of English in which candidates operate. English with a heavy Tanzanian accent is booed off stage, and Billings recounts a dramatic scene in which the lead contender for the crown catastrophically mutilates her otherwise well-rehearsed English speech and loses the contest to a girl whose superior English fluency was a result of years of education in the United States. The logic operates at two levels therefore: first, English is preferred over Swahili; and, second, fluent and 'international' English is preferred over non-fluent and locally accented English. We move from 'language' to 'register' here: the specific kind of language is what tips the balance, and the contest between registers shows the expansion and diversification of the sociolinguistic market in post-Ujamaa Tanzania.

We have seen this in the three vignettes presented in this chapter: Tanzanian society has moved from a monoglot and monocentric, Swahili-dominated sociolinguistic system towards a heteroglossic and polycentric system, in which a wide range of norms dominate specific social niches for communicative practices and identity construction, all relatively sovereign in the sense that they are not controlled (or even controllable) from above. From a strong emphasis on language – one language – we have moved towards a complex system of criss-crossing and overlapping registers, and the language ideologies have been likewise adjusted. Following the development of this polyglot complex is the challenge for sociolinguistics in Tanzania and elsewhere.

This has consequences, and one clear consequence is that we have to relocate the nation-state as one scale among many in a polycentric environment. State ideology under Ujamaa was a hegemony aimed at a monoglot society. In post-Ujamaa Tanzania, state ideology is no more hegemonic and certainly not monoglot in target: it is itself now incorporated in global frames for being a modern neoliberal state; it has adopted the key indexicals of that identity frame for the state – the businesslike and managerial register discussed in section 7.2. This new position of the state creates a vast space for the development of what we used to call 'subcultures' – consumerism, age peer-group identities, new middle-class identities, and popular culture identities.

The problem with the term 'subculture', however, is that it presupposes one dominant or hegemonic 'higher' culture. This we had under Ujamaa: there was a clear vision of a single hegemonic culture in Tanzania, even if this was an objective rather than a reality. In present-day Tanzania, the 'higher' culture, to the extent that we can identify it, probably consists of a set of global cultural and ideological templates that can be locally accented in a perpetual process of cultural production and reproduction. The 'dominant' culture, if you wish, is heteroglot and dynamic. From a monocentric model, Tanzania has moved to a polycentric model, and the continuous development of specific registers testifies to that.

So who is the Tanzanian? From an erstwhile singular definition, the *mwananchi* examined earlier, we have moved to a pluriform and polycentric definition allowing for tremendous diversity and continuous patterns of (re-)categorisation (Higgins 2007). These patterns of categorisation draw on new forms of sociolinguistic order, as semiotic and communicative resources are being perpetually reshuffled in new practices of enregisterment.

Language purists, language planners and language educators tend to abhor such perpetual patterns of innovation and change: a Tanzanian professor of Swahili once barked to his son, in my presence, that the language used by the teenage boy *siyo Kiswahili* ('is no Swahili'), repeating a responsive template which is probably universal and centuries old – the older generation's irritation about the fact that their children can't speak properly anymore (the 'complaints culture' described by Milroy and Milroy 1985). But in spite of their best efforts, such language guardians and experts cannot stop or alter the direction of these elementary sociolinguistic processes.

The contemporary Tanzanian will still be recognisable by the common use of Swahili. This achievement of Ujamaa stands, and will remain unshakeable as a sociolinguistic given. But the 'Swahili' that identifies Tanzanians appears in a thousand different shapes, some widely understandable and others understandable only among members of specific peer groups. This was probably always there; the previous chapter offered some early examples of this phenomenon. However, for a long time it was hidden behind a wall of monoglot discourse on Swahili, which denied (or at least disqualified) sociolinguistic diversification in the terms we encountered in earlier chapters.

As I argued in the first part of this book, it was this sociolinguistic differentiation that drove language planners and policy makers to despair and gave them the feeling that the Swahilisation efforts had failed. I argued then, and repeat here, that they were in actual fact hugely successful, and that the problem encountered by the planners and policy makers was an effect of their monoglot language ideology and of the sociolinguistic expectations they extracted from it. Sociolinguistic realism shows a phenomenal success: a complex of linguistic and communicative resources we usually denote with the label of 'Swahili' has been made available and accessible to almost everyone in Tanzania. The fact that all these people adopt these resources and start doing unplanned and unscripted things with them is a simple, normal and highly predictable sociolinguistic fact.

Further, it also points towards massive success: if we wish to apply the otherwise rather useless term 'ethnolinguistic vitality' to contemporary Swahili, it is not uniformity that indexes such vitality; the vitally is manifest from precisely the dynamics of change and differentiation within Swahili. The plethora of newly emerging registers is proof beyond reasonable doubt that this complex of language resources has become part of the deep fabric of an entire society. Since this society is not uniform, it follows that its languages will be plural too – even if one singular umbrella term 'Swahili' is used for them.

7.6 NOTES

1. The public education system, once the pride of Ujamaa Tanzania, has all but collapsed, forcing middle-class aspiring people to spend astronomical fees on private schools for their sons and daughters. One of my informants, for whose candidness I am grateful, reported that he spent 800,000TSh per year on secondary-school fees for one daughter and 1.6 million TSh annually on the secondary boarding school of another. His salary – a relatively decent one by local standards – amounted to 6 million TSh (3,000 euro) per year. The man took heavy bank loans to finance the education of his daughters. Access to the affluent middle class, consequently, has become even harder than before.
2. For the latter, see the excellent study from Fie Velghe (2012) on the use of a mobile chat application in townships around Cape Town.
3. Data available from *www.tcra.go.tz* (accessed 12 September 2012).
4. Data available from *www.tcra.go.tz* (accessed 12 September 2012).
5. I am grateful to Els Vandemoortele for granting me this glimpse of her household budget.
6. Data available from *www.ewura.com/electricity.html* (accessed 12 September 2012).
7. From campaign.dubib.com/news/10450_epiq-nation#.UFBhcKRdNHg , accessed 12 September 2012.
8. The fully globalised nature of marketing templates in Tanzania can also be judged from the extraordinarily frequent use of the greatest lie of global consumerist marketing: the suggestion that certain things are 'free of charge'. The Swahili word *bure* ('gratis', 'free of charge') occurs in every second advertisement, suggesting that a certain amount of prepaid airtime, SMSs or download megabytes is 'free' when you purchase certain package formulas (see Figure 2). Things are usually not 'free' when you have to pay for them, of course.

Chapter 8

Conclusions

The story of Swahili in independent Tanzania is narrowly intertwined with the story of the emergence and development of the local state ideology, Ujamaa. It is impossible to understand the adventures of the language without reference to the political developments and climate in Tanzania, and even if Ujamaa has been off the political-ideological scene for close to three decades now, its traces can still be found in Tanzanian society, most clearly in the field of language. Swahili in Tanzania was a highly politicised language, a political topic, a political target. It was both an instrument and an expression of Ujamaa: an instrument because it allowed ideological symbolisations that were fully in line with the basic principles of Ujamaa and because it was a handy instrument for democratic mass communication and political mobilisation; an expression because it could be said to express the new egalitarian socialist society, in which old social and ethnic divisions had been replaced by a new common identity.

The arguments I have developed throughout this book all revolve around processes of hegemony. The introduction of Ujamaa marked the beginning of intense nation-building activities, geared not to the cultural unification of the nation (and in that sense different from modern European nationalisms) but to the ideological and political unification of the nation. The new nation would be an Ujamaa-nation, in which citizens would see themselves unified by a common acceptance of Ujamaa. Swahili played a major role in this process of ideological hegemonisation; in turn, this hegemonisation was extended into the domain of Swahili itself. The discourse on Swahili strongly focused on what Swahili meant within the framework of Ujamaa. It was imbued with a number of functions, tasks and values, all strongly oriented towards macroscopic aims contained in Ujamaa.

But I also argued that this bid for hegemony in and on Swahili was fraught with contradictions. The idea of an ideologically unified nation was translated culturally as a nation unified by the generalised use of one particular standard variety of Swahili, whereby Swahili would retain all its politically correct associations of an egalitarian language, removing (or at least obscuring) ethnic as well as class distinctions.[1] In the eyes of those who made the bid for hegemony, the process would only be a success as soon as the nation accepted and adopted Swahili *in this particular way*. A generalised spread of an otherwise qualified Swahili – an 'impure' Swahili, a

Swahili associated with a historical Swahili ethnic community, or a Swahili expressing capitalist messages – would not be acceptable. Also, the *entire* nation needed to
be Swahilised, and in *every* aspect of social life. A functional superposition of Swahili
on top of the (already highly diversified) repertoires of the Tanzanians would not
be enough. In the eyes of (especially radical) supporters of the socialist national
culture, the specific kind of Swahili outlined above had to replace *all other* existing languages and varieties in the country. These were the benchmarks by means
of which successful hegemony (including a successful language policy) would be
measured; the aim was full Swahilisation with a doctrinaire set of ideological values
and messages attached to the language. Speaking the language was not enough, the
entire metapragmatic edifice of what the language stood for and what the use of
the language would mean culturally, socially and politically had to be accepted too.
The ambitions of the Tanzanian language planners had no limits, and these ambitions turned Swahilisation into an all-or-nothing game.

It is the use of these extraordinary benchmarks that accounts for the peculiar and
paradoxical situation that emerged in the late 1980s. From a purely distributional
sociolinguistic perspective, Swahili had become a hegemonic language – a level
of success in sociolinguistic engineering rarely matched elsewhere. Tanzania is a
rare case of a country in which Swahili is useful in almost all situations anywhere
in the country, and 'ownership' of the language is democratic: new generations
of Tanzanians have Swahili as their first and most central language, but have no
affiliations whatsoever with the historical 'core' Swahili communities. So Swahili
is democratised, generalised and de-ethnicised – and one of the ambitions of the
Ujamaa politicians has been brilliantly achieved. In addition, its introduction in
power domains such as politics and mass media (and to a lesser extent, science) has
turned it into a language of power and control too; Swahili occupied and continues
to occupy a very elevated position in almost every aspect of sociolinguistic stratification in Tanzania, even, as we saw in the previous chapter, in a society which has
undergone massive transformations due to globalisation and class restratification
(see also Billings 2006, 2013; Higgins 2009). Tanzania is and remains a case of
tremendously successful postcolonial sociolinguistic engineering; at least at the
pragmatic level of analysis, where we look at the actual scale and scope of language
usage, we are facing a case of highly successful hegemony.

Yet, and here the paradox emerges, local language planners, scholars and opinion-
makers have repeatedly declared full Swahilisation dead, and whenever the issue of
the hegemony of Swahili is raised, trouble talk starts. The reasons for this perceived
failure of the hegemonisation of Swahili must, as I argued, be sought in the parameters set for measuring the success of the exercise. The extremely rigorous *metapragmatic* conditions specified for the appropriate use of Swahili in Tanzanian society
have not been satisfied, and that failure prompts the trouble talk. Swahili has been
generalised, but it has not *replaced* other languages, and neither has its generalised
spread consolidated a socialist-political ideology among its users. Swahili is not only
the language of socialism – it never was. It was and is *also* the language of capitalism,
of the bourgeoisie, of the reactionaries, of the opposition, in short, of everyone.

Chapter 6 showed how, in spite of the massive adoption of Ujamaa among intellectuals and academics, the language use of these same academics revealed early processes of class restratification in Tanzania. And as we saw in Chapter 7, people whose political agendas are light years removed from Nyerere's socialism (or socialism in general) now find Swahili a fantastic medium of mass information and mobilisation, of advertisements and neoliberal propaganda, and thus ironically capitalise on the pragmatic hegemony of the language for attacking the ideological, metapragmatic complex that motivated its generalised spread and elaboration.

Theoretically, the different vignettes I have presented in this study should confirm, *pace* Bourdieu, that the state is an important actor in the field of language, even in an age of globalisation in which, according to some, the nation-state is on its way out (Blommaert 2010: 178–9, 182–96). In the case of Tanzania, it was the state that provided the conditions for the generalised spread of Swahili, the development of generic differentiation, linguistic innovation, creative literary production in Swahili, and so on. We saw the Tanzanian state shape an Ujamaa literature some decades ago, but we also saw it shape a neoliberal public management discourse in more recent years. The Tanzanian state is and remains an important innovator and regulator in the sociolinguistic field, even if that state now operates as a switchboard between intra-national and international forces and pressures (see Billings 2011a and 2011b for an excellent illustration).

But at the same time, as soon as the state launched its efforts at creating a particular pragmatics and metapragmatics for Swahili, it lost control over the process. The language and its meta-discourses were appropriated by a variety of actors in society, and these actors started doing all kinds of things with them that were not contained in the original plan. The 'official' ideological associations between Swahili and nationalism, Africanhood and self-respect and so on – as well as those between English and imperialism, and oppression, and so on – were *situational* associations, conditioned by particular topics and contexts of use.[2] Different associations could be made in different contexts, and a close observation of the language practices of people such as the academics described in Chapter 6 shows that a propositional expression of Ujamaa values may be carried out through linguistic structures that, in effect, indexically encode the opposite.

There is little unity in this domain, and this observation can serve as a caution against all too linear and across-the-board assumptions about languages and language attitudes (of the type 'Language X is the language of prestige'). This insight might also serve as a counterpoint to mechanistic and rationalist approaches to language situations and political decisions in the field of language, such as that of Laitin (1992). The rational calculations may dominate the public discourse about language, and they may be explicit statements of intent about what people *want* languages to do and to be. But an ethnographic inspection of language use in a variety of domains quickly reveals that there is more than one pattern, more than one line, and that state ideology and agency represent *parts* of a process of significant complexity, and that they possibly define just one among several scale-levels co-occurring in any sociolinguistic event (Blommaert 2010, 2013). Those who seek to understand language policy as a sociolinguistic factor, consequently, will benefit from addressing more than the mere scale-level of formal policy and institutionalisation itself. Language policy 'on the ground' appears to be controlled by more sets of norms than just those prescribed and proscribed in language policy.

A second but related theoretical point that emerged from the discussions in the previous chapters is that the history of language is not only a history of its use and its pragmatics (let alone a history of its *structure*), but also a history of its metapragmatic appropriation by power brokers, institutions and social actors. Rather than 'hard' figures of distribution and use, it is the particular set of debates about Swahili, especially debates between policy makers and intellectuals, that provides the clearest clue to understanding what happened to Swahili in the postcolonial period. The history of such debates in Tanzania is continuous but heterogeneous, and involves various and often unstable and shifting groups and alliances. The intellectuals – scholars and writers – are always at the forefront, constructing and disseminating expert discourses about Swahili and its role in society, incorporating political-ideological elements into their expert discourses, and feeding them back to the policy makers, who, in turn, respond with statements that are seen as either encouraging or discouraging by their interlocutors. I have argued that such discourses in which technocratic elements could be blended with political elements are important ingredients of the process of the formation of intellectuals as a particular socio-politically recognisable class in the independent state. It is through the politisation of Swahili that linguists, writers and literary scholars could become *important* intellectuals, whose work could be claimed to have socio-political relevance and validity. Intellectuals, thus, did not emerge solely as a social class in postcolonial Tanzania, but also as a Weberian status group.

But intellectuals were never alone. Politicians, journalists, teachers and other privileged voices also contributed significantly to the outcome of language policies, and continue to do so; for when such language policies land on the ground of actual society, the multitude of actors operating within, upon and against them is virtually endless, since any and every act of language can be measured and assessed against the norms specified by language policies and dominant interpretations of such policies. We have seen that such appraisals tend to be disappointing for language planners – not because of overt shortcomings in the policies and plans themselves, but because of a fundamental misjudgement of real sociolinguistic processes. These processes invariably operate within an environment we call *polycentric*, in which not just one normative focus occurs but several, and in which judgements by language users, thus, depend on more complex factors than those anticipated in political yes-no scenarios.

The historiographical outlook that defined the structure of this book is of major importance to me. Every language is a discourse, and carries with it the traces of its history of use. The discourse of Swahili is never a purely linguistic or functional discourse. It moves far beyond issues of efficiency, observable or measurable language use, or literary beauty, into domains moulded by colonialism, scientific traditions, political struggle, emblematic events such as the first Swahili speech in parliament, and so forth. Decoding these historical traces may look like the work of the historian; however, it is my firm belief that it is just as much the work of the sociolinguist. And, perhaps, the sociolinguist can contribute something to the work of the historian: an awareness of the complexity at the level of the everyday realities of sociolinguistic systems; an awareness of the nature of social systems with their feet on the ground, so to speak. Such systems have not just one single history – the chronological sequence we find in a good amount of scholarship. Instead, they are characterised by multiple histories coinciding into an – any – event, operating at different speeds, some slow ('structural' or 'conjunctural'), others fast. The event itself creates an illusion of synchrony and stability for the observer. In actual fact, whatever we can observe in such synchronic snapshots is a moment in a layered, complex and largely unpredictable process, a 'synchronisation' of several different forms of order and normativity, different speeds and historicities, becoming visible at moments of observation as *if* it were a unified and transparent object (cf. Blommaert 2005: 131–7, 2013: 10–14).

It is this understanding of complexity, involving different histories and speeds of development, that informed the analysis in this book. Ujamaa and its influence is a long and slow history, which continues to condition sociolinguistic processes even if overtly they appear devoid of any connection with the hegemonic Ujamaa of, say, the 1970s. Thus, the profoundly neoliberal discourses we encountered in Chapter 7 can be understood as a *non-linear* effect produced by the conditions for strong sociolinguistic-pragmatic hegemony shaped by Ujamaa in conjunction with globalisation effects that have a shorter and faster history and trajectory. Similarly, the class-stratifying code-switching styles of academics in the 1980s and 1990s documented in Chapter 6 can be understood as non-linear effects of some – then largely unnoticed – shortcomings in the imagination of sociolinguistic reality by the Tanzanian Swahilisation champions. These non-linear effects cannot be directly deduced from Ujamaa and the nation-building efforts it provoked in the 1960s to 1980s; in fact, they are their antithesis. Yet, they are entirely conditioned by the tremendous drive towards the generalised distribution and the prestige of Swahili under Ujamaa, which is, in Tanzanian postcolonial sociolinguistic history, the single most powerful *structure* in the system. I say 'structure' and many readers will instantly infer 'stability', 'dominant influence' and 'clarity' at this point. The 'structure' I am talking about, however, has none of those structuralist connotations; it is a slowly developing feature of a social system, present over a long period of time, but never *in itself* dominant, always operating in conjunction with other and often contradictory features, and never sufficient as an explanation for the specific character of the processes we study. Given the nature of our object of enquiry, I am afraid that these are the only kinds of structure we can empirically detect, analyse and explain. If we do that, however, and if we do that well, we shall have contributed a lot to the study of society.

8.1 NOTES

1. Comparisons with China are compelling. In a recent paper, Wang et al. (2013) demonstrate how the Chinese concept of 'harmony' was used by the Communist Party to ideologically centre a sociolinguistically superdiverse society around Putonghua and simplified character script. They also demonstrate how contemporary Chinese Internet discourses confront this homogenising tendency with a bewildering polycentricity.
2. The pattern is very similar to that described by Niloofar Haeri (1997) with respect to Arabic in Egypt.

References

Abdulaziz, M. H. (1971), 'Tanzania's national language policy and the rise of Swahili political culture', in W. H. Whiteley (ed.), *Language Use and Social Change*, London: Oxford University Press, pp. 160–78.

Abdulaziz, M. H. (1972), 'Triglossia and Swahili-English bilingualism in Tanzania', *Language in Society* 1: 197–213.

Abdulaziz, M. H. (1980), 'The ecology of Tanzanian national language policy', in E. C. Polomé and C. P. Hill (eds), *Language in Tanzania*, London: Oxford University Press, pp. 139–75.

Agha, A. (2000), 'Register', *Journal of Linguistic Anthropology* 9(1–2): 216–19.

Agha, A. (2007), *Language and Social Relations*, Cambridge: Cambridge University Press.

Akida, H. (1974), 'Language for the coming generations of the scientific age in Tanzania', *Kiswahili* 44(2): 1–6.

Akwilombe, R. A. (1988), *Dar Imenihadaa*, Dar es Salaam: Akajase Enterprises.

Althusser, L. (1971), *Lenin and Philosophy*, London: New Left Books.

Ansre, G. (1974), 'Language standardization in Sub-Saharan Africa', in J. Fishman (ed.), *Advances in Language Planning*, The Hague: Mouton, pp. 369–89.

Ansre, G. (1977), 'Four rationalizations for maintaining the European languages in education in Africa', *Kiswahili* 47(2): 55–61.

Appadurai, A. (1996), *Modernity at Large: Cultural Dimensions of Globalization*, Minneapolis: University of Minnesota Press.

Arap Moi, D. (1986), *Kenya African Nationalism: Nyayo Philosophy and Principles*, London: Macmillan.

Arnaut, K. and J. Blommaert (2009), 'Chtonic science: Georges Niangoran-Bouah and the anthropology of belonging in Cote d'Ivoire', *American Ethnologist* 36(3): 574–90.

Ashton, E. O. (1944), *Swahili Grammar (Including Intonation)*, London: Longmans.

Askew, K. (2002), *Performing the Nation: Swahili Music and Cultural Politics in Tanzania*, Chicago: University of Chicago Press.

Balandier, G. (1957), *Afrique Ambiguë*, Paris: Plon.

Balisidya, M. L. N. (1987), 'Adopted or adapted to? Neo-Swahili literature in Tanzania', *Kiswahili* 54(1–2): 14–33.

Bamgbose, A. (1994), 'Pride and prejudice in multilingualism and development', in R. Fardon and G. Furniss (eds), *African Languages, Development and the State*, London: Routledge, pp. 33–43.

Barthes, R. (1957), *Mythologies*, Paris: Seuil.

Batibo, H. (1987), 'Le statut morphosyntaxique du referent sujet en langues bantou', *Kiswahili* 54(1–2): 135–41.

Bauman, R. and C. Briggs (2003), *Voices of Modernity*, Cambridge: Cambridge University Press.

Bellamy, R. (1994), 'The social and political thought of Antonio Gramsci', in *The Polity Reader in Social Theory*, Cambridge: Polity Press, pp. 32–7.

Bertoncini, E. (1989), *Outline of Swahili Literature. Prose Fiction and Drama*, Leiden: E. J. Brill.

Bertoncini, E. (1994), 'Inland Tanzania: Swahili literature or literature in Swahili?', in D. Parkin (ed.), *Continuity and Autonomy in Swahili Communities*, Wien: Afropub, pp. 205–13.

Berwouts, K. (1989), 'Language and modernization: Kiswahili lexical expansion in the domain of the organization of the modern nation/state', *Working Papers in Kiswahili* 5.

Berwouts, K. (1991), *Le Sein de la Mère. Introduction à la Littérature Classique et Moderne en Swahili*, Bruxelles: ASDOC/CEDAF.

Besha, R. (1972), 'Lugha ya Kiswahili hivi leo; hasa katika siasa', *Kiswahili* 42(1): 22–38.

Billings, S. (2006), 'Speaking beauties: language use and linguistic ideologies in Tanzanian beauty pageants', PhD dissertation, University of Chicago.

Billings, S. (2009), 'Speaking beauties: linguistic posturing, language inequality, and the construction of a Tanzanian beauty queen', *Language in Society* 38: 581–606.

Billings, S. (2011a), '"And the winner is . . .": hierarchies of language competence and fashion sense in Tanzanian beauty pageants', *Crossroads of Language, Interaction and Culture* 8: 1–32.

Billings, S. (2011b), '"Education is the key to life": language, schooling and gender in Tanzanian beauty pageants', *Language and Communication* 31: 295–309.

Billings, S. (2013), *Language, Globalization, and the Making of a Tanzanian Beauty Queen*, Bristol: Multilingual Matters.

Biya, P. (1986), *Pour le Liberalisme Communautaire*, Lausanne: Favre; Paris: ABC.

Blommaert, J. (1991), 'Some problems in the interpretation of Swahili political texts', in J. Blommaert (ed.), *Swahili Studies*, Gent: Academia Press, pp. 109–35.

Blommaert, J. (1996), 'Language planning as a discourse on language and society: the linguistic ideology of a scholarly tradition', *Language Problems and Language Planning* 20(3): 199–222.

Blommaert, J. (ed.) (1999), *Language Ideological Debates*, Berlin: Mouton de Gruyter.

Blommaert, J. (2005), *Discourse: A Critical Introduction*, Cambridge: Cambridge University Press.

Blommaert, J. (2006), 'Language policy and national identity', in T. Ricento (ed.), *An Introduction to Language Policy*, London: Blackwell, pp. 238–54.

Blommaert, J. (2008a), 'Artefactual ideologies and the textual production of African languages', *Language and Communication* 28(4): 291–307.

Blommaert, J. (2008b), *Grassroots Literacy: Writing, Identity and Voice in Central Africa*, London: Routledge.

Blommaert, J. (2009), 'Language, asylum and the national order', *Current Anthropology* 50(4): 415–41.

Blommaert, J. (2010), *The Sociolinguistics of Globalization*, Cambridge: Cambridge University Press.

Blommaert, J. (2011), 'The long language-ideological debate in Belgium', *Journal of Multicultural Discourses* 6(3): 241–56.

Blommaert, J. (2012), 'Supervernaculars and their dialects', *Dutch Journal of Applied Linguistics* 1(1): 1–14.

Blommaert, J. (2013), *Ethnography, Superdiversity and Linguistic Landscapes: Chronicles of Complexity*, Bristol: Multilingual Matters.

Blommaert, J. and A. Backus (2013), 'Superdiverse repertoires and the individual', in I. de Saint-Georges and J. J. Weber (eds), *Multilingualism and Multimodality: Current Challenges for Educational Studies*, Rotterdam: Sense Publishers, pp. 11–32.

Blommaert, J. and M. Gysels (1987), 'Campus Kiswahili: language planning, language attitude, and the emergence of a mixed variant among Tanzanian academic staff', *Working Papers in Kiswahili* 1, Ghent University.

Blommaert, J. and M. Gysels (1990), 'On the functionality of English interferences in Campus Kiswahili', *Afrikanistische Arbeitspapiere (AAP)* 21: 87–104.

Blommaert, J. and K. Maryns (2002), 'Pretextuality and pretextual gaps: on de/refining linguistic inequality', *Pragmatics* 12(1): 11–30.

Blommaert, J. and B. Rampton (2011), 'Language and superdiversity', *Diversities* 13(2): 3–23.

Blommaert, J. and P. Varis (2012a), 'Culture as accent', *Tilburg Papers in Culture Studies* 18, Tilburg: Babylon.

Blommaert, J. and P. Varis (2012b), 'How to "how to"?: the prescriptive micropolitics of hijabista', *Tilburg Papers in Culture Studies* 30, Tilburg: Babylon.

Blommaert, J. and J. Verschueren (1992), 'The role of language in European nationalist ideologies', *Pragmatics* 2/3 (special issue on language ideologies): 355–75.

Blommaert, J. and J. Verschueren (1998), *Debating Diversity*, London: Routledge.

Boon, J. (1982), *Other Tribes, Other Scribes. Symbolic Anthropology in the Comparative Study of Cultures, Histories, Religions, and Texts*, Cambridge: Cambridge University Press.

Bourdieu, P. (1982), *Ce que Parler veut Dire*, Paris: Fayard.

Bulcaen, C. (1994), 'Kiswahili literatuur en de Arusha Verklaring', in J. Blommaert (ed.), *Taal, Interaktie en Kontekst in de Afrikastudie* (Antwerp Papers in Linguistics 77), Antwerp: UIA, pp. 69–101.

Campbell, H. and H. Stein (eds) (1992), *Tanzania and the IMF. The Dynamics of Liberalization*, Boulder: Westview Press.

Chiraghdin, S. and M. Mnyampala (1977), *Historia ya Kiswahili*, Nairobi: Oxford University Press.

Crawford, J. (2000), *At War with Diversity: US Language Policy in an Age of Anxiety*, Clevedon: Multilingual Matters.

Creese A. and A. Blackledge (2010), 'Translanguaging in the bilingual classroom: a pedagogy for learning and teaching?', *Modern Language Journal* 94: 103–15.

Denoon, D. and A. Kuper (1970), 'Nationalist historians in search of a nation. The "new historiography" in Dar es Salaam', *African Affairs* 69 (277): 329–49.

De Witte, L. (1996), *Crisis in Kongo*, Leuven: Van Halewyck.

D'hondt, E. D. (n.d.), *Le Lingala Pour Tous! Le Lingala Tel Qu'on le Parle*, Bruxelles: Editions L. Cuypers.

Doom, R. (1980), *Maendeleo*, Gent: Masereelfonds.

Du Gay, P. (2008) '"Without affection or enthusiasm": problems of involvement and attachment in "responsive" public management', *Organization* 15(3): 355–63.

Fabian, J. (1983a), 'Missions and the colonization of African languages: developments in the former Belgian Congo', *Canadian Journal of African Studies* 17: 165–87.

Fabian, J. (1983b), *Time and the Other. How Anthropology Makes its Object*, New York: Columbia University Press.

Fabian, J. (1986), *Language and Colonial Power. The Appropriation of Swahili in the Former Belgian Congo 1880–1938*, Cambridge: Cambridge University Press.

Fardon, R. and G. Furniss (1994), 'Introduction: frontiers and boundaries – African languages as political environment', in R. Fardon and G. Furniss (eds), *African Languages, Development and the State*, London: Routledge, pp. 1–29.

Graebner, W. (1989), 'Whose music? The songs of Remmy Ongala and Orchestra Super Matimila', *Popular Music* 8(3): 243–58.

Graebner, W. (1991), 'Ogopa Matapeli. Notes on a new lexical item', *Swahili Language and Society – Notes and News* 8: 67–72.

Gramsci, A. (1971), *Selections from the Prison Notebooks*, ed. Q. Hoare and G. N. Smith, London: Lawrence and Wishart.

Gurr, A. and A. Calder (eds) (1974), *Writers in East Africa*. Papers from a colloquium held at the University of Nairobi, June 1971, Nairobi: Kenya Literature Bureau.

Haeri, N. (1997), 'The reproduction of symbolic capital: language, state and class in Egypt', *Current Anthropology* 38(5): 795–816.

Hall, B. L. (1975), *Adult Education and the Development of Socialism in Tanzania*, Kampala: East African Literature Bureau.

Harries, L. (1968), 'Swahili in modern East Africa', in J. Fishman, C. Ferguson and J. Das Gupta (eds), *Language Problems of Developing Nations*, New York: John Wiley & Sons, pp. 415–29.

Harries, L. (1969), 'Language policy in Tanzania', *Africa* 39(3): 275–80.

Harries, L. (1972), 'Poetry and politics in Tanzania', *Ba Shiru* 4(3): 52–4.

Heine, B. (1970), *Status and Use of African Lingua Francas*, München: Weltforum Verlag.

Heller, M. (1992), 'The politics of codeswitching and language choice', in C. M. Eastman (ed.), *Codeswitching*, Clevedon: Multilingual Matters, pp. 123–42.

Higgins, C. (2007), 'Constructing membership in the in-group: affiliation and resistance among urban Tanzanians', *Pragmatics* 17(1): 49–70.

Higgins, C. (2009), *English as a Local Language: Post-Colonial Identities and Multilingual Practices*, Bristol: Multilingual Matters.

Higgins, C. (2012), 'When scapes collide: reterritorializing English in East Africa', in R. Rubdy and L. Alsagoff (eds), *The Global-Local Interface: Language Choice and Hybridity*, Bristol: Multilingual Matters.

Hobsbawm, E. (1990), *Nations and Nationalism Since 1780: Programme, Myth, Reality*, Cambridge: Cambridge University Press.

Hyden, G. (1980), *Beyond Ujamaa in Tanzania*, London: Heinemann.

Hymes, D. (1996), *Ethnography, Linguistics, Narrative Inequality: Toward an Understanding of Voice*, London: Taylor & Francis.

Irvine, J. T. (1995), 'The family romance of colonial linguistics: gender and family in nineteenth-century representations of African languages', *Pragmatics* 5(2): 13–53.

Johnson, D. C. (ed.) (2013), 'Ethnography of language policy: theory, method and practice', special issue of *International Journal of the Sociology of Language* 219: 1–140.

Johnson, F. (1939), *A Standard Swahili-English Dictionary*, London: Oxford University Press.

Jørgensen, J. N. (2008), 'Polylingual languaging around and among children and adolescents', *International Journal of Multilingualism* 5(3): 161–76.

Jørgensen, J. N., M. Karrebaek, L. Madsen and J. Møller (2011), 'Polylanguaging in superdiversity', *Diversities* 13(2): 22–37.

Juffermans, K. (2010), 'Local languaging: literacy products and practices in Gambian society', PhD dissertation, Tilburg University.

Kaduma, I. M. (1974), 'Twenty years of TANU "education"', in G. Ruhumbika (ed.), *Towards Ujamaa: Twenty Years of TANU Leadership*, Kampala: East African Literature Bureau, pp. 218–29.

Kaniki, M. H. Y. (1974), 'TANU: the party of independence and national consolidation', in G. Ruhumbika (ed.), *Towards Ujamaa: Twenty Years of TANU Leadership*, Kampala: East African Literature Bureau, pp. 1–30.

Kapinga, M. C. (1983), *Sarufi Maumbo ya Kiswahili Sanifu*, Dar es Salaam: Taasisi ya Uchunguzi wa Kiswahili.

Kassam, Y. O. (1979), *Illiterate No More. The Voices of New Literates from Tanzania*, Dar es Salaam: Tanzania Publishing House.

Kaye, H. J. (1984), *The British Marxist Historians. An Introductory Analysis*, Cambridge: Polity Press.

Kesteloot, L. (1972), *Intellectual Origins of the African Revolution*, Rockville, MD: New Perspectives.

Kezilahabi, E. (1975), *Dunia Uwanja wa Fujo* (*The World is a Chaotic Place*), Dar es Salaam: Tanzania Publishing House.

Kezilahabi, E. (1978), 'Kaputula la Marx' ('Marx's baggy shorts'), unpublished manuscript.

Kezilahabi, E. (1979), *Gamba la Nyoka* (*The Snake's Skin*), Dar es Salaam: Tanzania Publishing House.

Kezilahabi, E. (1980), 'The Swahili novel and the common man in East Africa', in U. Schild (ed.), *The East African Experience. Essays on English and Swahili Literature*, Berlin: Dietrich Reimer Verlag, pp. 75–84.

Khalid, A. (1977), *The Liberation of Swahili from European Appropriation*, Nairobi: East African Literature Bureau.

Khamisi, A. M. (1974), 'Swahili as a national language', in G. Ruhumbika (ed.), *Towards Ujamaa: Twenty Years of TANU Leadership*, Kampala: East African Literature Bureau, pp. 288–308.

Kihore, Y. (1976), 'Tanzania's language policy and Kiswahili's historical background', *Kiswahili* 46(2): 47–69.

Kiimbia, J. K. (1971), 'Uchunguzi wa maneno ya kisiasa', *Kiswahili* 41(2): 18–21.

Kirkpatrick, I. and S. Ackroyd (2003), 'Transforming the professional archetype?', *Public Management Review* 5(4): 511–31.

Kombo, S. M. (1972), 'The role of Swahili language in Tanzania as both national and working language', *Kiswahili* 42(1): 39–42.

Kroskrity, P. (ed.) (2000), *Regimes of Language*, Santa Fe: SAR Press.

Lacunza Balda, J. (1991), 'Tendances dans la littérature islamique swahili', in F. Le Guennec-Coppens and P. Caplan (eds), *Les Swahili entre Afrique et Arabie*, Paris: CREDU-Karthala, pp. 19–38.

Laitin, D. (1992), *Language Repertoires and State Construction in Africa*, Cambridge: Cambridge University Press.

Lambert, O. (2009), 'Dial growth', *Finance & Development*, September 2009: 48–9.

Le Guennec-Coppens, F. and D. Parkin (eds) (1998), *Autorité et Pouvoir Chez les Swahili*, Paris: Karthala.

Littlefield, E. (2009), 'An m-bank near you', *Finance & Development*, September 2009: 49–50.

Lodhi, A. Y. (1974), 'Language and cultural unity in Tanzania', *Kiswahili* 44(2): 10–13.

Loogman, A. (1967), *Swahili Readings*, Pittsburgh: Duquesne University Press.

Lwaitama, A. (1988), 'The Nyerere heritage', in M. Hodd (ed.), *Tanzania After Nyerere*, London: Pinter, pp. 19–26.

Mac-William, A. (1985), 'Research work in dictionary-making', *Kiswahili* 51(1–2): 102–11.

Madumulla, J. (1989), 'Another look at Kiswahili scholarship', *Kiswahili* 56: 10–24.

Madumulla, J., E. Bertoncini and J. Blommaert (1999), 'Politics, ideology and poetic form: the literary debate in Tanzania', in J. Blommaert (ed.), *Language Ideological Debates*, Berlin: Mouton de Gruyter, pp. 307–41.

Massamba, D. (1987a), 'The impact of politics in language development in Tanzania', *Kiswahili* 54(1–2): 180–91.

Massamba, D. (1987b), 'The effect of language modernization on the phonological system of the Kiswahili language', *Kiswahili* 54(1–2): 142–51.

Massamba, D. (1989), 'An assessment of the development and modernization of the Kiswahili language in Tanzania', in F. Coulmas (ed.), *Language Adaptation*, Cambridge: Cambridge University Press, pp. 60–78.

Mazrui, A. A. (1967a), *Towards a Pax Africana. A Study of Ideology and Ambition*, Chicago: University of Chicago Press.

Mazrui, A. A. (1967b), *On Heroes and Uhuru-Worship. Essays on Independent Africa*, London: Longmans.

Mazrui, A. A. (1978), *Political Values and the Educated Class in Africa*, Berkeley: University of California Press.

Mazrui, A. A. and A. M. Mazrui (1998), *The Power of Babel: Language & Governance in the African Experience*, Oxford: J. Currey; Chicago: University of Chicago Press.

Mazrui, A. M. (1983), 'The passive transformation in Swahili', *Kiswahili* 50(1): 19–28.

Mbuguni, L. A. and G. Ruhumbika (1974), 'TANU and national culture', in G. Ruhumbika (ed.), *Towards Ujamaa: Twenty Years of TANU Leadership*, Kampala: East African Literature Bureau, pp. 275–87.

McCarthy, T. (ed.) (2011), *Ethnography and Language Policy*, New York: Oxford University Press.

Mdee, J. S. (1986), 'Matatizo ya kuunda istilahi kama yanavyojitokeza katika Kiswahili', *Kiswahili* 53(1–2): 115–27.

Mekacha, R. D. (1992), 'Are women devils? The portrayal of women in Tanzanian popular music', in W. Graebner (ed.), *Matatu* 9: 99–113.

Mekacha, R. D. (1993), *The Sociolinguistic Impact of Kiswahili on Ethnic Community Languages in Tanzania: A Case Study of Ekinata*, Bayreuth: Bayreuth African Studies.

Mekacha, R. D. (1994), 'Language death: conceptions and misconceptions (review article)', *Journal of Pragmatics* 21: 101–16.

Metz, S. (1982), 'In lieu of orthodoxy: the socialist theories of Nkrumah and Nyerere', *Journal of Modern African Studies* 20(3): 377–92.

Mhina, G. A. (1972), 'Problems being faced in the process of developing African languages with special reference to Kiswahili', *Kiswahili* 42(1): 43–57.

Mhina, G. A. (1977), 'The Tanzanian experience in the use of Kiswahili in education', *Kiswahili* 47(2): 62–9.

Middleton, J. (1992), *The World of the Swahili: An African Mercantile Civilization*, New Haven: Yale University Press.

Milroy, J. and L. Milroy (1985), *Authority in Language: Investigating Standard English*, London: Routledge & Kegan Paul.

Mkelle, M. B. (1971), 'Kiswahili in the age of full commitment', *Kiswahili* 41(2): 72–83.

Mohiddin, A. (1981), *African Socialism in Two Countries*, London: Croom Helm; Totowa: Barnes & Noble.

Møller, J. S. and J. N. Jørgensen (2011), *Language Enregisterment and Attitudes*, Copenhagen: University of Copenhagen (Copenhagen Studies in Bilingualism 63).

Msanjila, Y. P. (1990), 'Problems of teaching through the medium of Kiswahili in Teacher Training Colleges in Tanzania', *Journal of Multilingual and Multicultural Development* 11(4): 307–17.

Mukama, R. (1978), 'On prepositionality and causativity in Swahili', *Kiswahili* 48(1): 26–41.

Mulei, C. (1972), 'The predicament of the left in Tanzania', *East Africa Journal* 9(2): 29–34.

Mulokozi, M. M. (1985), 'The present state of Swahili literature: a survey', in S. Arnold (ed.), *African Literature Studies: The Present State/L'Etat Présent*, Washington: Three Continents Press, pp. 171–88.

Mulokozi, M. M. (1986), 'Kiswahili as a medium of education in Tanzania: some observations on recent policy shifts', paper, International Symposium on Language Standardization, Mainz (Germany), March 1986 (mimeo).

Mulokozi, M. M. (1991), 'English versus Kiswahili in Tanzania's secondary education', in J. Blommaert (ed.), *Swahili Studies*, Gent: Academia Press, pp. 7–16.

Mulokozi, M. M. and K. K. Kahigi (1979), *Kunga za Ushairi na Diwani Yetu*, Dar es Salaam: Tanzania Publishing House.

Mushi, P. A. K. (2009), *History and Development of Education in Tanzania*, Dar es Salaam: Dar es Salaam University Press.

Mushi, S. S. (1968), 'The role of Swahili books in nation building endeavours', *Swahili* 38(1): 3–8.

Mutahi, K. (1986), 'Swahili lexical expansion: projects and problems', *Kiswahili* 53(1–2): 104–14.

Mwangomango, J. (1970), 'Kiswahili katika kujenga Utanzania', *Kiswahili* 40(2): 30–4.

Mwangomango, J. (1971), 'Ngonjera za Ushairi', *Kiswahili* 41(2): 67–71.

Mwansoko, H. J. (1990a), 'The dissemination of technical terms as a means of facilitating translation', in FIT, *Problems of Translation in Africa*, proceedings of the Round-Table Conference FIT-UNESCO, Dar es Salaam, 28–30 August 1989, Gent: FIT, pp. 77–86.

Mwansoko, H. J. (1990b), 'The end of Swahilization for post-primary education in Tanzania?', *Journal of Asian and African Languages* 40: 51–9.

Myers-Scotton, C. (1978), 'Language in East Africa: linguistic patterns and political ideologies', in J. Fishman (ed.), *Advances in the Study of Societal Multilingualism*, The Hague: Mouton, pp. 719–59.

Nazareth, P. (1978), *The Third World Writer. His Social Responsibility*, Nairobi: Kenya Literature Bureau.

Neke, S. (2002), 'English in Tanzania: an anatomy of hegemony', unpublished PhD dissertation, Ghent University.

Neustupny, J. V. (1974), 'Basic types of treatment of language problems', in J. Fishman (ed.), *Advances in Language Planning*, The Hague: Mouton, pp. 37–48.

Ngugi wa Thiong'o (1981a), *Writers in Politic*, London: Heinemann.

Ngugi wa Thiong'o (1981b) *Decolonising the Mind: The Politics of Language in African Literature*, Nairobi: Heinemann.

Nyerere, J. K. (1966), *Freedom and Unity: Uhuru Na Umoja*, Oxford: Oxford University Press.

Nyerere, J. K. (1969), *Nyerere on Socialism*, Dar es Salaam: Oxford University Press.

Nyerere, J. K. (1974), *Man and Development*, Nairobi: Oxford University Press.

Nyerere, J. K. [1962] (1975), 'Ujamaa – the basis of African Socialism', in G. C. M Mutiso and S. W. Rohio (eds), *Readings in African Political Thought*, London: Heinemann, pp. 512–15.

Nyerere, J. K. [1963] (1975), 'A United States of Africa', in G. C. M. Mutiso and S. W. Rohio (eds), *Readings in African Political Thought*, London: Heinemann, pp. 334–6.

O'Barr, W. (1976), 'Language use and language policy in Tanzania: an overview', in W. O'Barr and J. F. O'Barr (eds), *Language and Politics*, The Hague: Mouton, pp. 35–48.

Ohly, R. (1976), 'The conception of state through Swahili', *Kiswahili* 45(1): 25–33.

Ohly, R. (1978), *Language + Revolution = Swahili*, Dar es Salaam: Dar es Salaam University Press.

Ohly, R. (1981), *Aggressive Prose. A Case Study in Kiswahili Prose of the Seventies*, Dar es Salaam: Institute of Kiswahili Research.

Ohly, R. (1982), 'Report on the state of modern Swahili in urban Bukoba', *Kiswahili* 49(2): 81–92.

Okot p'Bitek (1973), *Africa's Cultural Revolution*, Nairobi: Macmillan Books for Africa.

Okot p'Bitek (1986), *Artist, the Ruler. Essays on Art, Culture and Values*, Nairobi: Heinemann Kenya.

O'Reilly, D. and M. Reed (2010), '"Leaderism": an evolution of managerialism in UK public service reform', *Public Administration* 88(4): 960–78.

Othman, H. (1994), 'The intellectual and transformation in Southern Africa', *Dar es Salaam Alumni Newsletter* 1(1): 9–10.

Pennycook, A. (2007), *Global Englishes and Transcultural Flows*, London: Routledge.

Pennycook, A. (2010), *Language as a Local Practice*, London: Routledge.

Pennycook, A. (2012), *Language and Mobility: Unexpected Places*, Bristol: Multilingual Matters.

Polomé, E. C. (1980), 'Tanzania: a socio-linguistic perspective', in E. C. Polomé and C. P.

Hill (eds), *Language in Tanzania*, London: Oxford University Press for the International African Institute, pp. 103–38.

Pratt, C. (1976), *The Critical Phase in Tanzania. Nyerere and the Emergence of a Socialist Strategy*, Cambridge: Cambridge University Press.

Rampton, B. (2006), *Language in Late Modernity*, Cambridge: Cambridge University Press.

Ransome, P. (1992), *Antonio Gramsci. A New Introduction*, New York: Harvester Wheatsheaf.

Robert, S. (1962), 'Swahili as a unifying force in East Africa', *Swahili* 33(1): 11–12.

Roy-Campbell, Z. and M. Qorro (1997), *Language Crisis in Tanzania: The Myth of English versus Education*, Dar es Salaam: Mkuki na Nyota.

Rubagumya, C. M. (ed.) (1990), *Language in Education in Africa: A Tanzanian Perspective*, Clevedon: Multilingual Matters.

Said, E. [1978] (1985), *Orientalism*, Harmondsworth: Penguin.

Samarin, W. (1982), 'Goals, roles and language skills in colonizing central equatorial Africa', *Anthropological Linguistics* 24(4): 410–22.

Samarin, W. (1984), 'The linguistic world of field colonialism', *Language in Society* 13: 435–53.

Seidel, A. (1900), *Suahili Konversations-Grammatik Nebst einer Einführung in die Schrift und die Briefstil der Suahili*, Heidelberg: Julius Groos Verlag.

Sengo, T. S. (1987), 'Towards maturity in Kiswahili scholarship', *Kiswahili* 54: 215–24.

Shivji, I. G. (1976), *Class Struggles in Tanzania*, London: Heinemann.

Shivji, I. G. (2008) *Pan-Africanism or Pragmatism: Lessons of Tanganyika-Zanzibar Union*, Dar es Salaam: Mkuki na Nyota.

Silverstein, M. (1996), 'Monoglot "standard" in America: standardization and metaphors of linguistic hegemony', in D. Brenneis and R. Macaulay (eds), *The Matrix of Language: Contemporary Linguistic Anthropology*, Boulder: Westview Press, pp. 284–306.

Silverstein, M. (1998), 'Contemporary transformations of local linguistic communities', *Annual Review of Anthropology* 27: 401–26.

Silverstein, M. (2003), 'Indexical order and the dialectics of sociolinguistic life', *Language and Communication* 23: 192–229.

Silverstein, M. and G. Urban (eds) (1996), *Natural Histories of Discourse*, Chicago: University of Chicago Press.

Spitulnik, D. (1992), 'Radio time sharing and the negotiation of linguistic pluralism in Zambia', (special issue on language ideologies), *Pragmatics* 2/3: 335–54.

Stans, A. (1989), 'Linguistisch onderzoek als politieke Aktie', unpublished licentiate dissertation, University of Ghent (mimeo).

Sumra, S. A. and A. G. Ishumi (1980), 'Development and trends in Tanzania's policies towards higher training and scholarships overseas', in T. L. Maliyamkono (ed.), *Policy Developments in Overseas Training*, Dar es Salaam: Black Star, pp. 38–57.

Tanzanian Ministry of Finance and Economic Affairs (2008), *Public Financial Management Reform Programme – Strategic Plan, June 2008*, Dar es Salaam: United Republic of Tanzania Prime Minister's Office.

Temu, C. (1971), 'The development of political vocabulary in Swahili', *Kiswahili* 41(2): 3–17.

Temu, C. (1984), 'Kiswahili terminology: principles adopted for the enrichment of the Kiswahili language', *Kiswahili* 51(1–2): 112–27.

Thompson, E. P. [1963] (1991), *The Making of the English Working Class*, London: Penguin Books.

Thompson, J. B. (1990), *Ideology and Modern Culture*, Cambridge: Polity Press.

Thompson, J. B. (1994), 'Ideology and modern culture', in *The Polity Reader in Social Theory*, Cambridge: Polity Press, pp. 133–41.

Topan, F. (1991), 'Réseaux religieux chez les Swahili', in F. Le Guennec-Coppens and P. Caplan (eds), *Les Swahili Entre Afrique et Arabie*, Paris: CREDU-Karthala, pp. 39–57.

Topan, F. (1992), 'Swahili as a religious language', *Journal of Religion in Africa* 22(4): 331–49.

Topan, F. (2008), 'Tanzania: the development of Swahili as a national and official language', in A. Simpson (ed.), *Language and National Identity in Africa*, Oxford: Oxford University Press, pp. 252–66.

Tordoff, W. and A. A. Mazrui (1972), 'The left and the super-left in Tanzania', *Journal of Modern African Studies* 10(3): 427–45.

TUKI (Taasisi ya Uchunguzi wa Kiswahili) (1981), *Kamusi ya Kiswahili Sanifu*, Dar es Salaam: Oxford University Press.

TUKI (Taasisi ya Uchunguzi wa Kiswahili) (2000), *Swahili-English Dictionary*, Dar es Salaam: Institute of Kiswahili Research.

Varis and X. Wang (2011), 'Superdiversity on the Internet: a case from China', *Diversities* 13(2): 69–81.

Velghe, F. (2012), '"I wanna go in the phone." Illiteracy, informal learning processes, "voice" and mobile phone appropriation in a South African township', *Tilburg Papers in Culture Studies* 40, Tilburg: Babylon.

Vertovec, S. (2007), 'Super-diversity and its implications', *Ethnic and Racial Studies* 30(6): 1024–54.

Von Freihold, W. (1979), *Ujamaa Villages in Tanzania*, London: Heinemann.

Wallerstein, I. (1961), *Africa. The Politics of Independence*, New York: Vintage Books.

Wallerstein, I. (1971), 'Conflit social en Afrique noire indépendante: réexamen des concepts de race et de "status-group"', *Cahiers du CEDAF* (Sociologie) 1971(8).

Wang, X., C. Du and K. Juffermans (2012) 'Harminy as language policy in China: an internet perspective', *Tilburg Papers in Culture Studies* 35, Tilburg: Babylon.

Wang, X., M. Spotti, K. Juffermans, L. Cornips, S. Kroon and J. Blommaert (2013), 'Globalization in the margins', *Tilburg Papers in Culture Studies* 73, Tilburg: Babylon.

Wanjala, C. (1978), *The Season of Harvest. A Literary Discussion*, Nairobi: Kenya Literature Bureau.

Whitehead, J. and L. F. Whitehead (1928), *Manuel de Kingwana, le Dialecte Occidental de Swahili*, Wayika, Congo Belge: Mission de et à Wayika.

Whiteley, W. H. (1968), 'Ideal and reality in national language policy: a case study from Tanzania', in J. Fisman, C. Ferguson and J. Das Gupta (eds), *Language Problems of Developing Nations*, New York: John Wiley & Sons, pp. 327–44.

Whiteley, W. H. (1969), *Swahili: The Rise of a National Language*, London: Methuen.

Whiteley, W. H. (1971), 'Some factors influencing language policies in Eastern Africa', in J. Rubin and B. Jernudd (eds), *Can Language be Planned? Sociolinguistic Theory and Practice for Developing Nations*, Honolulu: East-West Center Press, pp. 141–58.

Williams, G. (1992), *Sociolinguistics: A Sociological Critique*, London: Routledge.

Wright, M. (1965), 'Swahili language policies 1890–1940', *Swahili* 35(1): 40–8.

Yahya-Othman, S. (1997), 'Language and power in Tanzania', *LICCA Papers* 4, Duisburg: LICCA.

Young, C. (1982), *Ideology and Development in Africa*, New Haven: Yale University Press.

Young, C. (1993), 'The dialectics of cultural pluralism: concept and reality', in C. Young (ed.), *The Rising Tide of Cultural Pluralism: The Nation-state at Bay?*, Madison: University of Wisconsin Press, pp. 3–35.

Index